Anticipated

Lena Knight

A note from the Author

Please note that this is a work of fiction, created by my imagination. Naturally, some scenes were inspired by personal events. The story may also entail some triggering subjects, so be advised.

Thank you in advance for giving my story a chance. Hope you like it… Happy reading.

Trigger warnings: mention of loss, breast cancer scare

Lena

To all the girls who are scared to sing outside the shower - go ahead. Let your inner child free, it will forever be grateful!

Playlist

Available on Spotify

Stargazing - Myles Smith
The story of us (Taylor's version) - Taylor Swift
Strangers again - Matt Hansen
Too much - Dove Cameron
Good not Great - Jordy
Stuck with each other - Shontelle ft. Akon
Beautiful Lie - Voila
Nightlight - Livingston
Alone pt. II - Alan Walker, Ava Max
You feel like home - Lasso the sun
Reminisce - Saidthe Sky, Taylor Acorn
What would you do? - Tate McRae
Be mine - Kamrad
Combust - Lauv
Stars will align - Kygo, Imagine Dragons
Walk Thru Fire - Vicetone
Feelings - Lauv
Cliche - MGK
Mirrors - Natalia Kills
Troubled Waters - Alex Warren
MAD - Martin Garrix, Lauv
Mine (Taylor's version) - Taylor Swift
Versions of Forever - Matt Hansen
Loving myself - Eva Max

1

Lena Knight

Wait for you - Myles Smith
Carry you home - Alex Warren
There till the end - Jerub
Take my time - Kamrad
Wi$h li$t - Taylor Swift
My first Heartbreak - Myles Smith
Chasing Cars - Snow Patrol
Fix You - Coldplay
Bleeding Love - Leona Lewis
Sex is on fire - Kings of leon
Better than Revenge (Taylor's version) - Taylor Swift
I love you - Axwell, Ingrosso
Ready to be loved - St. Lundi
Dancing in the Flames - The Weekend
Messy - Rose
Turned into missing you - Max McNown
Wood - Taylor Swift
When your heart breaks - St. Lundi
Perfect to me - Michael Sanzone

Chapter 1

Aria

Fuck—my—life!

And add three exclamation points for emphasis!!!

"Oh, don't be so dramatic, Aria." John wiggled in his almighty leather chair across from me.

"You think that *this* is me being dramatic?" I took a step back to restrain myself from punching him in the face, no matter how much I loved the man.

John, also known as Mr. Wright, was my father's business partner and a long-time family friend, essentially my second dad. He had my utmost respect right up until about a minute ago, when he and my beloved ex-father laid out their plan.

My father and John were the CEOs of the W&B Corporation. They owned the majority of the mines around Boston and had businesses in almost everything. The company was listed on the Fortune 500; a plaque stating this was displayed on the wall behind me.

Yours truly was an only child in line to inherit half of the fortune, including my father's seat at the table. I was in my last year at Northeastern University's D'Amore-McKim School of Business, where I was learning everything there was to know about running one, even though my father had been preparing me for the role my entire life.

3

On the other hand, John had three children: two sons and a daughter, to be more precise. Mario was the oldest and set to inherit his father's seat, but one drunken mistake put that all in jeopardy, making the youngest child, Cillian, next in line. Their sister Helen had no interest in that world, which was a moot point since she was blissfully married with a third child on the way.

We've all grown up together, like a big, happy family, only to grow apart over the years. We spent every major holiday together, but other than that, we didn't see much of each other.

The dumb and dumber sitting across from me just informed me that they'd managed to "misplace" a large sum of money and were afraid of the board finding out. And that was not even the best part. The best part was their plan for a get-out-of-jail-free card in the form of a marriage contract. More specifically, an arranged marriage between Cillian and me would incline them to the other half of our trust. When we were kids, our family lawyer had drawn up the agreement, which was divided into two parts: one we inherited when we started college, and the other we would receive on the day we got married. Although it was never explicitly stated that we had to marry each other, the scenario was intended solely to double the money.

"You can't be serious?" Cillian finally yelled after being late to this spectacular charade of a meeting, but it was only 25 minutes, so no big deal—his words, not mine.

We exchanged disapproving looks as his frustration met mine. He'd rushed in late per usual—a fascinating fact considering he was a freaking soldier. The bastard defied nature, smelling awesome while also glistening with sweat. And I hated myself for even noticing it. He'd barged in, wearing a yellow t-shirt and navy shorts, with a golden eagle logo plastered on both.

"Oh, Hades, and to think you ran away from practice for this. Does the coach know?" I teased as if my life depended on it.

"Brooks, always a pleasure," he gibed, barely acknowledging my presence; no, make that my existence.

"Oh, come on now, say it like you mean it," I hissed, and his head flew to the ceiling with a frustrated growl.

Yes!

My life's mission was to make him as miserable as possible.

"Why would I, uh, m—" he waved his finger between us "—*we* ever go through with it?"

Cillian glanced at me, then back at our parents. "This was your mistake, deal with it like the adults you're supposed to be!"

I hated his voice, but agreed with his words.

Cillian was my age, but he acted way older, always serious… as opposed to me, who pretty much acted like a child, but in a good way. He was a marine, some big shot lieutenant on top of the world till about a year ago, when he'd risked his life to save his friend, injuring his back in the process. He was still in the Navy but not on active duty.

"Look, kids, we screwed up, we know, and we are asking for your help. This is our last resort. It is just for a year." My father stood up, setting his hand on his desk as Mr. Wright finished. "You've known each other your whole lives; you can make it one year faking a marriage."

They were oblivious to how much Cillian and I hated each other. The saddest part is that we used to be best friends. Now his ego sucked all the air out of the room, making it hard to breathe.

With that, my eyes betrayed me when they glanced at all of his muscles put on display. *Hey, I'm only human, and I do have eyes*, so naturally, they got drowned in the unmistakable eye candy. And despite Cillian's personality, his body was impossible to ignore, no matter how much my brain protested it.

Clearing my throat, I pointed a serious look at the two men sweating their asses off. "If, and I mean *if,* we decide to do this, walk me—us—through everything."

Cillian choked on my request but listened to their plan without making a single move.

They took turns laying out the groundwork; it was a matter of two signatures, and just like that, we would be inclined to $2 billion—each. There was some talk about a big, fancy wedding to show how strong the families are, but I tuned out a bit at that point. It was relatively simple, not that hard to do. I mean, I could smile for the camera and pretend I didn't want to kill the groom. The problem with it all was the year we had to pretend to actually like each other, love each other, in order not to raise any suspicions. The pretending part would also entail living together for a whole year, and that was something I couldn't be persuaded into, no matter how much I loved my dad or John. The mere thought of being under the same roof as him disgusted me to my very core.

"How did you 'lose' the money?" I air-quoted the word

lose.

"That is not important," John said, enraging my already boiling blood.

"This is unacceptable," Cillian said before storming out.

"Wow, his future wife is one lucky hell of a gal. Oh, wait!"

Sarcasm was me, me was Sarcasm. I lived by it, to it, and for it. Without it, I don't think I could cope with a mere act of blinking, as it was the only thing that saved people from me killing them. Cillian being on top of my kill list.

"Look, Peanut, I don't think you understand how much trouble we could potentially be in. We could lose the company altogether or face prison. It's just a piece of paper, and it's only a year. Please think about it." My father stooped so low that he resorted to the puppy-dog-eyes trick on me. And it almost worked. Almost.

It wasn't lost on me that my father's nickname for me was the one thing that had the power to kill me in an instant, even with his endearing tone.

"Aria, don't you dare eat that, it has nuts," my dad shouted, Mario's hand mid-air with a cracker ready. Cillian jerked it out of my hand, making it fall to the ground, and I burst into tears. My dad ran to me so quickly that the first tear didn't even get the chance to touch my lips. "Come here, Peanut, don't cry," he gasped, dropping his pipe on the grass. "Cillian, why would you do that?" my dad yelled at my best friend, then focused back on me. "You have to be careful, you can't go around taking food without knowing its contents." He grazed my hair and held me tight, the mix of mint and tobacco filling up my nostrils.

I snapped out the memory that should've been my first indication of Cillian's true nature.

"I'll think about it, but I can't make any promises," I said, losing my energy.

"That is all we ask. Thank you." John pulled me into a hug, and I took a whiff of his scent,   letting the nostalgia hit.

Chapter 2

Cillian

This was not how I'd imagined my day going. One minute, I was doing push-ups, and the next, I was being pushed into a fake marriage with *her.*

Aria was the bane of my existence, the reason why every hair on my body was familiar with the term piloerection, as the mere sound of her voice made my skin itch with repulsion.

I'd rushed from my training session when I got the 911 text from my father. Never in my wildest imagination could I have pictured the severity of the emergency.

Growing up in my father's office, there was nothing more majestic than watching the two CEOs conduct their business. They'd always had my respect. But oh, *how the mighty have fallen*. Disappointment couldn't even cover it.

"What are you still doing here?" Aria's voice annoyed me like a nail scratching a blackboard.

"Waiting for you."

She narrowed her eyes and crossed her arms, unbothered.

"Assuming you want to get out of this as much as I do, you must have a plan?" I formed it as a question even though I had no doubt about it.

"Your assumption is correct, and no, I do not. Y*et*!"

The sun grazed her porcelain skin as she covered her ocean blue eyes with a set of dark glasses. Aria had always been a part of our family, and as much as I'd wanted her far, far away, she stuck like some disease I couldn't shake off.

"I have to get to class, but I will brainstorm. Do you need a ride?"

A nice gesture from the devil herself? I looked up.

"What are you doing?"

"Just checking for pigs flying," I snarked, raking my fingers through my wet hair.

She tried to push me away, and I laughed my ass off at her attempt.

Muscle wall right here, baby, you can't touch me.

"So that's a no?"

"Actually, if it is not much of a trouble…" I swallowed. "I ran here from base and don't feel like running back."

She nodded, then, exasperated, "Wait here, I'll bring the car around."

Aria was known for her love of cars. She had a decent collection, but it was nothing compared to mine. I've made it a point to one-up her in everything, even something as petty as better road pets.

Her blue McLaren 720S convertible stopped in front of my feet, and I got inside, noticing the top was up on such a warm and sunny day.

"Afraid you'll ruin your hair?"

She stepped on the gas with a loud snarl. "And here I was doing something for your benefit." She pushed the button that commanded the top to lower. "But hey. I'm not the one at risk of catching pneumonia."

Hell must be freezing over because no way in hell would Aria ever do something for my benefit. I tried my best to think up a retort, but my mind couldn't do any constructing. Maybe that was her intention all along, to bewitch me into a state of blank.

In trying to avoid looking at her, something shiny reflected right into my left eye. I quickly glanced at the culprit—a key chain dangling from the ignition.

She still has it?

"Come on, Aria, make a wish," my mom said. *The birthday girl smiled and blew out the candles, all 13 of them. She took the wishing process very seriously and never allowed people to clap after her blow, saying it was bad luck. Something to do with the wishing spirits. She opened all the presents and politely thanked everyone. My present always came last, with her reminding me it was the only one she truly cared about. Nerves rushed through me, but when she opened the little box, her eyes spoke volumes. "I love it, thank you so much." She jumped into my arms, squishing my pipes. "It is now my most prized possession." She looked at the simple padlock, grazing her finger over the letters C&A 4ever.*

"You're welcome," her raspy voice snapped me out of memory lane when I noticed her pulling in front of the gate.

"Yeah, thank you." I opened the door, waiting for it.

"Oh, come on. Say it like you mean it."

Right on cue, and with that tone—God, I hated that condescending tone of hers.

"Yeah, yeah." I waved goodbye and showed my

11

credentials to the guard, never looking back.

"Lieutenant Wright." The guard lifted his chin in salute. I nodded, waiting for him to buzz me in. "Officer Chase," I said back and entered the base.

"Where did you run off to so abruptly?" Marco shouted the moment I stepped into the locker room to find all my men getting dressed.

"It is a long story, one that requires a lot of alcohol," I answered in passing, "but first I need to hit something, or someone." I took the steps two at a time to find Ray and Cade from the other platoon, knuckles deep in a bloodbath. Cade's arcade was split; so was Ray's lip. The pit was a boxing ring in the base's basement. Many of the Marines were fighters of some sort before they'd enlisted and used the ring for actual sparring, while others used it for therapeutic purposes. And I was in desperate need of a session.

In the corner, I sat my ass down on the bench and started wrapping up my fingers with the elastic band and waited. Everyone knew the reason I came down, and it was pointless to even ask if anyone wanted to get in the ring with me. I was the leading champion, so everyone wanted a piece of me. But to my dismay, the only person who dared to confront me today was none other than my best friend.

Two rounds in, I was barely standing on wobbling feet.

"Come on, finish him," the crowd yelled as another punch collided with my ribs. I lost my balance and fell right into the ropes.

"Damn, Wright, you're off your game," Marco stated the obvious, offering his hand. I brushed it off, not needing any assistance.

"Funny! Don't get cocky; you caught me on an off day." I took off the gloves and stepped out of the ring only to watch all the guys patting Marco on the back. I will never hear the end of this. But at least my mind had been clear for the past thirty minutes.

Despite being in a room filled with sweaty men, there was a stench of Chanel No. 5 I had to get rid of and pronto, so I beelined to the shower.

"The Eagle?" I heard Marco's question echo around the stall.

The Eagle was a bar located near the base, essentially a private establishment given the scarcity of civilians.

"You know it," was all I said before I let the cold water wash away any remnants of the woman who always seemed to find a way to get under my skin.

Only when I was sure I couldn't smell the devil was I out of the stall and in the locker room. I got dressed and stepped outside to find Marco waiting for me. We walked the small steps to the bar side by side, not sharing a single word. When we entered, we nodded at Perry, the owner-slash-bartender, and before we took our seats in front of him, two amber-filled glasses awaited us.

The whiskey slid down my throat with ease, washing away the sting of my father's words.

"Uh, that bad? Do tell?"

Marco was one of the officers who worked with me, but was on active duty, unlike me.   About a year ago, while on a mission to secure another unit's vessel, one of the M4s had backfired, fallen to the ground, and misfired. I'd practically tackled Marco to the ground, but the bullet managed to find my spine.

Luckily, there was no real harm, but a lot of my nerves had gotten damaged, preventing me from staying fully active. I remained a lieutenant commander, still important, but it wasn't the same.

"My father wants to marry me off," I gulped my fourth whiskey.

"Okay, so? Just decline, what's the big deal?" He was oblivious.

"I don't think I can! That's the deal and the problem!" Down went the fifth, along with the story behind the conundrum.

After I laid it all out, Marco turned on the charm. "Is this your way of asking me to be your best man?"

I choked on a laugh. Marco wasn't a people person, except when it came to me. For some unexplainable reason, he took a liking to me.

"I can't say I do without you, man," I mused, or at least I tried.

"Aw, shucks. I think I'm gonna cry," he teased, and I pushed my elbow into his ribs.

"Hey, hey, no violence necessary. I'll be honored. And if you want my two cents, you could do far worse than Aria."

I cocked a brow. He grinned.

"It makes sense. You've known each other your whole life; no one would suspect a thing."

"Why does everyone keep saying that? You've seen us together. We can't stand each other."

"All I see is fire when you two bicker," he deadpanned.

And I must be drunk because I didn't fight him on it.

My head buzzing, I nodded to Pierre, the concierge, on my way to the elevator when he handed me an envelope. My head was hurting like hell as I opened it on my ride up. I lived in a penthouse with a sky view on the top floor of The Imperial. It was a private building with all things luxury money could buy.

I got inside and poured myself another whiskey, slid the paper out, then read the heading: 'Prenup.'

The fuck?

Chapter 3

Aria

My whole day sitting in classes had gone by in the most blurriest of blurs. Nala had kept shooting a specific look at me the entire time, but I'd just nodded her off. I couldn't bring myself to tell her anything, at least not yet.

Nala was one of my best friends in the world. We've known each other for a couple of years now, but it felt like we'd known each other in each reincarnation. As much as I loved her, I wasn't in the mood for her analyzing it all and then fishing out some books that had the same tropes or whatever she called them. I was more of a screen person, unlike Nala, whose nose only saw the pages of books. Additionally, she would point out that every movie or story about an arranged marriage ultimately ended with the couple falling in love.

All of a sudden, that became my biggest fear.

We stepped outside the building, and I took out my phone, cursing under my breath when the screen lit up: 11 missed calls from Dad, six from John, and one from Loren, aka Mrs. Wright.

Shit!

I'd lost my mother to breast cancer when I was ten, and Loren had been there, holding my hand through it all. She'd become an essential part of my life simply by being there for me. With how much my father had loved my mother, he took it pretty hard, and it killed him seeing her life slowly extinguish. For a long time, he'd refused to look at me because I reminded him so much of her.

I picked up my phone and dialed back. She answered on the first ring, breaking my eardrum as she yelled, "We need to talk! When will you be home?"

I could try to get out of it, but Loren had this sixth sense about me, something I hated most of the time. It was like she could read me, even when I tried my best to hide whatever I was burying deep down.

"In twenty minutes."

"I'll wait for you."

And that was it, and even though her voice was all kind and fluffy, I could hear the threat in it.

"I have to go," I told Nala, who was looking at me with curiosity.

Nope, not gonna work. My mouth is staying shut.

"Okaay," she dragged, "but don't think you're getting out of this."

"Out of what?" I feigned ignorance, knowing it wouldn't do shit.

"Oh, there's a story there, and you're gonna spill it. I am not afraid to get out my big guns," she threatened, and I shook my head. Her form of big guns was over-talking with impressive speed about the newest read. I pretended to hate it, but in truth, I loved her ability to babble pointlessly and her stories.

"Do your worst," I deadpanned. We kissed goodbye, and I started to walk to my place, each step getting heavier. Living near campus, I rarely drove, using my feet for transportation.

When I walked up the street, Loren was already waiting for me in front of my building. We went inside together, and I beelined to the kitchen to open a bottle of wine and pour us both a glass.

"I don't know how they allowed this to happen. What were they thinking?" she snarled, tapping her finger when the glass was half-full.

"I don't know, never in a million years would I have imagined them to do such a thing."

I honestly couldn't comprehend it. What went through their heads to play with money when they had so much of it? They had a thriving business and owned several properties, ranging from garages to commercial buildings, and everything they owned was profitable. So why would they need to play with any of it?

"I don't know, and frankly, right now, I don't care. I don't like that they are dragging me into it!"

I chugged my wine like it was water and poured another one.

"Honey, you know I love you like a daughter, and I will respect any decision you make, because it is *your* decision. Ok?"

Her reassurance made all the difference regarding the tension in my stomach. She caressed my hand the way she always had, something that always brought me comfort. I traced her features, taking in the wrinkles that formed around her face, her eyes that still sparkled with love, and my heart instantly warmed and grew fuzzy.

The woman was beautiful; her hair naturally brown and

curly, with a couple of grays emerging here and there. She carried that classic, everlasting beauty, but it was her heart that made her the wonderful person she was. Her physique was impeccable for a fifty-year-old - fit, her skin tight, never touched by any needle. I admired her for it; she had all the money in the world, but it never changed her. She never underwent any surgery, not even a simple Botox injection - always herself. And John loved her all the more for it. Their love was too suitable even for the movie screens. They were high school sweethearts, and everything they'd accomplished, they did so together. It was the kind of love I had always aspired to find one day. And now I was being forced into a marriage with the person that I hated most, the person that hated me even more.

"Thank you," I said under my breath, and I meant it. I was always thankful for her.

An hour of bitching and one empty wine bottle later, Loren left me alone with my thoughts. Deciding to turn the day around, I took a shower and slipped into my favorite pair of skinny jeans and a strapless, gold-sequined shirt. I put on my most comfortable ankle boots and headed out. I never liked dressing up, but I loved a good pair of heels—my favorite accessory. With one quick text to Sabrina, I headed out.

The moment I entered The Brick, my eyes were transfixed by the lights. Nala worked here as a bartender and was on tonight, but I didn't care; I needed to lose myself in the music and a high percentage of ethanol. Sabrina texted back that she couldn't make it, so I was left alone with my vices. Sabrina was my childhood friend; we were cut from the same cloth, but she was more adventurous—always pushing me out of my comfort zone. Not that I minded it.

I got to the bar, and Nala's smile widened when she noticed me. It amazed me how her face wore a genuine smile as a default setting. I smiled back as she handed me a glass of pure vodka with ice.

Fuck, she knew me so well.

The bar area had no speakers, so it was easy to talk, but I wasn't in the mood for talking. The dance floor and I had some business to attend to. I nodded to Nala, and she understood my intention, blowing me a kiss in return.

In the middle of the crowd, I closed my eyes and started to dance my ass off in an effort to lose myself. I didn't care that I was alone; I never did. I just danced and sang like no one could see or hear me. A gentle tap on my shoulder made me turn around to face a tall, handsome man asking for a dance. With a soft smile, I engaged with him in a wavy movement. I didn't bother mapping out any of his details; being easy on the eyes was good enough for me. One-night stands were not my forte, but some heavy groping was more than welcome. And let me tell you…his hands—grope city. His intentions were clear when he whispered in my ear, asking if I wanted to go to the bathroom.

Been there. Done that. Won't be repeating it ever again.

The disgust on my face must've been enough of an answer because the guy bolted so fast, I was sure his shadow had trouble keeping up.

Right back where I started, alone on the dance floor, my mood downshifted. Not even the loud pumping of the bass could bring it back up. Trying to salvage the night, I exited the place, typing out a quick text to Nala, letting her know I'd bolted.

Turned out, all I needed was a long walk with the right soundtrack. I took the longer route and inhaled the city while the songs in my ears hit just right.

One hundred ninety-five countries in the world, and I was stuck in the most perfect corner of it. I'd traveled the globe, seen most of its beauty, but Boston was my second-favorite place in the world—an ideal combination of modern and classic, with the smell of the river giving it life.

I loved walking in the night, taking in all the lights surrounding me. But I loved driving more. It felt liberating, free. The day I got my license was the day my freedom was forever stamped. But right now, for some reason, the weight on my chest felt like I was trapped, and I didn't like it one bit.

Chapter 4

Cillian

A hard knock on my door woke me right up. I looked at the clock—7 AM.

Fucking hell!

Without bothering to check through the peephole, I flung the door open. And there he was, Peter Brooks, Aria's father and my dad's best friend-slash-partner. His unexpected presence at my doorstep was a shock I couldn't believe.

"I am sorry to barge in without notice, but we need to talk!"

I stepped aside and allowed him in. "Coffee?"

"Thanks." He grabbed a seat at the kitchen island.

"So, did my dad send you?" There was no need to be polite or beat around the bush with Peter. He was like my second father; sometimes he was more of a father than my own could be. Our shared history, intertwined with our families and business, hung heavily in the air.

"No, son. I wanted to talk to you on my own." He cleared his throat. "I know you don't understand the situation, but in order to save our families and our business, we honestly believe this is the only way."

So, if he came to push this on me, that means he wasn't the one who left the envelope.

Interesting.

I slid him his coffee and poured mine next.

"Think about it. It makes sense. You've known each other your whole lives; you are both in line for the CEO positions, so no one will ever question the marriage."

It was a good idea on paper, but in practice, it was far too complicated, given our history.

"Yes, they will, when they see us together and realize how much we despise each other. It's as clear as day, even from the moon," I shot back, my defiance ringing in my voice.

"What happened to you two? You used to be glued to each other, and now we have to sit you on opposite sides of the table at dinner."

It was a question I had been asking myself for the past eight years. The question I hadn't managed to get an answer to. The memory of our past closeness only served to highlight the stark contrast of our current estrangement. I didn't know what was worse, being in the same room with her, or not at all. The thought prompted me to think about all the times the latter had occurred, stirring up a storm of emotions within me.

"She's not coming." My mother appeared beside me as I looked out the window.

"I have no idea what you are talking about!"

Denial, pure denial. No way could I hide the disappointment, not from my mother.

"Don't play dumb with me. She is spending the holidays with Sebastian's family."

Ugh. Sebastian the prick. I hated her boyfriend of two years. My whole family, on the other hand, loved him, as he was the picture-perfect son-in-law. I disagreed with their opinion. He didn't deserve her. No one did. He was tall, but not taller than me; I had a good 6 inches on him, and his stupid blond hair. They looked like twins more than a couple. But I couldn't lie and say that he didn't make her happy, no matter how hard I wished it wasn't true.

"What makes you think that I care? We can't stand each other, remember?"

"Any feeling is better than no feeling. There is not much difference between love and hate, you know?"

She grabbed my shoulder and squeezed it. "I always thought that you two would end up together." She sighed, "She won't share her reasons either!"

"Reasons for what?" I knew what she meant, but still had to say it.

"For you two hating each other," she sighed, "I always ask; she always shuts down."

That sounded about right. Aria did a whole 180 on me without a single warning shot. She'd closed the doors and all the windows, not leaving a single crack.

Powering off the movie of the past, I simply stated, "I know."

"Please talk to her and figure it out. Everything depends on the two of you," Peter said, standing up.

"It's not fair to put that kind of pressure on both of us!" I slammed the countertop, my frustration boiling over. Peter flinched at my outburst. "What you did is unacceptable, but one wrong slip can't overpower everything you did for me. So I will talk to her, and we will figure something out."

"Thank you, son." He pinched my cheek like he always had, and I walked him out.

Right after Peter left, I got dressed and went on my morning run. When I hit the 4-mile mark, I turned back; my head still spinning with all the development. I picked up my pace, disregarding the tingle in my lower back, hoping it would help clear my thoughts.

When I got home, I drank my protein shake and took a shower. The second I stepped out, the doorbell rang. I slipped on my shorts and opened the door, shirtless, thinking it was Pierre with my mail, but I was surprised by the sight of a certain champagne blonde.

"Do you mind?" she scoffed, "not everyone enjoys looking at your skin." She circled her palm between us.

"My dad?"—the reason for her being here.

"Worse, your mom!"

Fuck!

I stepped aside to let another Brooks into my home. Must be the theme of the day. Thank God she had no other siblings. I swallowed my thoughts.

Idiot!

"As much as I hate to admit it, the marriage plan is quite genius."

She looked at my expression and continued, "I know. But if you exclude the fact that we are the sacrificial lambs, we could use this to expand the business." She stepped into my kitchen and opened the first cabinet.

"Second door on the left," I said, pointing my finger in the direction of what she was looking for. She opened the right one and turned on the coffee machine. Facing me, she motioned with a cup. I nodded.

"Would you care to elaborate?" I took a seat at the island across from her while Aria roamed my kitchen and made the coffee.

"I stayed up all night and came up with the whole plan. We use the wedding to get into the hotel business, something John always wanted to add to the portfolio," she pointed out. "I found this place." She unlocked her phone with a quick swoosh and held it out for me, a photo of something called 'The Coral'.

I nodded, and she handed me the first coffee.

Hmm? Interesting.

"This is a high-end resort located in the Seychelles. They have practically no social presence and no marketing."

My eyebrows rose higher.

"Imagine *the* social wedding of the decade, a merging of two of the most powerful families in the Commonwealth. Then, imagine all the free publicity."

I fought off a smile, realizing where this was going.

"We can make up an agreement for the free publicity, invite influencers to help raise their online followers, all that in exchange for a partnership."

Intrigue rose, and despite it being a good idea, it benefited our parents, not me.

"What do I get out of it?"

I knew the look she just gave me; she was waiting for me to ask that question, and I stepped right into it.

She dabbed her phone again, and then she slid the thing over the counter until it reached my waiting hand, revealing a website of The Admiral. It was a well-known casino and resort in Majorca, one I frequented often.

"For the honeymoon." The discomfort in her voice was so loud, I had to swallow a lump in my throat. "We could use it to partner up. I was thinking of a VIP high roller, featuring monthly games with high-level players, exclusive to invited members. I'll leave the concept to you since you always wanted to be in the casino business."

Now, how did she know about that?

"Again, this would be great publicity for them and an easy business transaction."

The wheels in my head started spinning with ideas, but I pushed them aside for now, far too interested in what else she had to say.

Damn, I knew she was smart, but this, this was diabolical. My expression must have given it away because she scoffed, "Oh, don't be so surprised; I do go to business school."

I wasn't surprised; that was the funny thing.

"As for what happens after," she hesitated, taking another sip of her coffee, "we would have a signed contract with demands. For example, what public outings would we attend together, and how would we act? Also, I propose we condole in a truce—in public, of course. Behind closed doors, we would do our own thing and try not to get in each other's way."

Something unsettling roamed in the pit of my stomach, and for the life of me, I couldn't figure out what it was.

"You can list your own rules, demands, whatever you want to call it, and if we can both agree on everything, we'll simply get divorced in exactly one year. That's it."

I almost wanted to stand up and do a slow clap, even

bow with worship at the amazing brain that this woman possessed. Hell, at everything she possessed. Then she straightened her posture, reminding me of who I was staring at, and my blood turned to ice.

Chapter 5

Aria

He has to stop looking at me like that. It's giving me the creeps.

"How about we give each other 24 hours to think of the demands, and we can do the rest via email?" I offered, finishing my coffee to the last drop while trying my best to keep my knees from giving out.

"Is there room for negotiations?" He stood up, and my eyes followed his movement, despite my head not wanting to. I caught a whiff of his scent as he passed by. It was the same spicy aroma he'd had since we were fifteen. I could never quite pinpoint it, but it was a mix of wood and something sweet that blended perfectly.

Curiously, I watched him raid his fridge and had to contain a gasp when he took out a slice of vanilla cake, my favorite. I gritted my teeth, hearing the clanking of silverware behind me.

The ruler of hell sat back down, dug his fork into a delicious piece of art, and, without breaking eye contact, slid a piece into his mouth.

"I can do negotiations," I said, not bothering to acknowledge his smirk. I would not give him the satisfaction.

"Fine," he mumbled with his mouth full. When he swallowed, he deliberately licked his lips. My heart skipped a beat for some reason, reminding me it was time for a check-up.

"Fine," I sassed, trying hard not to snatch the fork from him and stab that stupid grin off his face.

With our parting words, I walked myself out of his penthouse and released a breath I had been holding for the entire time I was inside. As I drove back to my condo, I tried to make sense of everything that had happened in the last 24 hours. But Cillian, looking at me with what seemed to be admiration, was the thought that occupied me the most. The way he'd known what I was looking for when I'd roamed his kitchen, the way he'd always read my mind...

Stop it!

I screamed to the confused version of me and pushed myself out of this gutter, not allowing my mind to digest it any longer. He was not going to ruin my favorite day. I won't let him.

I loved Sundays. Not because there were no classes, but because I could indulge in being a couch potato for one whole day. I liked school way too much, with its intellectual stimulus, but I loved getting lost in the fictional world of TV more.

Excited to enter my Sunday mood, I parked my newest Rolls-Royce Doptail next to my Porsche and turned off the ignition. It was funny, really, how my personal parking lot was bigger than my entire one-bedroom apartment. Hey, I had to spoil myself somehow, and what better way than buying out the whole garage to store all my cars in? Collecting cars was a passion, as was having them custom-foiled in various shades of blue.

Locking my car with a beep-beep, I strode to the elevator as if I were on a runway. The door slid open, and I hummed my way to the third floor. The building was nothing special, but the streets were quiet, and all my neighbors were friendly. I got out of the elevator and walked the small hallway to my door. Each floor had three apartments, and mine was right there in the middle. Unlocking the door, I pushed it open and snapped into action.

With my favorite snacks on my little tray, a glass of Merlot, and a white Kit Kat to top it all off, I got comfortable under my blanket and turned on the big screen. Tonight's screening was the continuation of last weekend's showing of Veronica Mars. I was deep into the third season when my phone dinged, indicating I had an email from the one and only Cillian Allen Wright.

It should not come as a surprise that he addressed his demands so quickly, given his tendency to be an overachiever. With a large portion of anticipation, I unlocked my phone and opened the email.

From: wright.c-w&b@office.com
To: brooks.a-w&b@office.com
Subject: Rider

1. We'll live in my apartment

2. You won't wear my mother's dress, no matter how much she begs you to

3. You are not allowed to entertain the opposite sex in our apartment

4. My room is off-limits

5. No eating together alone—ever

6. No dancing

I couldn't stop my body from reacting to two specific words—SEX, even knowing it was not mentioned in *that* context, and OUR.

I immediately pressed reply.

From: *brooks.a-w&b@office.com*
To: *wright.c-w&b@office.com*
Subject: *RE: Rider*

What is wrong with my apartment?

Another ding, this time a regular text

Hades: *First of all, my apartment is bigger, and second, it has an extra room—unless you are interested in sharing one?*

Me: *Have you already forgotten about your own rule? A little reminder, it's no. 4*

Hades: *Funny. I will even free a parking space for one of your cars*

Me: *Tempting!*

I bit down on my lip, reading the terms one more time before I started typing.

Hades: *Two*

Me: *Three*

Hades: *Fine*

Now, which one of my pets will I pick?

Me: *Fine. I accept your demands. I have only two*
1. No getting caught while fraternizing
2. Every Sunday, I get the ownership of the screening room, which is a nonnegotiable

The three little dots poked my eyes for exactly four minutes, just enough time for me to empty my bag of chips.

Hades: *Is no. 1 for your benefit or mine?*

I reread his text five times. Why was he acting oblivious, as if he didn't know?

Me: *I don't want to get embarrassed and have the words beautiful heiress cheated on by a douchebag plastered on every front page.*

Hades: *You honestly think I would do that?*

I once trusted the old Cillian, my best friend. But that trust had shattered the moment he'd broke it, and I'd be damned if I ever let myself in that position again.

Me: *Your reputation is no secret. I don't care what you do or who you do it with as long as it doesn't blow up in my face.*

Cillian's reputation didn't bother me. I never cared about the pictures of him with flawless supermodels and actresses in the tabloids. Ok, that was a lie. His nickname was NDA for crying out loud. Whenever a new article came out, I felt a small sting inside. I wasn't sure where it was from, but it was definitely noticeable. Looking at the women who were under his arms brought up all the insecurities a girl could gather. Every woman he was involved with fit the same pattern. The shiny dark hair, long legs, double D's, tight dresses, and eyelashes that could blow you away—both literally and figuratively.

Hades: *I accept your terms.*

Me: *Fine!*

Hades: Fine

A beat passed, and then another text pinged. I took a chug of my wine, preparing myself.

Hades: *What's the second of all?*

I honestly forgot the point I tried to make or create earlier. I got back up to the mail, and then remembered the reason I forgot. Two words, both containing three letters.

Me: *I forgot*

Hades: *So do you have a date in mind? For the wedding I mean?*

My stomach coiled at that. We were talking about our wedding, or the possibility of one. I wanted to vomit.

Me: *We are still in negotiations*
Me: *oh, I remembered… the dancing. You might want to scratch that one, since you know our parents are going to push on that, and there is also that thing called 'The First Dance'*

Hades: *Fine, no, 6 is of the table*

Me: *Fine*

Hades: *Fine!*

A second passed, and another text popped up.

Hades: *I have an addendum*

Playing with words, I decided to test a theory. Our earlier interaction got me thinking if his ability to read my mind was still strong, so I let my fingers do all the work.

Me: *I'm reading*

Hades: *Nice! You should move in before the wedding so that it looks more convincing*

The fuck?! Oh, hell NO! That is the worst idea ever.

And as expected, Cillian got what I was putting down. I'd forgotten how easy it was to carry on a conversation with him.

Oh Dionysus, what was I doing? I can't live with him for a whole year.

You hate him, remember? You will kill each other. Or worse…

I was far too young to go to jail.

Me: *Fine*

Hades: *Fine*

Me: *Good night*

Hades: *Look at us, being all civil and shit*

Me: *Don't get used to it. It's only because I'm not looking at your smug face.*

Hades: *Fair enough. Good night, Ice Queen*

I ignored the ping at the nickname and focused on the paused screen. It was ironic, knowing what was about to happen. Veronica would soon say her famous words: "I hope we're still friends after I taser you."

What the hell had I gotten myself into?

Chapter 6

Cillian

It had been 5 minutes since she last texted, and what had I been doing in that time? Scrolling through the entire conversation over and over. It was our first decent interaction in the past eight years, a glimpse of the old Aria, the one I could actually stand—the one I used to like.

Bringing up my reputation hurt more than I wanted to show. But the real pain was her belief that I would risk hers. That felt like a knife in the gut. Despite our differences and the feud we were having, she was still family, and I would never hurt my family.

The image of her getting all flustered when I'd taunted her with her favorite cake snuck up without a warning shot. Aria's weakness (not counting her nut allergy) was anything sweet, but mostly vanilla cake. I couldn't help but tease her with it. And the satisfaction I'd felt when her death glare pierced through me—fuck. I had the biggest grin on my face.

Turning our situation into a business opportunity was brilliant. It was no surprise, as she was always the smartest person in the room. She already knew everything there was to know about business, and it didn't stop her from attending business school. Now she was just a couple of months away from a freaking master's degree. We had a clause in our trust fund that required us to attend college to receive half of it, but she could've chosen something easier, as I did. I'd picked the one with the best basketball team and the most leniency for student-athletes.

My college life at Duke hadn't lasted long, though. It all came crashing down when my brother ended up in jail for punching some guy in the face, putting him in a coma in the process, forcing me to take his place as the next Wright on top.

Mario was the oldest of the three of us, and our father had been preparing him to take his place since he was old enough to sit at his desk. The pressure had all been on him, and he liked it that way. He was meant to fill our father's shoes, and I? I couldn't even fill his socks.

The day I got the call about Mario's arrest was our last game of the season. It wasn't just any game; it was the championship game. Scouts from all over the country were there to see me. Our team had been undefeated throughout the season, and my game was on fire. Every ball I'd pointed at the basket flew in like a breath to a lung. And then, in the last quarter, everything turned around. I couldn't keep the ball in my hands if it were glued to it. We'd lost by 2 points, and my whole world had shattered.

After the game, my father informed me that Mario could no longer be the CEO and that it was my responsibility to take his place. I'd never wanted to be a corporate man, but I would do anything for my father. My only condition was that he let me enlist until it was time to take his place. I'd dropped out of college, moved back home, and replaced my basketball jersey with a marine uniform. Peter had pulled some strings to get me into the Boston base, but the rest was all my doing.

I was good, fuck that, I was great at orchestrating it all. I always had a knack for strategy, and it was the main reason I rose to lieutenant so fast. It usually took people years, and I managed it in less than two. The memory of the day I got the promotion flashed by.

"What the hell are you doing here?" we both yelled over each other when I stepped into my parents' living room. She was sitting on the floor, playing with my niblings, all smiles and giggles.

"This is my house," I pointed out.

"You don't live here anymore," she rebutted with a scoff.

Point Aria.

"And you never did, so I'll ask you again—what are you doing here?"

I came here to celebrate with my family, only for my mood to shift. Another great day ruined. I tucked my newest epaulet back into my jeans pocket.

Her face turned red, and I swear I could see the steam coming from her ears.

"Not that it's any of your business, but I had a bad day and needed my fix." She pointed at the two kids looking at her, all lovey-dovey. I wasn't a jealous person, but the fact that my sister's kids loved Aria more than they did me stung.

What happened?

The words almost slipped out, but thankfully, my brain remembered that I didn't care.

"Where's Mom?" I pointed the question at my sister, who was resting on the couch, feet propped on the table.

"In the kitchen," she answered with one cocked eyebrow. "What? No kiss?"

Chuckling, I dropped my head and kissed my sister on her cheek, then got on the floor and hugged Lana and Karl. Aria's presence consumed me so thoroughly that I forgot how to be an uncle.

I blinked, anger consuming me at the recollection. That day was supposed to be one to remember. My hard work earned me recognition and a reward. All I wanted was to share it with my family. I wanted to make them proud. I was a great commander. I knew how to build a team, play to their strengths, and hide their weaknesses. It wasn't lost on me that I was never able to mask my own. I only had one, though, and it was Aria. She had the power to ruin my day with one breath.

I went to bed mulling it over…calling a one-year truce, the marriage, living under the same roof, and the possibility of her killing me in my sleep. Hell, she would do it while I was wide awake.

Hell! I don't think I can do this.

Chapter 7

Aria

"So you're telling me that you're gonna marry that hot ass of a man we saw on that yacht a year ago?" Nala glared at me, and I completely forgot about that little encounter.

"Unfortunately," I deadpanned.

"I don't see a problem there. Just add to the contract that he must walk around shirtless," she mused, "problem solved."

"I will do no such thing. What is the matter with you? I am literally shaking here," I whisper-shouted. We were in our favorite little bistro across campus, and my nerves were working overtime.

The deadline to sign our contract was exactly thirty minutes away, and I was supposed to meet Cillian here to go over it. Before I could sign it, I had to come clean to Nala. So far, it wasn't going well, and all because my best friend had hearts in her eyes.

"Oh, boohoo, poor you! You get to have an extravagant wedding and live with a living, breathing sculpture. Sorry if I'm not joining the pity party."

My best friend, ladies and gentlemen.

"You are supposed to be on my side here," I pointed out, adding a pout. I took a sip of my coffee, glaring at her.

"I am on your side," she noted, "and I know how this thing will end."

"And how is that?"

Why the hell did I even ask?

Don't say it! Don't say it! Don't say it!

"With you two in love by the end of the year."

She said it. And now it was out in the universe. Damn my mouth for bringing any of it up.

"Are you fucking kidding me?" I shirked.

She kept her composure; I had to hand it to her.

"No. It's inevitable."

"I hate you," I frowned. Those thoughts were not going to get to me.

"You love me, and you know it."

Much to my dismay, she wasn't wrong. I loved the woman far too much, and that was the only reason why I restrained myself from punching her in the gut.

"Debatable," I retorted.

She gathered her stuff and stood to leave, giving me a pointed look. "You've got this."

No, I don't!

She crunched down, kissing me on the cheek. Crossing my arms over my chest, I overdid my pout.

"Oh, don't give me that. You know I have to go, and you don't need a buffer. You're a tough cookie. Make him sweat."

I was more than a tough cookie; I was a straight-ass bitch in a power suit.

"Now that I can do."

With a gleam, she waved goodbye and left me alone with my thoughts.

My stupid leg kept jumping up and down, and the fourth coffee I just ingested didn't help one bit.

The sleepless night had been spent putting together this contract, one that would save my sanity. It was ironclad, and Sabrina would've been so proud. My BFF was a law student, so naturally, I'd picked up a few things. Not to mention, spending all my free time at our family company got me fluent in most legal aspects of running a business. And that's what this was, a simple business transaction.

I felt him before I saw him close in, and my leg froze, fuck, my whole body froze. He was wearing jeans and a green t-shirt with some words splattered on it.

"Hades!"

"Ice queen," he said back, sliding down into the chair across from me.

He represented my personal hell, so his nickname made sense to both of us, but the one he gave me stung a lot more than I let on. Getting comfortable in his chair, he ordered us both a cup of coffee while he smiled at the waitress.

There it was, another slight ping inside, somewhere.

"So?"

"So?"

Awkward smiles were plastered on our faces as we just kept looking at each other. I broke the locked stare and pulled out the contract. It listed all the demands and the rules governing our public outing, etc. This contract was our attempt to set boundaries and navigate our complicated relationship. He skimmed through it and extended his hand. I gave him my pen, and he signed it.

Just like that.

He turned the paper over to me with the pen on top; I took it and signed it.

Just like that.

"Nice doing business with you!" I reached for a handshake; he smiled, grabbed my hand, and motioned up and down to seal it. Something sparked at the contact, moving from my palm down to my toes.

"Right back at ya!"

Crickets could be heard during the two minutes of dead silence and eye contact avoidance.

"So, I had the guest bedroom prepared for you to invade whenever you want."

He did what?

Oh, right, we were going to live together.

There went the legwork again. When I stayed mute, he quipped, "What, you don't want to move in before Sunday?"

I tilted my head, narrowing my eyes.

"For the screening room?" he clarified, and I blinked.

"Right…" I swallowed. "Does Saturday work for you?"

"Don't care. And don't expect me to help you with anything."

"Wouldn't dream of it," I bit back.

An awkward silence made me bite my cheek. Then he turned all serious, "Here, I already talked to Pierre. He knows you will be coming, and he can help you with anything you need. The same key card opens the garage; you have three spaces reserved."

It was all too weird. His words sounded harsh, but his tone was the complete opposite. My other leg joined my anxiety, but a simple act of him standing up froze them both in an instant.

"I gotta go. I'll see you when I see you."

And puff, he was gone before I even had the chance to say goodbye.

The waitress set a plate of white profiteroles in front of me, and I looked up at her with an apologetic smile. "Sorry, I didn't order this."

"The gentleman who was with you did. Enjoy!" she exclaimed, and I thanked her, or at least I thought I did. I was too hypnotized by the white chocolate slowly dripping over the balls of pastries that my future husband had ordered for me.

This isn't going to end well.

I was way over my head with all kinds of scenarios, none of the good kind. My mind spiraled with the thoughts of sharing a space with the one person that had the power to hurt me, or at least hurt me more than he already had - the same person that knew me better than anybody on the entire planet. Our past was filled with love, betrayal, and heartbreak, and it was hard to forget. Playing with my mother's tennis bracelet, I fought away the tears.

"Don't go there."

"How do you do that?"

"I can read your mind, and you know it. It's my one superpower," he said matter-of-factly.

"What's mine?"

"Your heart, Aria, your heart is your superpower."

Sitting outside the room where my mother prepared herself for her last breaths, I allowed my mind to shut down the thoughts of a life without her. Feeling safe with his arm wrapped around me, I knew I would not be alone during the upcoming grief I was bound to face. That notion itself gave me all the hope and strength needed to get through it all. Cillian had always been there for me, and I knew he always would.

"Don't let go, ok?" I squeezed his hand.

"Never," he said so assertively that my heart fluttered.

I wiped away the tears and the memory. That ten-year-old girl prepared for the loss of her mother. She had no idea she would soon face another loss, one that would change her forever. She had an entirely different future planned out, one that, to her dismay, never happened. That girl was lucky and would be for the next six years.

Chapter 8

Aria

Early Saturday morning, I'd called reinforcements on my quest to pack up my life for my move to Hell.

"What about this?"

Sab and I were practicing the Marie Kondo method of closet cleansing, a technique we had both read about and found intriguing. It was all about keeping only the things that truly sparked joy and getting rid of the rest. We thought it was a good way to start my new life at Cillian's penthouse. This whole week, I had been dreading this day, and it was safe to say I was doomed. If my lack of sleep thinking over us living together were any indication of what awaited me, I was in for some severe sleep deprivation.

"Does this spark your joy?"

Sabrina, or Sab for her loved ones, held up a simple black dress with long sleeves that I had never worn, and I saw the look in her eyes—it sparked joy...for her.

"You can take it."

You'd think that someone who grew up having everything would have trouble converting to a simple life, but not Sabrina—she thrived in it.

Last year, her life had turned upside down. She'd been on top of the world, a model, heiress to her family's fashion empire, up until she'd walked away from her fortune. The reason: love and revenge. She'd uncovered her corrupt judge father's secrets to the world, forcing him to face justice, but not before her family disowned her for falling in love with someone outside our social circles. Despite it all, she had never been happier, and Mateo, her now-husband, was the reason for that.

"Thank you, you're the best!"

"You damn right I am," I wisecracked.

Two hours later, I was packed. All the items that sparked joy were now neatly folded into one large suitcase, while the rest were left for my BFF to use. One positive aspect of this ordeal was that I was able to offer Sabrina and Mateo my place for the duration of my new living arrangement. At the moment, the two of them were living in The Port, with Mateo's mother and three brothers. And to say that she was ecstatic to have a place of their own would be an understatement. By the time the charade of the marriage would be concluded, Sabrina and Mateo would have completed college, secured jobs, and could afford a place for themselves.

I eyed my suitcase and frowned.

The irony was not lost on me that my whole life fit in one large travel bag. Well, that plus a smaller one containing my shoes. This girl couldn't live without her collection. The hardest part of this whole move was deciding which three cars to take with me. Sabrina came up with the idea of drawing keys from a hat. The hat was a box since no hat could fit them all. The fates had spoken, and it came down to my Aston Martin, the Bentley, and my Rolls-Royce.

"Here's to you! To make it a whole year without ending up in prison!" Sab raised her wine.

"Hear! Hear!"

A second later, both our glasses were empty.

When I arrived at The Imperial, I was greeted by Pierre, who helped me with my suitcase and rode the elevator with me up to Cillian's penthouse.

"Is Mr. Wright home?"

"No, he stepped outside about an hour ago," the old man answered in a French accent.

Thank Dionysus.

I took out my key and froze.

This was starting to get all too real.

With a smile, Pierre took the key from my hand and unlocked the door, slowly pushing it open. I still couldn't move. Stepping over that threshold meant no going back.

You already signed the contract; there is no going back.

Taking a step forward, I sighed. I fully expected to get burned or something, but the only flames brewing were in the pit of my stomach.

"If you need anything, there is a phone on the wall next to the door that is directly connected to my desk, so please don't hesitate to use it."

I took a moment to look at Pierre, who probably knew more about the man I was moving in with than I ever could. He was middle-aged, maybe in his mid-forties, and coincidentally resembled Jean Reno. However, he was extremely kind for a Frenchman, and his kindness was greatly appreciated.

"Thank you for your help," I said with a shy smile.

"You are most welcome, Miss Brooks."

The second he closed the door behind me, leaving me alone, my gut started working overtime. I forgot how amazing Cillian's place was, and it had been featured in a lifestyle magazine last year. The entire penthouse was surrounded by glass windows, offering a view that overlooked the entire city. A view to die for, where you could see every part of Boston, including the water. The furniture included a large black leather couch facing a fireplace. Above the fireplace was a TV. An elliptical glass coffee table sat in front, with two gray lounge footstools on each side. An all-black bar was in the corner, with all the best liquor hanging from the well rail.

A tall partition wall with an aquarium in the center divided the living room and dining room. A round glass table sat in the middle, surrounded by simple black stools. Another partition wall, this one a bit wider, purposely served to hide the kitchen. It was all white, with a black countertop, and two sets of black leather bar stools accompanied the island table across it.

All the walls were covered with art, and it immediately reminded me of Nala. She loved art and aspired to open her own gallery someday. She would love this place.

According to Hades' text he'd sent me this morning, my room was across the hall from the living room, and that was the direction I was headed.

It was a simple guest room, nothing special, but it did have a king-sized bed, a walk-in closet, and a private bathroom. I tossed my suitcase on the bed, unzipped it, and opened it with a flop.

But first things first—music.

I loved music and everything that came with it. I loved how a single note in a song could change a whole mood, how it could transport you to a specific place and time. I loved how I could easily lose myself in a heartbeat.

I hit play, Griff's 'Vertigo' fading in as I started personalizing the space. A picture of my family on the nightstand, my favorite DVDs on the shelf above the bed, and my stuffed animals arranged around them. I conquered the bathroom next, stacking all my makeup and feminine hygiene products neatly in the mirror cabinet.

I left the closet for last because I took my closet organizing very, very seriously. The process took about one hour and one bottle of Merlot. So far, we've gathered that I was a sucker for cars, sweets, and music, but right there with all that was my love for wine. We'd go to Martha's Vineyard every year to try all kinds of varieties. I had the ability to smell each aroma, feel the sweetness with my tongue, and pinpoint the region of origin with one sip. When it came to drinking at home, I wasn't particularly picky about the quality, as long as the bottle had a label that said 'Merlot'. But I did love a good Château Margaux, my favorite. It wasn't the most expensive one or the best, according to some people, but it perfectly stimulated my palate. Wine was not just a drink for me; it was an experience, a journey through different flavors and regions.

Giving my work one last once-over, I hummed in approval and slumped on the bed. The mattress was the perfect type of soft meets firm. And the sheets... Oof, like I was wrapped in cotton candy. Buzzed, I stared at the ceiling, the same ceiling I would be looking at for the following year.

Something heavy pressed down on my chest, a sensation I was unfamiliar with, when a knock sounded at the door.

Chapter 9

Cillian

Pierre informed me that Aria had arrived two hours ago. I rode the elevator up with a large knot in my throat. With dread, I stared at the increasing numbers on the dash, each one drawing me closer to my personal hell. When I opened the door, her scent immediately flared through my nostrils.

Great, two hours and the air was already invaded. I would need to get the place fumigated after the charade.

It was around 9 pm, and I was tired of steering clear of my own penthouse. She'd never specified the time of her hostile takeover, just the day, so I'd done everything I could to avoid being here when she eventually decided to show up. Marco had poked at me, saying I was a coward; truth be told, he wasn't far off the mark. Despite having an entire week to prepare, it wasn't nearly enough. My mindset was far from ready for any of it.

Careful not to make any noise, I strode to my bedroom, but my feet went in the opposite direction. Faded music sounded from her room, growing louder with each step. I froze in front of her door.

What the fuck am I doing?

My hand rose of its own accord and knocked on the wood. It swung open, revealing Aria as I had never seen her before. A long, oversized shirt fell down her body, barely covering her knees, with a messy bun on top of her head. No makeup. Signature death stare.

"I wanted to let you know I'm home and to say welcome." I turned on my heel to walk away, but was stopped by her soft voice.

"Uhm. Sorry, I took one of your wine bottles from the bar. We never discussed my, uhm," a beat of hesitation, "limitations." I faced her; she gaped at me, clearing her throat, "I forgot to bring one and desperately needed a glass. I'll replace it first thing in the morning."

I pinched the bridge of my nose and turned back around. "I have a housekeeper, Meg. She comes three times a week to clean, cook, and do the groceries. There's a list on the fridge. If you need something, write it down, and she will get it for you."

"Oh, ok." She sounded disappointed.

You don't care.

"What?" I huffed.

"I like doing my own shopping."

Of course you do.

"Do whatever you want, Aria, as long as you stay clear of my room."

"You got a body hidden in there or something?"

Or something.

"That is none of your business. So as long as you stay clear, we will have no problems!"

"Noted." There was a bite to her tone, and despite her messy appearance, she still exuded power.

"I'll be in the gym; don't let the weights' crushing noise

scare you."

"There is a gym here?"

Right, she hasn't seen the whole place.

Reluctantly, I sighed, "Come on, I'll give you the tour."

"You don't have to; I can explore it when you go to work on Monday."

Somehow, that thought unsettled me; I didn't want her to snoop or explore anything. This was my space.

Except now it was ours.

Ours? Fuck, I'll have to get used to that.

"This is my only offer. If you want to take it, follow me."

With a single nod, she stepped forward.

I showed her the gym, the sauna, the storage room, and we stopped at the screening room. Her eyes lit up like it was Christmas morning.

She started biting her inner cheek, a habit she often had when thinking something over.

"I know I demanded Sundays, but could I maybe invade it now?"

I didn't miss the little wordplay, even if it came out all playful and innocent.

"Whatever, I never use it anyway," I said matter-of-factly.

"Why not?" she shrieked, like I somehow offended her. "You know what, it doesn't matter. Do you have any snacks?"

Rolling my eyes, I waved my hand for her to follow me. The kitchen had a hidden door at the far end next to the oven, and I clicked it open. Her jaw dropped at the sight of my stocked pantry.

"What the fuck is this? You have a whole store in here! And all the good stuff too, color me impressed!" she exclaimed.

"I didn't know that all it took to impress the Ice Queen was a room full of junk food."

She didn't react to the ice queen mark.

I must be losing my touch.

"Funny. Luckily, I can't hear you from all the chunkiness I will devour."

She started grabbing everything, but not before checking the ingredients. Aria had a deadly nut allergy and was rightfully cautious regarding what she ate. While she was busy double-checking, I went to the hidden wine room and took out a bottle of red. When I got back, I found her scanning the upper shelf, her hands overloaded.

Her tiny, delicate hands.

Without thinking, I grabbed a corkscrew and popped the bottle open. The sound startled her, causing her arsenal to drop to the floor.

"Shit. Sorry," she mumbled.

Why the hell was she apologizing?

I let out a groan and helped her carry the insane amount of snacks into the screening room. She grabbed a seat, and I set all the stuff down on the bar cart in the corner before I rolled it to her feet. Eyeing the junk load, I wondered, "You expecting company?"

She gawked at me. "Sorry to disappoint, but I intend to stuff all of this by myself."

The rest was muttered, but I heard every single word. "With all those models you hang around with, you probably have never seen a woman eat anything other than a salad."

She had me there. And for some reason, the words

stung.

Before exiting the room, I switched off the lights and closed the door, leaving her in pitch black. In the kitchen, I poured the wine down the drain and tossed the bottle in the garbage. Footsteps heavy, I stomped to the gym, hoping the weights would get rid of the tension.

Aria

My loud, frustrated growl echoed in the darkness. I wasn't afraid of the dark by any means, but that didn't mean I would restrain myself from killing him for leaving me in it.

Just as I thought Cillian had a nice bone in his body when he'd helped me with all the stuff, he went and showed the only color of his I was familiar with—black.

I grabbed my phone to turn on the flashlight, which helped me find the remote control in the wall holder. I turned the screen on, and I immediately regretted it. Releasing a breath, I dragged my feet until I reached the gym door, hearing clanking sounds.

I knocked—no answer.

I banged—no answer.

Swallowing hard, I took another deep breath and opened the door. I found Cillian working out on the lat machine. Thank Dionysus, he was wearing a shirt. He flinched when I got in front of him. That was a first. He pulled his head up and took out one earplug.

"I'm sorry, I knocked. Is it okay for me to log you out of Hulu so I can sign in with my account?"

"I already told you to do whatever you want. And... new rule, don't bother me, ever!"

Fucking prick.

"My mistake." I bowed my head and turned on my heel.

Guess the nice Cillian from before was gone. I much preferred to hate this version of him. Before hitting the screening room, I went to the kitchen to get something to drink when a familiar scent hit me. I sniffed harder, following its intensity to the sink. There were remnants of reddened liquid, and I would know that smell anywhere—Château Margaux. Pinching my eyebrows together while simultaneously working on a hunch, I walked to the trash can. When I opened it, sure enough, an empty bottle of my favorite wine was staring right at me.

What the actual fuck?

The popping sound... that must have been him opening the bottle. Where did it come from? It wasn't in the bar when I ransacked it earlier. And why did he waste it down the drain?

Puzzled, I walked into the dark, slummed in the most comfortable seat imaginable, and signed into my account. Resuming where I had left off last weekend, around the time Veronica was taking the PI exam, I clicked ok.

Movies and shows with puns were my favorite. Those types of characters, like Buffy, Sabrina, and Veronica, were my whole vibe.

I watched the rest of the season in one sitting, then

decided to retreat to my room. I cleaned everything up, threw the trash away, and opened the door. Relieved when I didn't hear any clanking noises, which meant my path to my room was clear, I tiptoed through the hall.

In the safety of my room, I brushed my teeth and got under the covers.

My first night in someone else's bed since Sebastian and I broke up.

Damn it.

It was the first time I thought about him in a while.

"What do you mean you can't do this?" I started hyperventilating.

"I can't, Aria. I can't live like this. This is your third scare in the last six months."

The coward couldn't even look at me.

"You knew the risks. I explained everything at the very beginning, and you said you could handle it." My heart slowly started to crack with each word.

"I know you did, but I didn't realize it would be this hard."

"You know what's funny? The fact that it could all have been prevented with one snip… one snip I didn't undergo because of you."

Sebastian finally looked at me, anger on display.

"Don't you dare put that on me," he snapped, nostrils flaring.

"Oh, I'm sorry, is the truth hitting you where it hurts?"

"Fuck you and your sarcasm right now. This is serious!"

"No shit. I thought we were doing stand-up comedy," I snarked, crossing my arms over my chest in an attempt to

keep myself at bay.

"You know what, I'm done with this. I'm done with you."

"Fine, you have until 3 pm tomorrow to get all your shit, or it goes up in flames."

The door slammed shut, and I broke down into pieces, adding another loss to the mix.

The memories served like caffeine, keeping me awake as I spent the night replaying them over and over.

Chapter 10

Cillian

I'd barely slept last night, knowing I had an imposter so close. If I weren't so damn hungry, I would've stayed locked up in my room the entire day. I sucked it up and went to the kitchen to make myself a coffee. Noticing a washed mug beside the sink, indicating Aria already had hers and was probably out and about, I sighed with relief.

Thank fuck!

I made a quick sandwich and ate it with my coffee before I went for a run. It was a frisky morning, with an added breeze that gave my back a bit of a push. I always took the same route when running, one by the water. Something about following the current calmed me and kept my breathing steady. Hitting the 2.5-mile mark, I turned and ran back along the same path. My watch beeped when I reached my building, and I noticed my BPM returned to normal quickly as my breathing steadied.

Having played sports my entire life, not to mention my hard Marine training, I was well above average in condition despite my injury. And even with the pain shooting down my back, I couldn't... wouldn't stop running.

Passing by Martin with a nod, I picked up my mail and took the stairs to my penthouse, prolonging the inevitable.

Martin was the other concierge, too old to be working if all the times I caught him snoring behind the front desk were any indication.

One cold shower later, I slumped on the couch and turned on my PS to play some Assassin's Creed when my phone rang. The display showed 'MOM,' and I answered with a sigh.

"Sweetheart, just wanted to remind you that it's Mr. Davenport's birthday tonight."

As if I needed a reminder. It was in the contract Aria drew up—our 'coming out' party.

Mr. Davenport, or Tom to those he deemed worthy, was a member of the board of directors and a close enough friend to make his birthday a significant occasion. I had to kiss everyone's ass after my brother had screwed everything up. The entire board had opposed my stepping in, doubting my knowledge of the business. They didn't expect me to be a fast learner.

I wasn't the biggest fan of the corporate parties, but they served top-of-the-shelf whiskey, so at least there was that. However, no amount of alcohol would be enough to get me through tonight.

"See you there, mother," I drawled, knowing damn well that pouting wouldn't solve anything.

"Good boy."

I hung up and opened my message thread with the Ice Queen. I was about to hit send when the front door swooshed open, revealing Aria with two sets of garment covers.

She handed me the black one. "Loren sent me your measurements. I thought I would save you the trouble."

"You rubbed it with poison ivy or something?"

"Damn, why didn't I think of that?" She snapped her fingers with a tsk.

Shaking my head, I unpaused my game and went about ignoring my new roommate. She disappeared without another word, and I heard her bedroom door close more forcefully than necessary.

Not even a minute had passed before she tiptoed back into the living room. With my eyes fixed on the screen, I grumbled, "What?"

"You mentioned a Meg, and her making lunch..." she trailed off.

"Yeees?" I dragged.

"Am I also privy to the said lunch?"

"Yes, she's aware that she'll be cooking for two from now on and doing your laundry, changing your sheets, and cleaning your room."

"Oh, that's not necessary; I can do my own laundry, as well as the cleaning."

I paused the game, turning to face her with a cocked brow.

"What? I've been living alone for three years now."

Not entirely true.

"So?"

"I didn't have a housekeeper, Hades. You know damn well we never had one growing up, not even after Mom..." her mouth quivered, but she quickly pulled it into a straight line.

"You can work it out with Meg. She's free on weekends. I've ordered lunch already."

She swallowed. Blinked. Swallowed again. Hovering.

I cleared my throat. "I doubled the order."

"Oh." A long pause, followed by the well-known "Fine."

"Fine."

I got back into the game, but I turned it off when I heard her door slam. My concentration was nowhere to be found.

Gym it is.

I thought to myself and beelined to my indoor setup. My personal gym was small, but it had everything I needed, including a punching bag I desperately needed to hit. I wasn't a violent man, but the built-up tension mixed with anger had to be released somehow. I did a quick workout, focusing more on knee stabilization before wrapping my knuckles in tape. The second I released the first punch, I felt lighter. And the more I hit, the more relaxed I got. By the time I finished, there were a couple of broken stitches at the seam. I'd just gotten it last month. A new one was imminent at this rate—thanks to Aria.

Releasing a grunt, I swiped a towel over my face, letting it soak in my sweat, and walked into the sauna. The steam opened my pores, allowing my body to release its toxins. I only wished it could do some magic to rid me of a certain blonde one.

The timer beeped, and I stepped out of the wooden cabin and paced until my body adjusted its temperature before I took another shower.

All, clean and dry, I pulled on my sweatpants, hearing the intercom buzz. I jogged to my front door and picked up the headset.

"Sir, your delivery is here."

"Thank you, Martin; let them through."

Swinging the door open, I leaned on the frame and waited for the Uber Eats guy. The elevator dinged, and I watched a young Asian-looking girl close in. She handed me two bags, and I gave her a nice tip with a smile. She returned one of her own and waved goodbye.

Hands full, I closed the door with my foot and placed the bags on the island. Breathing in the smell, my mouth watered when I opened all the containers. While I stretched my hand to grab a plate from my upper cabinet, Aria's door creaked, and I heard her soft footsteps approaching.

"Almighty Greek god, I'm starving. It smells amazing." Her soft voice never ceased to make me cringe. Ignoring her, I walked around the counter and took out one fork and one knife.

She scoffed. A rebuttal was coming, but she stopped her train of thought when her eyes landed on the food. "Is this Pad Thai?! That looks good."

I nodded, and her face turned gentle all of a sudden. "Thanks. It's my favorite."

Yeah, I know.

She then double-checked the food, and I let out a sigh.

"No peanuts; I made sure. I'll leave you to it."

Despite her belief, I wasn't a complete monster. Noting her surprised expression, I grabbed my food and backed away. No way in hell would I be eating with her. Guess my bed was now my dining table.

"Thank you for the suit," I slipped. Damn my good manners.

"Don't get used to it!"

"Wasn't planning on it!"

"Good!"

"Good!"

"Fine!"

"Fine!"

Forced out of my own kitchen.

"Unbelievable," I mumbled to myself.

With that, I slammed the door behind me shut.

Chapter 11

Cillian

With my shirt still unbuttoned, my tie hanging around my neck, I stepped out of my room with only my suit pants fastened. Barefoot, my feet made soft thuds on my way to the bar. I had it custom-made; it was small, but had everything I needed, down to the ice machine that produced the perfect cubes. I poured some of my second-favorite whiskey and twirled the tumbler in my hand. Behind me, I heard footsteps, and when I turned, a vision of Aria appeared. She was wearing a tight, long red dress that accentuated every curve of her body.

With her feet also bare, she wiggled toward the hall, all the while putting an earring in her ear. Her hair swung with the movement, and I couldn't remember the last time I'd seen it loose. Honestly, Aria was the most beautiful woman I'd ever seen. Her hair, free from the tight bun she paraded around with, made her even more stunning. Not that I would ever admit it out loud, especially not to her. I was a man after all, with eyes and perfect vision, but I also had common sense and a gut that hated everything about her.

The Ice Queen hadn't even noticed me, apparently searching for something.

"Cillian?" She yelled out for me, and my name sounding

from those lips got me to tighten my grip around the glass.

"At the bar," I echoed back, making her stop in her tracks.

"Oh, didn't see you there. Could you help me with the zipper? It's stuck, and I can't seem to shake it."

Not waiting for an answer, she positioned herself in front of me, pulling her long hair forward over her shoulder to give me access. Her bare back was exposed; fair, light, flawless skin. I lifted my hand, noting the contrast—light and dark; day and night. I swallowed at the sight of one birthmark placed above her gluteal cleft. She moved an inch, causing her shoulder blades to pop out, and I quickly covered it all with the red silk, making sure my annoyed grunt was loud and clear. I could feel her eye roll, but she managed to whisper a "Thank you" before she sashayed away.

I returned to my whiskey, sending the burn down my throat until there was no drop left in my tumbler. Pouring another one, I worked on my buttons and then finished tying the leash around my neck.

Another glass of liquid courage later, and I was all ready for fake smiles and salutations when Aria stepped out again, her hair up in a tight bun and high heels that made her legs look longer. She had very little makeup, but her lips were covered in devil-red lipstick that would make any other man fall to his knees. Her eyes, ever so obvious, traced my entire height, and I didn't even bother to hide my smirk.

"You ready?" Her eyes met mine, and I shrugged.

"Ready as I'll ever be!"

Both of us knew we needed alcohol to get through the night, so we took the town car. I didn't bother opening the door for her, but the driver stepped up. She slid inside, and I followed, the tie around my neck tightening.

"I have something to ask?" She sat at the far left side of the seat, turning to face me. "I was thinking about September 21st."

I sighed out a breath at the date; it was my parents' anniversary.

"I understand completely if you don't like the idea. I thought that it would be nice if we switched the charade to them celebrating their accomplishment; I mean, 35 years is a big deal."

It was a nice sentiment. But I didn't want to tarnish their day.

"I'll think about it," was all I could say.

The car pulled out of the driveway and turned onto the busy street. The sun set, and it grew dark; the city's lights replaced its rays.

I pulled a small box out of my pocket and slid it across the leather seat to her.

"What's this?" She looked up at me, not bothering to take it.

"We can't announce anything with your ring bare."

She looked down at her hand and snorted a laugh. I cocked a brow.

"Sorry, my mind went somewhere."

I knew exactly where her mind had gone, and I hated every second of it.

"Barney and Robin?"

There was a scene in a show where an engaged couple fought over the pronunciation of the word 'ring bearer/bear'.

"Smart ass!"

"I'll take that as a compliment," I retorted.

"You always do."

With a loud sigh, she opened the box, and then her mouth fell open.

"Wow."

She stared at the ring without blinking, then shook her head, closing the lid with a snap.

"You didn't have to do this. I could've switched one of my rings to the finger. As much as it is wow, just wow!" she exclaimed.

I had managed to stun Aria once again. Something was clearly cooking down in hell.

She handed me back the box, but I waved my hand.

"It was no big deal; I went to a store, pointed my finger, took out my AMEX, and they wrapped it."

It was an 18K white gold ring with a distinctive oval-cut aquamarine diamond, surrounded by a halo of smaller sparkling diamonds; or at least that was what the woman behind the counter had told me.

"Well, your finger sure knows how to pick them!"

She pulled the ring out of the box and slid it onto her finger by herself; the fit perfect. Maybe I should've offered to do it for her, but it was better this way.

"I think the 21st is a great idea."

She nodded and continued to look out the window for the rest of the drive.

We arrived at the Mirage in time to be greeted by my parents.

"Honey, you look beautiful as ever," my mother said, stepping out and hugging Aria first.

The traitor.

"Thank you, but look at you…" Aria gave my mother an appraisal, "You look gorgeous." She spoke the truth. My mother was a vision in a sapphire dress that effortlessly fell to the floor.

"Oh my god! Look at that!" My mother grabbed Aria's hand and examined the finger. "It suits you perfectly."

"It was my thought exactly." Aria pulled out a smile, and they headed inside, hand in hand.

My father pulled me in for a handshake. "Thank you, son; you have no idea how much I appreciate it."

"Oh, I will find a way for you to show your appreciation, with interest." We laughed it off and went inside, where Peter was waiting for us at our table. I opened my arms, and we both emerged into the half-hug, half-shoulder-slap embrace. He topped it off with a gentle smack of his palm on my cheek, trying to appear intimidating, but failing. The guy had a heart of gold and almost never raised his voice at any of us.

After half an hour of ass-kissing, I finally stepped to the bar, placing my elbows on the cold surface.

"Old Rip?" the barmaid asked, remembering my go-to. I was about to nod, but stopped myself before confirming.

"Old Forester, 1910," I said instead. She cocked a brow, surprised; albeit, she made good on my order. Tumbler in hand, I slowly savored the aroma, vanilla taking over. The red-haired woman pouring the drinks kept eyeing me, but the honey-colored liquid in my hold transfixed me. I turned away and scanned the room, stopping when a familiar laugh hit my ears. My head snapped toward where Aria was talking to one of the board members; I forgot his name, but he was younger than the rest, maybe just a couple of years older than us.

I gripped the glass that was on the verge of breaking when the barmaid tapped my shoulder. I turned around, and she handed me a piece of paper. "I get off at 11," she whispered with a wink. I crumpled the paper in front of her and made my way back to the table. Before I took my seat, my mother's hand stopped me.

"You can't spend the entire night on opposite sides of the room. Go dance with her. People need to see that you two are together."

Releasing an aggravated breath, I bobbed my head and made my way toward the future ball and chain. She was still talking to the same guy, so I plastered on my best smile and cleared my throat.

"I'm sorry to bother you. May I steal my fiancée for a second?"

The surprised expression on Aria's face at my offered hand felt like a reward. The guy nodded, and she placed her hand in mine before I guided us to the middle of the dance floor.

"What are you doing?" she gaped at me, her hand trembling in mine. I was making her nervous. Good.

"My mother ordered me to dance with you."

"You could've waited; you didn't have to drag me away from a conversation?"

"A drop-dead boring conversation, by the looks of it."

"Well, you couldn't be more wrong," she turned all business. "We were talking about the contracts for everything. He is our legal director," she pointed out, then cocked a brow. "You should have known that. Or is it your male ego, the testosterone that doesn't allow you men to share?"

"Don't get full of yourself. I don't care who you talk to, but we do need to start acting like we're together if we want this whole thing to work," I deadpanned.

She sighed, "Fine."

"Fine."

We both noticed that every eye in the room was pointed at us, and it wasn't because of the discussion. It was because we were dancing—her arms around my neck, mine around her waist, full on swaying.

How did I not register the movement?

When the song faded, we pulled away too quickly, like both of us couldn't wait to run away in the opposite direction.

Chapter 12

Aria

I'd dived into planning mode since we had decided on a date that was too close for comfort. The date made sense; it would make everything more believable for the public since we had to do it as quickly as possible.

With Sabrina's help, I've accomplished most of the tasks in a week. I've successfully negotiated with the Coral manager and secured the venue for the weekend surrounding the 21st. I left the talks for The Admiral to Cillian since that was his forte. I've even gotten Sabrina to tip the Boston Herald about the wedding, so it could generate good buzz.

On Wednesday, I had the pleasure of meeting Meg, a nice woman with short gray hair and soft brown eyes. Our interaction had been sweet, and so was her heart. Although it was her food that sold me, her humor sealed the deal. We ended up with something in common. We both loved taking jabs at Cillian. She called him a robot, and I called him the ruler of hell. We'd laughed, and the rest was history. It had taken some hard convincing for her to let me do the cleaning. We ended with a compromise: she would do the cooking, I would do my own cleaning, with the same pay and fewer hours, all without Cillian knowing.

By Friday night, my checklist was two-thirds done, a testament to my control over the situation. Thank you! Thank you! No need for applause.

Lists were my thing. I went all in, and the wedding one was no exception. Handwritten? Yup. Custom stationery paper? Damn straight. Color-coordinated? Heck yeah.

1. Venue—check—color yellow
2. Flowers—check—color burgundy
3. Rings—check—color black
4. Photographer—check—color orange
5. Band—double-check (one for the reception, one for the ceremony)—color purple
6. Bridesmaid dressed—check—color sky blue, and yes, so were the dresses
7. The invitations—check—color beige

The last items on the list, unchecked: the dress, the tux, and, per the band's request, a song for the first dance.

Cillian was right; his mother had offered me her dress, but I'd politely declined, and she didn't mention it again. I'd reached out to a newbie stylist on the rise, and we made an appointment at a cute little boutique for tomorrow morning.

It was amazing how easy it was to plan a wedding when you didn't actually care about any of it. Cillian had joined in on the 'Don't care' party, leaving pretty much everything in my capable hands with no argument from me whatsoever. The less we saw each other, the better it was for both of us.

Over the week, I'd only seen him twice in passing, and even that was two times too many. Our form of communication: post-its.

On a warm Saturday morning, I walked into a charming atelier. It was filled with flowers and dresses on the racks, offering a mix of pastel colors. I brought Sab with me for a second opinion. The owner was a petite woman with an honest smile and the voice of an angel. We made our introductions, and the woman showed me to the fitting room.

I lost count of how many dresses I'd tried thus far, but I could tell you it was nothing like the movies. No montage with a hit pop song with best friends all giddy and shit. Nope. It was a jawn fest. I wanted to bail, but Sab and Iona (the wedding stylist) wouldn't allow it, waiting for me to find *'the one'*—their words, not mine.

Their faces brightened when I came out of the fitting room and stepped onto the podium, wearing the embodiment of spring. I turned to the mirror and stunned myself with a gasp. It was a stunning ivory and prosecco gown. It burst with colors, showcasing frosted floral appliqués in sky blue, beige, and wine red. The sweetheart bodice and off-the-shoulder sleeves, paired with a mermaid tulle silhouette, worked well with my body type, accentuating the hourglass shape.

"Dare I say we found it?" Iona clapped her hands, and I swear, Sab had tears in her eyes; her hands covered her mouth as she gasped, "I hate how beautiful you look in it."

The dress fit me perfectly, the blues matched my ring and eyes, and the reds expressed my love for wine. But it was the name of the dress that sealed the deal for me.

Persephone.

Oh, the irony. I mean, she was forced to go live with Hades down below. If this was not kismet, I didn't know what was.

After purchasing the dress, Sab and I decided to celebrate over brunch. She knew all the best spots in the city, so I followed her like a hungry little puppy until we reached a hidden gem of a bistro. We sat outside, and before my ass even met the chair, Sabrina had already puffed enough smoke to make me go blind. Thankfully, over a decade of friendship had gotten my lungs used to her cigarettes, so it wasn't such a choking hazard. We ordered the day's special with a side of coffee. While we waited for our food, Sabrina decided to torture me by showing me photos of my apartment. Or better yet, proof of her remodel, down to a large bookcase covering half of my old living room.

As I swiped on, the waitress brought out our orders; the scent of freshly baked goods hit all the right spots.

Midway through my delicious croissant bite, a familiar voice called out my name. My whole body recognized it by the way it stiffened.

This is not happening right now.

No, I was going to handle the unexpected encounter with grace.

"Sebastian, what a surprise."

His blue eyes locked on mine and stayed there, making it hard to breathe.

"It sure is. How have you been?"

I hated how good he looked—the same, yet different somehow. Even the sun played in his favor, making his golden hair glow. My heart pumped loudly in my chest, reliving the heartbreak all over again.

I flinched. Something hit my shin under the table. Sabrina.

Right. Concentrate. Be the bigger person. Win the breakup!

"I've been great, almost done with school. Just need to finish my thesis, and the torture will be over."

Way to go! I mentally patted myself on the back.

"Good for you." Without breaking eye contact, he cleared his throat, turning his attention to my friend. "Sabrina, you good?"

"Always," she said with spite. Sab was not his biggest fan and had made her disapproval known—loudly.

"Anyway, it was nice to see you. Maybe we could grab a cup of cof—" His sight fell on my left hand, interrupting his thought. "Oh, wow. I guess congratulations are in order," he stuttered a bit, surprise undeniable. "Who's the lucky guy?"

I eyed the ring, and a pang of guilt took over. Not too long ago, it had been his ring that covered the same finger. Unlike this one, which suited me perfectly, the one Sebastian had given me had been gold, the wrong size, and the opposite of my style.

I hesitated to answer, so Sab chimed in, "It's Cillian."

"As in Wright?"

There was a slight tick of his jaw, followed by his Adam's apple contracting.

"Yes, as in Wright," I confirmed, and one of his brows flew higher than the other.

"I thought you hated him?"

Ain't that the truth.

79

"Things change, people change, not all, but most do," I drove straight to the point, hoping it would hit where intended, my resilience shining through. The look on his face confirmed the strength I had shown in that moment, and I found myself beaming with pride.

"Right, well," he shuddered, losing his cool for a beat. "Congratulations again. I wish you all the best," he recovered with reservation in his voice, but I chose to ignore it and keep up with the graceful facade.

"Thank you," I faltered. "And same; truly."

He smiled and walked away, taking a piece of me with him.

"Well, that was certainly unexpected," Sab stated the obvious. "You okay?"

Sabrina and Nala were the only ones, aside from Sebastian and me, who knew the whole story behind our terminated engagement. The rest of them got the old 'we were too young' spiel.

Seeing him brought it all back, and I had to wash it away.

"Barely! Can we turn this brunch into happy hour?"

Her hand flew in the air before I even got a chance to bring out my puppy eyes. And Greek goddess, how I loved her for it.

"I thought you'd never ask."

She flagged the waiter, who wasn't our server, and ordered us the house cocktails. All hell broke loose. It started when the poor kid politely pointed out that alcohol wasn't served before 9 PM. It ended with a colorful array of cocktails after the manager realized who made the request. These days, Sabrina wasn't recognized as a model. Instead, she was known as a badass who took down her own father and blew up the justice system. Being her friend came with perks, and alcohol was by far my favorite.

Chapter 13

Cillian

"Hi," Aria murmured when she opened the door, finding me on the couch, deep in my game. I paused and turned to face her. She looked… tipsy?

"Hi."

"I got complimentary steaks, still hot."

I waited for the punchline.

"One word—Sabrina."

And there it was.

"Enough said," I barked.

She set a bag on the island with a thud. "There's enough for two if you want to join." She shook her head, then smacked the side of her head. "No! Shit. Rule No. 5," she reminded, but it felt like it was more for herself.

My jaw clenched.

"Right, I'll take mine in my room; you can eat the rest of it here."

During our first week living together, I'd followed the rule of taking my meals in my room while she ate hers in the kitchen.

I stood up, saved my game, and walked to the island to investigate the offerings.

"Hade—" she stopped herself, clearing her throat. "I

mean, Cillian. Maybe there's room to negotiate the rule. For example, we can eat together if we talk business."

It was a tempting offer, especially since I feared I would be housing a family of ants if I kept eating in my bed.

"I can go with that," I deadpanned, shrugging one shoulder.

"Fine."

"Fine."

I took a plate out of the cabinet and placed it on the counter. Next, I grabbed a fork and a knife and slid them over to the plate. So I wouldn't pass by her, I took the longer route to the other side. The two chairs were too close for my liking, so I dragged mine a bit further before I took a seat.

"This one's medium rare," she pointed at the box with an X crossed over it. My mouth watered.

Just how I like it!

I ignored the obvious—how she knew my preferences, and how she brought me food when she didn't have to.

"Let's talk business, shall we?" She grabbed her own set of utensils from the drawer, took a plate from the drying rack, and rounded the island. She almost missed the chair, but quickly recovered, grabbing the end of the countertop to keep her balance. Taking a seat, she blabbered, "I pretty much took care of everything regarding the wedding."

Yup. Aria was definitely a robot.

"In a week? I thought that I was the overachiever of the family."

She rolled her tongue, unamused.

"It kind of clicked together, and since my classes are over, I have way too much free time."

She rummaged through her bag, took something out, then slid it across the surface. Our wedding invitation. It was simple, off-white paper with roses in the corners. I scanned it, read it, and nodded in approval.

"So what's left to do?" I mumbled with my mouth full, the meat melting around my tongue.

"The tuxes and the song for the first dance." She worked her knife, cutting her steak into small, bite-sized pieces.

"I see. I'll handle the tux, and you do the song. Music is your thing anyway."

I was more of a podcast person, while Aria liked to blast her playlist as loudly as possible for everyone to hear.

"So generous," she quipped, "sure you don't want any input?"

"I'm sure; surprise me."

I regretted it the moment I'd said it because her whole face lit up, making every hair on my body rise—pure mischief coloring her skin.

We can't have that.

"Keep it clean."

"Dammit. So close," she mumbled, taking a bite. "Fine!"

"Fine."

We fell into that awkward silence until we both emptied our plates. She cleaned the dishes, and we went our separate ways, Aria to her room and I to the gym. After not seeing her for nearly a week, it felt strange to be in her company. I broke my own rule because, for some unexplainable reason, I didn't want to leave her side.

I doubled my training tonight, not wanting to go to sleep and clear my head, but it was impossible as I started looking back at the last time we shared a meal.

"Happy Thanksgiving," Aria's voice echoed from the main entrance.

"Oh, honey, what a surprise." My mother rushed and squeezed her in a hug, and everybody else followed; our dinner forgotten.

"Happy Thanksgiving," stupid Sebastian. I could hear the condescending snarl before I even got a chance to see his smug face.

"Sorry to barge in, but the dinner at Sebastian's ran short, so we decided to come. I wanted to see you all."

"Ariiii," my niece Lana jumped at her.

"Hey, butterfly. My God, how you've grown."

"Aunt Ari," Karl followed, tackling her on the ground. "Hi, slugger. How are my two favorite little humans?"

"We missed you," they said in unison.

"I missed you too, so, so much." She hugged them both, not bothering to move from the floor.

"Come on, leave Aunt Ari alone, give her some air," my sister Helen to the rescue.

"You know I don't mind," Aria said, standing up, and they hugged. My whole family loved Aria, but my sister's kids loved her even more. And she loved them right back. Last Christmas, they'd asked Helen what she was to them, and no one knew how to answer. So Lana had stepped forward and demanded that Aria be their aunt. It made sense when she'd said it, so everybody had agreed.

"Come in, sweetie. There is a lot of food left. Sebastian, please make yourself at home." My mother guided them into

the dining room. The polite trust-fund prep Ken doll shook everyone's hand, including mine. Aria hugged both her dad and mine, leaving a simple nod for me. "Hades, happy Thanksgiving."

"Happy Thanksgiving, Ice Queen."

The happy couple sat at the table, and I handed Aria a bowl of roasted Brussels sprouts. She eyed the offering as if it were poisonous or something. It was her favorite; she'd said it reminded her of her mom because it was the dish her mom would prepare before we'd lost her. Aria didn't bother to look at me but took the bowl anyway.

I blinked with a grunt. Why did my mind keep doing this to me? This back-and-forth memory was giving me whiplash. And then I noticed the darkness. How long had I been working out? I checked my watch: 10:52 PM.

Fuck.

I suppose I had to incorporate some brain training into my workouts, given that this whole memory lane stuff was unacceptable. Half a day lost on it. I ran a hand over my jaw and headed to the bathroom. I stripped, stepped into the shower, and turned it on. The showerhead started making a weird sound.

Double Fuck.

I needed to wash off badly.

Then a thought came to mind. There was a bathroom in Aria's room.

*I could take a quick one—*I thought… It won't bother her. With nothing but my boxers on, I made my way to her door.

I knocked—no answer. Thinking that she might be

sleeping, I decided to go in anyway.

I'll pass her and take a quick shower; it won't be a big deal.

I opened the door to check and found her under the covers, pitch-black and way too quiet. So, I tiptoed to the bathroom but stopped when I heard the bed creak.

"What do you think you're doing?"

Shit.

The light turned on, revealing Aria cooped up in a blanket with earphones on her head, wide awake.

I'm so screwed.

"Sorry," I croaked, "I thought you were sleeping!"

"And that gives you the right to come in? What the fuck, Cillian?"

There goes my name out of her mouth, doing something to me.

"For what it's worth, I knocked first."

She was giving me that *'I'm going to kill you'* face she liked so much.

"My shower is broken, and I just worked out."

I made a point of showing all the sweat and zeroed in on the way her throat bobbed, but then her clenched fist took the focus away. Since I wanted to live, I raised my hands as if approaching an angry animal and lowered my voice. "I really need to wash off." I gave her an innocent little shrug, but the death glare stayed put, tearing through me.

She stood up, sans blanket, and now it was my turn to work the throat. Her bare legs were right there, her long pink shirt doing nothing to cover anything up. Suddenly, I wanted to feel the softness of her skin.

Nope, not gonna happen.

"Do you have a toolbox?"

I gulped, "What?"

She crossed her arms over her chest, the snob in her voice loud and clear. "A box that stores tools. Do you have one?"

"In the pantry," I murmured, scratching the back of my head.

Was she going to kill me with a hammer or something?

She passed by me, her shoulder grazing my upper arm. I turned on my heel to follow her.

"What's happening?" I asked, confused as hell.

She opened the pantry, took out the red toolbox, and headed right for my room before she stopped at the door, turning to face me. "If I go straight to your bathroom, that wouldn't technically be breaking any rules. Right?"

"Right?" I dragged it out, uncertainty in my voice.

"Good." It was way too chipper for someone who wanted to kill me a minute ago.

She beelined to the bathroom, my steps right behind her. The box was set on the floor by her gentle hands. She opened it and rummaged through until she took out a set of pliers and went straight for the shower, while I watched, muddled and curious. She had to stretch a bit higher, her shirt lifting in the process, revealing black fabric covering her ass cheeks. The room temperature went boiling. Using the pliers, she unscrewed the showerhead. Next, she took something small and black out of it, then tossed it into the box. My manhood be damned, I had no idea what she was doing, but I was enjoying every second of it. She scraped the little holes of the head with her thumbnail before she screwed it back. Going back to the toolbox, she took out a screwdriver. She used it to unscrew a small metal plate on the wall, which I never even paid much attention to. Behind it were pipes and two valves. She turned both all the way, then screwed the plate back in. When she finished twerking, she put the tools back in the box and closed it. This woman never ceased to amaze me.

She stepped into the enclosure and grabbed the wrong tap.

"The fuck," she shrieked, and I couldn't contain my laugh.

She was soaked, thanks to the rain showerhead on the ceiling.

"A warning would've been nice," she sneered.

I couldn't stop laughing even though I knew my life depended on it.

"Good news is your shower is temporarily fixed; bad news—you're dead," she threatened, making my knees wobble.

What in the actual fuck? What am I? Afraid of her now?

"How did you do that?"

"It's called Google. It's there for a reason. You should use it," she hissed, water draping all over her.

"Noted."

I handed her a towel, and she took it—reluctantly.

"Your showerhead is clogged. I increased the water pressure, but you should tell Meg to soak it in vinegar."

"Thanks," was all I could say, hypnotized by the droplets sliding down her skin.

"It wasn't for your benefit, trust me. I don't want you

coming into my room ever again."

"Addendum?"

"Addendum."

"Fine."

"Fine."

She lingered for a moment, something far too scary flashing in her eyes.

"Wait, if you have two showerheads, why didn't you use the ceiling one?"

Screaming in the back of my head, I bit my lip. "I forgot it was there; I never use it."

She scoffed, did her famous eye roll, then stormed out, finishing it off with a loud slam of my bedroom door.

For a long minute, I couldn't move, unable to get the picture of her in that shirt out of my head—the way it clung to her body after it got wet, revealing the outline of her breasts and her pink nipples.

Fuck.

I stepped into my shower, turning the water to ice cold. It did nothing to extinguish the fire of my imagination. Before I knew it, my hand took control, the water washing away my release.

Chapter 14

Aria

Fuck! Fuck! Fuck! With Calvin Klein on top.

That eight-pack, the deep V, those meticulously defined muscles—the Navy had done him good.

No. We're not going there.

But it was already too late.

I was soaked, and the rain had nothing to do with it.

Back in my room, I took a shower and made the mistake of closing my eyes. The image was so clear. Those green shiny eyes, the thick dark lashes, the coily curls of his hair, the biceps, all the ceps, his chocolaty chestnut skin. Then the damned image of his tight briefs blew up, the happy trail right above the waistband. And my stupid mind started to pull them down, as I began to envision his touch with every new drop. I had never hated my imagination more.

I turned off the water and dried out every part of me. I pulled a new sleep shirt from the closet and covered my naked body, hiding my throbbing core with underwear before I went under the covers. The image of his lips appeared, full and wide. And my hand just slipped under, down my shirt, and into my undies. I imagined him biting his lower lip as I slid a finger inside.

Holy…

That was all it took, one finger and a set of vivid images

produced by my mind, for me to crumble and fall into the abyss.

In the morning, I woke up to an unread text from Sabrina.

Sab: *Free for breakfast?*

It was as if she knew how much I needed to escape this place...

Me: *Yesss!!! Bonjour? 9:30?*

Sab: *Works for me... See ya... wouldn't wanna be ya...*

Neither would I, but unfortunately, I had no choice in the matter. On a scale from one to full-on crazy, how weird was it that I was sneaking out of my room in order not to bump into my fiancée—again?

Don't answer that...

It was like a bad sitcom, and I was the punchline.

Every move I made, every step I took, was careful and silent. I only relaxed when the front door clicked behind me, and I started walking like a normal person. If boots were made for walking, my limited-edition baby blue Alexander McQueens were made for running away from Cillian.

When I got out of the elevator into the lobby, Pierre greeted me with his white teeth on display. This building was a peculiar one... Since I'd moved in here, I had never run into a neighbor, not even a courier—no one—none. Only Pierre, and once, the other concierge who worked nights, but I didn't catch his name. He was older than Pierre and looked as though he could pass out at any minute.

I walked to the small café that Sabrina and I often frequented together after an alcohol-induced night out. I spotted her at the corner table, under the parasol. Smoke rose from the cigarette dangling between her fingers.

"Sabby Darling," I mocked in my fake British accent, one she'd used whenever talking about some famous photographer.

"You must think you're sooooo funny." She pulled her sunshades on top of her head, showing her full death stare…

The waitress came and took our order. By the time Sab put out her cigarette, the house breakfast had sat before us with two coffees on the side.

I took an invitation from my bag and handed it over. "You can bring the whole Hart clan if you want."

I'd met her husband's family and hung out with them a couple of times. They were good for her, better than good. The found family she deserved more than anything.

"Oh God, no," she feigned disgust. "I love them, remember… Why would I want to put them through that?"

Ok, so she had a point. These kinds of things were more of a business than a pleasure within our circles. It all had to be serious and poised. Greek god forbid actual fun.

"So, when are you planning on asking me to be your maid of honor?"

This woman… I'd been there at her impromptu wedding, which she'd organized in just fifteen minutes. Full disclosure, I had trouble deciding between Nala and Sabrina… both were important, but Sabrina was more familiar, not to mention more comfortable within the social circle. And I couldn't put pressure on Nala for the sake of my sanity.

"You can have Nala for your real wedding," she said through a laugh, but I imagined the situation was weird for her as much as it was for me.

"Yeah, I doubt that would ever happen."

"Thinking about sticking with Cillian?"

"No! What? Where did that come from?"

Why was I panicking right now?

"Okay, that reaction was uncalled for... unless..." she hissed.

"Nothing to read into. You just threw me..." I waved it off.

My life was beyond fucked up. One failed engagement, one fake one, and a marriage in the making that would end up in flames. I was a walking punchline.

"Are you catching feelings for your fiancée?"

"If you mean disgust, anger, repulsion..."

Desire, lust, arousal...

Dammit, Aria, snap the fuck out of it!

"Then yeah!"

"Still avoiding him?"

Like the plague.

"I avoid him because my temper around him goes from zero to life in prison in less than three seconds," I snapped.

"Rowr. Retract the claws; it's only me."

"Sorry."

Cillian got under my skin, invading my imagination, not to mention some other places. And now I was taking out all my frustration on my best friend. That man was not worth any of my anger, nor any other feelings.

You hate him, remember!

Like I needed the reminder…

Your fingers sure do!

Was it possible to bitch slap a voice in my head? She was being a hormonal little bitch with an attitude problem all day! One thing she had going on was that she sounded like Emma Stone… Yeah, my conscience was narrated by Emma freaking Stone, making it hard to hate her.

"Do you honestly think you two will be able to pull it off?"

I sure hope so.

"I don't know. Right now, we are trying to be civil, though my hand is always at the ready to grab his neck."

Sabrina's brows went skyward, and I had to work fast on killing that spark in her eyes.

"Oh, Sab, come on.. You little perv!"

"I can't help it." She shrugged, batting her lashes.

I crossed one leg over the other, taking a sip of my coffee.

"You've gotta cut back on the smut."

Both my friends were open about their sexuality, but Sabrina was extremely loud about it. I, on the other hand, kept it in the dark. And yes, that had a double meaning.

"It's not smut, it's called cliterature," she enunciated the last word loudly and proudly.

"My Dionysus, you're diabolical," I snickered, shaking my head.

"And damn proud of it."

"How does your husband feel about it?"

"Who do you think stimulates the clit?"

"Dude, please, let's keep it PG-13, at least till my divorce."

She cocked a brow, eyes narrowing as she dragged the question out. "Whyyy?"

I choked... I should've kept my stupid mouth shut.

"Aria, you're not planning to go celibate, are you?"

I mean, I've been doing a fine job of it so far; what was another year?

"Kind of. I mean, I can't go around having sex in public bathrooms with a ring on my finger, now can I?"

"Oh, honey, I am so sorry for your VA-jay-jay."

How strange was it that my best friend felt more compassion for my lady parts than for anything else? Don't answer that either.

"Don't worry about her... I've got my fingers and know how to keep her satisfied."

Yeah, with images of your future husband.

Dammit Emma!

I slumped back in my chair, and Sabrina took out another cigarette, mischief gleaming in her eyes. I didn't know why, but the look on her face scared me... She was cooking up something, something bad, shameful, and possibly perverted... I was sure of it.

"Do you think he is going to extend the same courtesy?"

That question I couldn't answer.

"I don't care," I lied, and Sabrina saw right through it.

"You could put it in the contract."

There was a brief moment when I'd considered it, but thankfully, it was short-lived.

"It's already in. Though it's more in the line of keeping it behind closed doors and on the down low."

"What?" she shrieked, making the other patrons of the

place snap their attention to us. Sab, per her usual, couldn't be bothered by it. "You gave him a hall pass?"

I wouldn't call it that.

"Come on, Sab, this whole thing is fake. I can't expect him to be faithful when we're not even together."

"So let me get this straight. You'll turn all prude while he goes around dipping Junior wherever he wants?"

"Yup," I popped the P, trying to hide the unease.

"Aria, I love you. But that's a recipe for hurt."

"Hurt only comes when feelings are involved. Fake, remember," I reminded her.

"Yeah, keep telling yourself that."

"Can we drop this?"

"Your wish is my command," she said sheepishly, focusing back on her breakfast.

Chapter 15

Aria

The Fourth of July came way too quickly, and I wasn't prepared for it. After successfully avoiding Cillian, I was now about to spend a long weekend with him, our family, and friends while trying to play nice.

Gag!

Stupid Independence Day on a Thursday... that meant four days... Four days of fake smiles. We'd driven to Nantucket separately, with me making excuses about some wedding-related appointments... it was a total lie, but no one seemed to care.

Every year, our famous CEOs made a big deal out of it... A big party for close friends, followed by an over-the-top fireworks display. The best part was the bonfire on the beach, which catered to the younger crowd. This year would be no different, and I was overly excited to see all my friends.

We were having a heated chat about vendors with Mr. and Mrs. Smith (and yes, I had to bite my tongue to keep from laughing as I greeted them). Then, Cillian put his hand on my bare back. Skin-to-skin contact right there. My entire focus was on keeping my hair from rising at his touch. He kept up the polite talk, working the crowd, offering fake smiles as he shook hands. He said all the right things, and I was right there with him, my face spasming from overworked muscles.

After our parents gave us approving nods, meaning our work here was done, we all headed to the beach. With some heavy group effort, the fire was lit, drinks were set out, iced cups were passed around, and music blasted from a Bluetooth speaker.

This year, the atmosphere was different. Maybe it was because the last bonfire I had been with Sebastian. Or perhaps it was Cillian's change in behavior. He stopped acting like my fiancé and started flirting with Chrissy, one of his past hookups. On the upside, the vodka was good, burning at all the right places.

"You okay?" a guy who looked familiar but I couldn't quite place stood in front of me, all 7 feet of him. My neck hurt from the angle I had to tilt my head to meet his gaze.

"Is that your way of telling me I look terrible?"

"God no, Aria, you always look beautiful."

So he knew my name, meaning we definitely knew each other. Was he a famous athlete? I wasn't sure... His calves were on the thinner side, his figure more defined than bulky, and his shoulders were not broad... a soccer player?

"Thank you, I guess!"

"Been a long time…"

Has it?

"Yeah. What have you been up to?"

"You know, same old same old, just got home for the holiday."

Come on, dude, give me a breadcrumb.

"You miss home?"

"Yeah, I mean, Europe is different, and the language is so

hard."

He had that camera-ready smile, all white teeth with a sparkle in the corner. He stuffed one hand into his pocket, while the other held the red cup.

"What's the first thing you learned to say?"

"Arschloch and Scheisse!"

Now we're getting somewhere.

"Naturally, the swear words!"

"It's like a law," he stated, and I nodded, not sure why... I wasn't even sure why this guy was talking to me, but here we were.

"You speak German?"

Yes.

"No," I lied. Frankly, I didn't want to go through a tutoring session. The guy was still standing in front of me while I sat on the log when the cat dragged the devil in.

"Wow, Aria, is that you?" The sound of her voice made me want to vomit.

"Chrissy, to what do I owe the pleasure?"

I looked up at her, in a bikini, covering her privates. Her fake boobs were in my face, taunting and making fun of me. I recoiled for a breath, but then her voice snapped me out of it.

"Oh, you know me; I like to make my rounds and say hello to the little people."

The snark did its job, making me straighten my back.

"Well, thank you for gracing us with your presence. We are so blessed to have your inferiority," I derided.

"Oh, come on, Aria, why so hostile?"

"Whatever do you mean?" I acted offended, making my lashes do all the work.

"You always have the same expression during our short conversations."

How she managed to keep her tone annoying was beyond me, but I wanted to strain it out of her. I stood up, getting in her face. "And yet, despite the look on my face, you're still talking."

"That was kind of harsh," the maybe soccer dude spoke, and I wish he hadn't. Not that we were friends or anything, but I could really use an ally here.

"I hope you are talking to her," I snapped at him. Damn, the guy was tall, too skinny for my taste. Lovely eyes, though. Now that I look at them more, they seem transfixed...on me?

"No, actually, that was pointed at you."

"Are you serious? You did hear her condescending tone, right?"

"What's going on here?" Cillian stepped up, and honestly, this whole scene felt so high school.

"Ice queen was being rude to me," the damsel pouted.

Every hair on my body pricked upward at that name, the one *he* used. Did they use it often, talking shit about me while they were naked?

At this point, my fists were clenched and ready to hit.

"You're the one who started talking about my expression... Sorry, Chrissy, I am not responsible for what my face does when you talk."

Cillian chuckled, and for a second, I thought I had imagined it.

"Are you going to allow her to talk to me like that?" The She-devil crossed her arms over her chest and glared at a very confused Cillian.

I cannot believe this!

Was she being serious?

"What do you expect me to do?"

Like I knew he would, he took her side.

"I don't think she likes me very much," I told him, tapping my hand on my chest.

"If you think I don't like you, let me make myself clear... I don't!" Chrissy barked, obviously not aware of my bite.

"When I googled who gives a fuck, I didn't see my name pop up in the results!"

Even though I thought it wasn't my best work, both the soccer guy and Cillian laughed, so I naturally joined in. Even so, she kept her eyes firmly on Cillian, licking her lower lip like he was the most delicious piece of cake.

Something possessed me, this strange urge to mark my territory. I had to be subtle, inconspicuous...but how?

Luckily, I didn't have to do a thing; my maid of honor swooped in like the best knight in shining armor. "Let me see it," she yelled while striding toward me. She pushed her way through the crowd I hadn't even noticed gathering around us, and went straight to my left hand, lifting it. She inspected the ring as if seeing it for the first time.

"Damn, Cill, you did good!"

I swear, I could hear Chrissy's jaw drop, and it felt so good. Petty? Sure, but good.

"You two are engaged?" She gawked, her eyes playing ping-pong between Cillian and me.

"Yeah, didn't you know? It's all over the tabloids," Sab took over the entire conversation.

"I don't read that."

"Right, probably only like seeing your name in them, not that it's there often." Damn, my BFF's bitch face was perfection.

"Neither is yours," Chrissy tried to hit low, but was unsuccessful.

"By choice, darling, not for the lack of offers."

Mateo came to her side, and Chrissy's eyes went full prowl, with some heavy drool.

"Don't even think about it, sweetie, this one's also claimed!"

"Excuse you?" Chrissy's whole face wrinkled with confusion, and Sabrina took Mateo's hand, lifting it next to hers to show off their matching rings.

"Come on, Hank, let's go!" Chrissy grabbed soccer's, I mean Hank's hand, and they both stormed off, leaving us at the verge of a blow-up laugh.

I hugged Sabrina, mumbling a soft "Thank you" in her ear before I extended my hug to her husband.

Chapter 16

Cillian

This year's bonfire was the worst one yet, and it wasn't all due to the bad company. I'd spent most of the night trying not to punch Hank fucking Shaw in his stupid face. The dude wouldn't stop flirting, even after Sabrina not so subtly pointed out Aria was engaged—to me. And Aria... she was so ignorant. For a woman who exuded confidence, she was oblivious to the impact she had on men. For example, right now she had three guys staring at her ass, one checking out her entire profile and one boring the breath out of her. The guy checking her profile had been trying to get in with her, but Hank monopolized all her attention. He had been doing that all damn night, and for reasons unknown to me, I couldn't look away. Not when he'd walked up to her, not when she'd seemed uninterested, not when Chrissy had decided to poke the bear.

We'd all gone to high school together, and Chrissy was Aria's enemy number two. I had used that notion to get on Aria's nerves by letting her cling to me on occasion, up until she spread the rumor that I deflowered her after prom.

Tonight, she'd come to me with googly eyes and hair twirls, but I made it clear I was not interested. Still, she wouldn't budge; that was until she saw Aria. During our teenage years, those two were your regular mean girl enemies; guess the bickering never stopped.

I was on the other side of the bonfire, talking with Cole, a former teammate of mine. We were in the middle of recollecting one of the best games when Hank brushed Aria's shoulder.

Yeah, he was definitely eye-fucking her.

My fists clenched of their own accord, making me spill my drink. "Fuck," I muttered, to which Cole chuckled. He waved at someone, said something to me I couldn't pick up, and walked in the direction of three girls wiggling their fingers at him.

"You just gonna stare all night, or are you going to do something about it?" Sabrina nudged me with her elbow. I flinched, not noticing her sneak up on me.

"I don't know what you are talking about."

"Riiight…" she drawled, "don't worry, your secret is safe with me!"

What secret

"You'll owe me," she quipped over her shoulder, going straight to Aria.

She whispered something in her ear and then dragged her away from the stupid soccer player to the made-up bar.

"You know she'll collect on that?" Sabrina's husband came up to my right, handing me a beer. I took it and nodded, knowing damn well the price would be high, but so fucking worth it.

"Sorry, man, we never properly met," I extended my hand, and he took it, shaking it with a smile. "Yeah, those two aren't very good with manners," he remarked, his sight never leaving his wife. "I'm Mateo."

"I'm Cillian," I muttered, following his line of sight, my focus on the blonde in the duo.

They chugged down one, two, three shots before someone yelled, "Skinny-dipping!"

I couldn't tell you how it happened; all I knew was it went down fast. Clothes were discarded, people started running, and in less than a minute, the beach was in chaos, with the water overcrowded. People splashed around, chicken fights broke out, and some people danced. It was absolute pandemonium. The only married couple couldn't be bothered by the rest of us, as I was pretty sure they were doing the nasty in front of everybody, water being the only thing hiding their public display of affection.

Why are you jealous?

I shook that thought away and got in with the guys playing ball in the shallows. We played for a while, jumping all over the place to keep the ball from dropping.

Sabrina and Mateo were the first to get out, followed by Aria. They lay down on a blanket, and I knew Aria was staring at the sky. I knew because it was something we used to do together.

"There!" She lifted her finger, and my eyes followed. "That's Cassiopeia." It was the only constellation she knew; however, she always managed to find it.

"God, how beautiful this is."

You have no idea! *I thought while watching her gaze at the night sky. The moon was my best friend that night, as it shone over her face, illuminating her.*

Wow, she is breathtaking.

Those were my thoughts the entire time she made up names for shapes she found in the sky. I tried; I did try to concentrate on what she was saying, but all I could hear was her breath and see her shiny skin, while ignoring the need to touch her lips.

That night had been the first time I'd seen her for her beauty, the first time I'd realized how uniquely beautiful she was—the first time I'd wanted more.

"Hey, Aria," Hank walked right past me on my way out, and Aria propped up on her elbows, looking up at him. She was still in her underwear, like the rest of us, except for Chrissy, who went into the water commando-style.

"Dude, you did see the ring; you do know she's taken," Sabrina sneered at him.

That made me like her some more.

"Her finger was already occupied once, so I wanted to keep her options open."

Oh no, he didn't!

"Oh no, you didn't," Aria snarked out in frustration, then she stood up, looking like a fireball. "You know what, even if I weren't engaged—*Hank*—I wouldn't go there. I kind of have an irrational fear of being bored to death," she jeered, saying his name with a loud twirl.

Damn… By this rate, there won't be any witty remarks left for her to use on me!

The guy scoffed and left. Like left, left, from the premises, into his car, and hopefully far, far away.

"You look like you need anger management." I closed in

on her, fixated on her red face.

"What I need is for people to stop pissing me off!"

Yup, the jab was aimed at me, but I didn't care. I was too happy she still had enough to dart at me.

"How about a round of never have I ever?" Chrissy got out of the water, swaying her hips as she passed me by.

"You'll be drunk in 5 minutes," Sabrina darted, and Chrissy got in her face. "You calling me a slut?"

"Don't worry, honey, I'll be drunk in two!"

Chrissy choked on air, and Sabrina puffed out her chest. Mateo came behind her, removed the hair from her shoulder, and sucked on her neck.

Aria clapped her hands. "Come on, no need to show off."

Over a dozen of us made a circle next to the fire, drinks in hand, with Chrissy and Sabrina exchanging eye daggers.

"Never have I ever gone down on someone on the beach." Chrissy's eyes never left mine while she chugged from her cup. Sabrina, Mateo, and I followed. Aria looked at her bare feet, drink intact.

"Wow, Aria. I didn't know you were so conservative," Chrissy ribbed, but Aria sat up straight.

"Just so I don't disappoint, how do you want me to react?" Aria poked back, and Chrissy choked.

"My turn," Sabrina stepped in, "Never have I ever tried to steal someone else's man."

Chrissy took a sip, taunting, "It's not stealing when they come willingly."

Aria and Sabrina both rolled their eyes—no comment necessary. But I did notice the slight twitch in Aria's throat.

"Never have I ever done it on a motorcycle on the side of

the road," Mateo blurted next, taking a swig. His gaze twinkled as he watched his wife take her cup to her mouth. She made a point of licking her lips after she drank, making him smirk.

"Never have I ever made out with the same sex?" a guy whose name I couldn't think of challenged. The two best friends yet again shared a look, and both took their swigs at the same time, never breaking eye contact. I couldn't help but notice all the guys fixing their crotches, myself included.

By the time the sun started to set, I had learned that both Sabrina and Chrissy were great multitaskers and that Aria lost her virginity on a beach. Aria had learned I was in a threesome, had sex in an elevator, and that I joined the Mile High Club. We'd both had sex in a public bathroom, and we both had one-night stands.

Yeah, this was definitely fun!

Fun! Fun! Fun!

Chapter 17

Aria

I'd slept for half of Friday, which was logical, since I got in around 6. A small number of people had stayed for the sunrise, including Sabrina, Mateo, Cillian, and yours truly. Cillian and I had walked back together, two feet apart, with crickets the only sound filling the silence.

Our Nantucket 9.8-acre estate was my second favorite. Aside from our homes in Boston, the Wrights and Brooks held all our real estate 50-50. This one was our summer getaway—a timeless, elegant 10-bedroom home designed by a renowned architect. From the grand foyer to the post-and-beam living room, the entire space exuded sophistication. There were over a dozen fireplaces and a rarely used state-of-the-art kitchen. Our time here was usually spent at the outside grill. This residence was a haven with so much greenery surrounding the gray beauty. There was a pool, a tennis court, a basketball court, a golf course for the dads, and a boat landing. The best part was the private beach where I'd spent the night, drinking and fighting my inner thoughts.

Vodka had stayed by my side the whole time, washing away all the nasty things taking over my mind, most of them regarding Cillian's sexual expeditions. Not the best thoughts to have in his proximity. I was far from a prude, and though I was more of a serious long-term relationships type, I had my fair share of smut, as Sabrina would call it. Still, hearing about Cillian's escapades made me feel like Mrs. Grundy. The sunrise had been lovely, at least.

When I woke up around one, I went outside and found everyone scattered all over the place. My dad and John were at the grill, tongs in hand and their aprons proudly tied around them. They were a gift from Cillian and me—all black with big white letters that said 'I like big buns, and I cannot lie;' below that, in smaller cursive, it read 'Your opinion wasn't in the recipe!'

Helen was soaking up the rays while the kids played tag football on the grass with Cillian. I had a front-row seat to a shirtless, sweaty, glowing Cillian in the sun.

Images of him and Chrissy reappeared, all that vodka too, so with quick work, I ran to the bathroom and emptied my stomach.

On my way out, I told Helen to let everyone know I was heading to town, a fake excuse for a shopping spree. Driving around in circles was pointless, especially since the radio had an agenda to get on my nerves. Every station I turned to taunted me, like it was handpicking songs to further mess up my head. When I couldn't take it any longer, I ended up at a local Stop & Shop, and as if last night wasn't enough of a blow, I just had to run into *him.*

He looked good, in his pretty-boy way. He had that clean lines, gorgeous face thing going for him, with a set of full lips completing the picture. With a tennis racket bag over his shoulder, wearing a set of white tennis attire, and a wristband—one I had given him for his last birthday, with his initials sewn in blue to match his eyes, he stood tall in the sweets aisle.

It still hurts! I realized…

"Aria?" He walked toward me, stopping when he hit the two-step distance mark.

"Sebastian." I waved awkwardly. "Missed you at the bonfire!"

"Yeah, I just figured…" he trailed off, his hand scratching the back of his neck, showing off his muscles flexing. Even though he didn't finish, we both knew very well what he was about to say. It would be awkward, and by the look on his face, he thought it would be worse for me.

"You look good," he broke the silence, and I couldn't help but notice his eyes roaming my physique.

"So do you," I admitted.

He zoomed in on my ring, one that I've been unconsciously playing with.

"Are you really with that guy?"

"Sebastian I…"

"I miss you," he blurted out, interrupting my chain of thought. I couldn't say it back, though, not that I didn't miss him... We had been together for two years and had lived together for one. We'd had plans, a whole future set up, and with one quick *puff,* it had all vanished.

"Do you love him?" It came out more like a whisper, but loud enough to snap me out of my stupor, surprising me with the direction this whole conversation had taken.

I stayed silent, unsure of how to respond. His eyes penetrated mine, looking for an answer. He must have gotten it because, without a single word, he turned on his heel and passed from sight. I just wish I knew what he saw.

Back at the house, I avoided everyone by locking myself in my room under the pretense of working on my thesis. Although I should be working on it, I chose to lie in bed with earbuds in and let my brain rest.

I emerged for lunch, a grill feast spread out in the yard with the kids eating on a picnic blanket and the grown-ups at the big table.

"How's the thesis going?" Helen asked from across the table, handing me the salad.

"Inefficiently," I blurted. "I spent an hour staring at a blank page."

A recurrence at this point. I had ideas, but I had trouble verbalizing them.

"What's the topic?"

"Family Business Succession Planning and Challenges."

"Are you doing your own research?" this time, Loren asked.

I nodded. "I already have the necessary data; now I have to explain it with words," I emphasized the last part.

"Oh, come on, words have always been your forte," Cillian ribbed from the seat next to his sister. Drained of all energy, I sent him a look, one that would be the equivalent of a middle finger. He smirked back, and I chose not to retaliate.

My little rascals saved me from whatever was happening. "Auntie, let's go for a swim!" Karl pulled on my dress.

"Sure, little dude. Go get your trunks on and meet me at the pool, you too, Lana!"

They both fist-bumped with a "Yes" and bolted inside. I kissed both John and my dad as I passed by, then went out back to the pool.

The kids and I did the usual: we tossed the weight and dove in, splashed some water, and held a diving competition. We ended up relaxing in our flamingo floaties when my dad came out back, his phone in hand.

"Kids, we have to go," he yelled, and we all froze. He looked like he had seen a ghost.

"What happened?"

"There was an explosion in one of the mines. We need to do damage control." He sounded so defeated, and I hated how it aged him. I navigated the floatie to the edge and got out with my father's help.

"What can I do?"

"Deal with the press?"

I was well-connected with the press, having friends in the right places who could keep certain stories out of the headlines. It all got started with Mario's arrest. I'd worked my magic, clearing the air, not allowing anyone to twist the story. Also, I'd swept a lot of Cillian's sexcapades under the rug, something he wasn't aware of.

"Of course. I'll get right on it," I deadpanned, trying to keep it cool for my father's sake. I draped my beach towel over my shoulders and headed inside for a quick wardrobe change. It was time to get into the role of the Ice Queen.

Chapter 18

Cillian

Today we had a big fundraiser gala we all needed to attend, mainly to show people our feet were firmly on the ground, not sinking. Word had spread in the corporate world, but thankfully, it stayed whispered.

During the week, I've helped Dad and Peter with the aftermath of the mine explosion as much as I could. Fortunately, no one had gotten hurt, but for safety reasons, we'd shut down the entire operation. Aria had done her best to keep the story hushed; so far, there were no leaks, making it easier on us all. We didn't need another hit with the stock market. We'd had a similar incident last year when one of the workers hit a pipe, flooding a whole tunnel. Stocks plummeted, but we'd recovered quickly thanks to Aria's idea to blame the city for failing to provide the correct pipeline plans. Our legal team had nipped it in the bud, and we were back on top in no time.

I hadn't seen her much in the past couple of days; our communication was over post-its. I'd been wrapped up with work, training the fresh meat into submission. Every day I'd get home, tired as fuck, to find the place empty. At times, I'd thought it was a good thing; at other times, there was this emptiness in the pit of my stomach that bugged the shit out of me. Dissecting it was pointless, so I hadn't even dared to try.

Nodding my head, trying to concentrate on whatever the person I was in the middle of a conversation with was trying to say, I felt my hand slip once again. It was a black-tie event, so I wore my black tux, and Aria had a long, tight, green backless dress. The front was completely covered, but the fabric seemed painted on, leaving little to the imagination. She was a vision, and her bare back was pure temptation. My hand kept finding her lumbar region, covering her naked skin with my warmth, and the mere thought of it got me hard.

Despite my hatred of her for the past eight years, my dick and I always seemed to be at odds when it came to her. No matter how much she irritated me, the traitor in my pants had different thoughts. Tonight was no different. She kept her distance, snapping at me every chance she got, and that throb kept on pulsing, hardening.

In the middle of our rounds of fake pleasantries, I noticed Sebastian in the corner, staring at us. She hadn't seen him, and I didn't want her to. The way he was looking at her made me feel a bit threatened. The questions kept coming to me... Was she still in love with him? What happened? Did he still love her? The last one was obvious; I could see the longing screaming out of his eyes. The first one bugged me more than I would like to admit. She'd sold us the fake spiel that they'd decided to call it quits because they weren't ready for marriage, but I always felt there was more to it.

When she finally spotted him, I was sure of it. Her whole body stiffened, and she retreated into herself almost instantly. I hated who she became around him, not that I'd spent much time with them, but whenever that happened, she'd become reserved and pulled back. Aria was the person who captivated a room, could talk to anyone about everything, and rarely used a filter. But under Sebastian's arms, she'd stayed quiet, disengaged.

"I have to go to the bathroom," she said before beelining to the ladies' room in the back.

Don't ask why I followed her…

Don't ask why I stayed in the hallway listening for any signs of distress…

Don't ask why I cared…

Because I didn't! I was playing my part, nothing to read into, right?

This wouldn't be the first time I did something like this… sadly, it wouldn't be the second either. So just like that, my mind went back.

Loud music hurt my ears while I squeezed through the crowd. It was Aria's 21st birthday. Sabrina had the whole club closed down for the party, complete with a karaoke setup. Usually, I wasn't invited to her birthday parties, but this one had the whole family participating. It was a surprise party, and I figured Sabrina had mistakenly invited me. I wasn't sure why I came, but there I was, eavesdropping on the happy couple.

"What's the big deal? It's only karaoke," Aria went on the defensive.

"It's embarrassing; that's what it is." His condescending tone made my clenched fist twitch.

"It's my birthday, and it's a karaoke bar. What did you expect was going to happen?"

Sabrina got between them, pulling Aria to the stage, where they performed their rendition of the over-the-top, goofy, choreographed 'Wannabe'. It was amazing. The smile on their faces was captivating and contagious as they lit up the stage with their presence, but as always, I couldn't keep my eyes away from the blonde. My heart kept pounding during each turn, hip bump, and laugh. It was impossible not to stare at her, the way she glowed. And for a moment, I forgot we hated each other.

When the two vixens finished, Aria ran into Sebastian's arms, but he pulled back, snapping at her. I couldn't hear what he told her, but I did see the water in her eyes.

I found myself following her to the bathroom, but I quickly turned away. It wasn't my job; it was his.

For some reason, that day always stuck with me. How I'd stayed outside in the hall, waiting… when she'd finally passed by me, she did so with her poised, pulled-up self. Fresh makeup covering whatever she wanted to hide. Not long after, I'd found myself in a similar situation.

"So did you two set a date?" Helen asked when we all got seated. We got front-row seats for Lana's recital. The family's presence was mandatory, and Lana kept reminding us of this every day for the past month.

"No, but we're thinking Christmas, since Ari loves it so much," the pompous ass answered.

She doesn't like the cold, you idiot! *I yelled at him with my inner voice, fist ready for the punch.*

Helen cleared her throat and gave me a side look,

matching my thoughts.

"Did you find a dress already?"

"No, but I found this short one for the reception; it's like a ballerina dress with glitter on it that glows in the dark." Her eyes twinkled, and her smile was so wide as she described every detail of the dress to my sister.

Sebastian's voice turned it into a frown. "You're not seriously thinking about wearing that to the reception?"

"No, I was joking," she faltered, and something inside me tightened.

"Our wedding is not a joke." His voice made me want to rip out his vocal cords. Trust me, I had a lifetime of knowledge of all the different ways to rip him apart.

"That's not what I said."

Why the hell was she explaining herself to him? He was the one in the wrong here.

But I bit my tongue, reminding myself that it was not my place; not anymore. Maybe it never was.

"Whatever," he brushed her off as the curtain pulled up. During the intermission, she bolted for the bathroom, and I went after her. I heard the sobs but never spoke to her about them. I got back to my seat before she exited the stall.

The door finally opened, and she froze when she saw me standing, waiting.

"What are you doing?" She glared at me, makeup intact. Perfect.

"My marital duties," I said matter-of-factly.

She crossed her arms over her chest, cocking a brow. "We're not married yet. And I don't need you to take care of me; been doing fine on my own so far." She tried to bite, but failed. And I knew damn well she was not some damsel in distress, but I hated her ex and wanted to flaunt his loss in his face.

"Come on, let's dance." I took her hand, but she snatched it right out.

"No! And don't touch me. Ever!"

The Ice Queen was back!

Chapter 19

Aria

This whole thing was a complete mess... Hell, I was a complete mess. I'd been snapping at Cillian ever since the stupid bonfire where I had to watch Chrissy all over him. It was not like I expected him to go celibate, but did he have to do that kind of stuff in front of me? And now, in the big ballroom, with the sexy bartender behind the bar, all smiles and flirtatious. It made me sick.

Another thing that was not helpful was that Sebastian was here with another woman. It was a low blow, seeing him holding her hand, attached to a slender body, long legs, curly red hair, and watermelons for breasts. Hurt more than it should have, not to mention the instant dig into my self-confidence, which somehow ceased to exist whenever I was around him.

It wasn't just that I had small tits; it was what they carried. And Sebastian knew all about it, had made it a point whenever the topic came up. Unfortunately, that had mostly happened in the bedroom.

The small of my back felt the familiar touch, the one that had been there for most of the night, the one I couldn't stop thinking about, no matter how much I tried.

"You ok?" His low voice felt like a brush to the skin, prickling my nerves.

"Why do you care?" I snapped, not sure why. Right now, I wasn't angry at Cillian, despite it being weird that he was playing nice. It was out of character for him, regardless of the public truce.

"Come on, dance with me, show him you're better off."

"And you think that my being with you makes me better off?"

"Damn right!"

"Egotistical bastard much?"

"Hey, what can I say? I happen to like my ego." He shrugged, gently pushing me to the middle of the room. The venue was nice, with the lights dimmed around the dance floor, a mix of blue and white spotlights moving in circles. I noticed a couple of people swaying, wrapped up in each other.

"I bet you do."

He pulled me into a twirl, my mouth inches apart from his. I could smell his breath. There was something different; no usual nutty odor.

Wait a minute!

I took another sniff.

Was that... vanilla?

Stop smelling him!

"You're prettier than her," Cillian whispered in my ear, his lips brushing against the outer rim of it. He took my left hand into his hold.

On its own accord, my free hand went around his neck, almost like an instinct, but before I could pull it back, he pushed me closer. He led the first step into the waltz, and I followed. We had mastered all the classical dances at a very young age. He'd been my partner at my first debutante ball and ever since. We moved together in perfect sync, the steps coming ever so naturally.

"You don't need to lie, I am not blind. She's gorgeous and has the perfect body." That last part was supposed to stay silent, but it escaped my mouth without thinking.

"So do you," he said, and I scoffed, brushing it off with a loud "pfft."

His talking, or even thinking about my body, was not something I needed on my mind, not now, not ever. A visual of both our bodies colliding, naked, was right there with the thoughts, not allowed!

NOPE!

Delete! Delete! Delete!

Oddly, the entire time we were dancing, I hadn't glanced in Sebastian's direction once. Instead, I had been eyeing the sexy mixologist—black long hair, amber eyes, a nose ring, and a set of full lips painted devil red. She had a tattoo on her neck, roses and thorns, suiting her perfectly. She was focused on Cillian, giving zero fucks about the fact that he was dancing with someone else. She knew what she put on the table, and I was no threat. I wondered if he would get it with her; she was his type after all. The thought sent a lump to my throat, and suddenly I forgot how to breathe.

"Deep breath." He squeezed my lower back, maybe to reassure, maybe to freak me out... I wasn't sure. "Stop looking like you're constipated for fuck's sake. You want to make him suffer, not thinking that I make you sick."

If he could see the entanglement in my mind, he would understand. But he didn't deserve my explanations, nor did I want him to. He was the one who forced me into the spotlight. I didn't have to be a good sport about it. So, with one quick clearing of the throat, I quipped, "Well, you being near me makes it hard to hide the truth."

"Don't be an asshole; I was trying to help."

I couldn't decide whether he was being sincere or messing with me, but I chose to play along.

"Hey, I'm the nicest asshole you'll ever meet," I bantered, but it only made his smile wider.

"And yet you seem calm in my presence." And there came the cocky grin. I hated how good it looked on him.

"I may look calm, but in my head, I've slapped you about three times already."

"Only three, I must be losing my touch." He added a brow twitch to his smirk. Ugh, he was frustrating. But I knew what he was doing. And it was working. He got me out of my head and into our usual back-and-forth. It was then that I noticed his line of sight switch from me to the bar. My chest tightened, my palms got sweaty, and I stepped away from his hold, the same song still playing.

"Thank you." It came out more as a whisper, but I didn't even check if he had heard me, too busy walking away without an explanation.

How was I supposed to live like this for a whole year? Knowing he would be doing God knows what with God knows who. As I tried my best to compose myself, all the mini quiches I'd nibbled during the night threatened to reemerge. I swallowed them down right before I got to our table, plastering on my best smile as I joined in on the conversation about the current rise in gold prices. One thing I was always grateful to have inherited from my father was the ability to switch into business mode at any given moment. But it didn't mean there wasn't something looming in the back of my mind.

Chapter 20

Cillian

Shifting my weight slightly on the rubber mat, I pressed my M27 tight into my shoulder—the sling cinched just right, high and tight. The room smelled like machine oil, and I never understood how they managed to get the smell.

This week was the indoor simulated marksmanship training, ISMT for short. The system was designed and utilized as a tool to support the training of all the organic weapons of an infantry battalion. We had one of the best setups here on base. It provided a realistic, interactive environment for refining marksmanship, weapons handling, and tactical decision-making. It used interactive audiovisual systems that simulated realistic scenarios, and it was the closest thing I got to real action. It included moving targets, and it was just the distraction I needed after what happened this weekend. I still had trouble getting certain images deleted from my brain cells, mostly ones of a pompous ass in the leading role. The way he'd gotten under Aria's skin. The way they both got under mine.

The commanding instructor stepped up, clearing his throat. "Targets will appear at random intervals, and you will engage center mass. Take immediate action if you get a malfunction." I glanced at Marco, his M9 at the ready.

Yeah, we knew the drill.

The screen flickered to life, revealing a dusty urban street—busted windows at the side of the building, a burning car in the center, trash all around. My pulse slowed, everything else fading.

Beep.

The simulation started, and the first target appeared on the right, a male with an AK raised. I fired twice, right in the center, and he dropped to the ground. I checked my chamber, took a breath, and continued scanning. Another one appeared on the left, behind a dumpster, but this time it was moving. No weapon in sight, so I waited, focusing on the hands. Then I zeroed in on the pistol.

Crack - miss. Another one, this time a hit, and he dropped.

Adjusting my stance, I leaned into the rifle, the air conditioning doing nothing to keep the sweat away. My finger twitched off the trigger as I reset.

Another target came front and center, a hostage scenario—a civilian, hostile behind with a pistol to the head. My breath caught when a strand of blonde hair blew out in the air.

Nope.

Time was of the essence, and I didn't need my imagination to bring real people into these scenarios. And why the hell were my protective instincts overstimulated all of a sudden?

I took a deep breath, my finger hovering over the trigger, front sight post over the threat's shoulder. A controlled exhale right before the crack—clean headshot.

The screen registered it, spelling out 'neutralized'.

"Maintain the discipline," I heard Marco's voice over the headset.

Roger that.

I prepared for the rest, taking another deep breath. Every soldier loved to shoot, but this simulation wasn't about loving it; it was about perfecting it. Discipline under pressure, consistency. Responding to the chaos with control. This was where others got ready for the real thing, but it was where I got all the action. That notion sent a sharp ping somewhere deep inside. For a moment, I'd forgotten I was out of active duty.

I shook it off when another target popped out, a familiar golden speck causing my blood to boil. I hit the trigger too quickly.

The screen beeped red, revealing a blinking *"Civilian hit."*

"What was that, Wright?"

That was my messed-up head occupied with thinking about the prick clouding my control. And I never lost control.

Tapping out, I reassembled my weapon and headed outside, where my officer was waiting for me, shaking his head in disapproval. "What the hell happened in there?"

Should I lie or tell the truth?

"I had unfinished business with a SOB who looked a lot like the civilian whose head I blew up."

I gave him a shrug of the shoulder to let him know I didn't give a damn. He knew I would never do such a thing in real life, but it didn't make it any less wrong.

"Don't make it a habit," was all he said before Marco spoke through the communication system. "The Eagle after

I'm done?"

"Sure," I said, knowing damn well alcohol wasn't going to solve any of my problems. Maybe some distance would. And then it hit me—my best idea yet. So before I indulged in some fine-tasting whiskey, I made a stop on the way.

My base commander kept on begging me to lead a boot camp in New London. Luckily, there was one starting next week—no time like the present, or something like that. When I entered Captain Michelson's office, he welcomed me with his full support. I filled out the necessary paperwork; the mere act made my shoulders feel lighter.

"So, what's eating you up?" Marco spoke the moment we took our seats at the bar - a bottle of whiskey's finest and two tumblers set before us. Marco poured, and my stupid heart tried to do the same.

"Nothing."

"You shot a civilian," he pointed out.

"He deserved it," I snapped.

"Ouch. What did a graphic design ever do to you?"

"Fuck!"

I was the image of desperation, my elbows on the bartop, my hands holding my heavy head. I only had myself to blame, since I allowed her to get into my head. Again. And after all the years fighting it off. It was my personal form of torture, all the emotions mixing up right there in the center of my chest.

"I'm going to take a wild guess and say this has

something to do with Aria."

I stayed silent, letting it do all the talking. Marco's head bobbed next to me.

"And by the way, thanks for the invite."

I turned to face him, confused.

"Yeah, good thing your fiancé's got the brains…" he trailed off, swiping out his phone and turning the screen to me. A digital invitation for an engagement party stared at me. I completely forgot about that, and I'd approved the damn thing, down to the guest list.

"Shit, man, sorry. I'm all up in my head," I grumbled.

"Yeah, I can see that. So who did you actually neutralize back there?" my friend wondered, looking at me like he already knew the answer.

"Her ex."

I took out the stupid-douchebag-prick part, but he got the gist, hissing before taking a long swig. Another person who got under my skin, and all because of *her.* All my problems had one denominator—Aria. The bane of my existence, the one that got away without ever being mine.

"So what? You're jealous now?"

"No!"

I don't do jealous. Never have. Never will.

"Wow," he gibed, "she really did a number on you, and you haven't even walked down the aisle."

You have no idea!

Funny thing, neither did I.

Chapter 21

Cillian

"Congratulations. We always knew you'd end up together," Tina and Ian, my aunt and uncle, smiled as they shook my hand. Aria was across the room, next to Sabrina and Nala, giving a performance of a lifetime, looking drop-dead gorgeous in a blue cocktail dress. I'd had the pleasure of meeting her other best friend last night while she was helping Aria set up the venue's decorations.

It was the night of our engagement party, and Aria had organized the whole thing. She got The Brick closed down for our closest friends and family. It was a nightclub where Nala worked, so it wasn't hard to pull the strings. The place had all-brick walls, hence its name, with a giant fake bonsai tree standing right in the middle of the dance floor, surrounded by large blue balloons. The music echoed from the speakers, soft and lyricless as champagne trays worked their way through the room. The atmosphere was good, with people engaging in conversation, all smiles and pleasantries.

I made my way to the bar, noticing Marco transfixed. I ordered another glass of whiskey and turned to check his line of sight. The three best friends were laughing, drinks in hand, screaming trouble. While I focused on Aria, Marco was all in on her partner in crime.

"I see Nala has caught your attention."

My soon-to-be best man hummed, not blinking, as if he would miss something with the action.

"She's nice, different," he spoke almost in a whisper.

"Different how?"

"I don't know. Just different."

I was about to pry when a large screen lit up, causing a lump to appear in my throat. A slideshow. A fucking slideshow of baby pictures of Aria and me. A timeline of our buried friendship. Each new slide felt like a knife to the gut. The beam on our faces while we looked at each other, the innocent hugs. People around us gushed with audible 'Aaaw's.'

I glanced to the corner where Aria was fully into her nail biting. She'd asked me via text if I'd thought it would be a good idea to do the whole presentation, to make it more believable. At the time, I'd thought it was a great idea, but now I wasn't so sure. Seeing the past blown up on the big screen didn't make me nostalgic—it made me angry.

Before I got lost in my thoughts, a video started to play, making something turn in my stomach. The two of us were under her favorite tree in Martha's Vineyard on her tenth birthday, spinning in circles while holding hands. She had flowers in her hair and looked like the epitome of innocence. The video's sound was off, but I remembered every single word we'd spoken.

"Promise you'll always be my best friend," she demanded, her nose wrinkling.

"Only if you promise the same."

"Done. Easiest promise ever." Gleaming at me, her eyes sparkled in the sun.

Who would have thought that both of us would break that promise so effortlessly? Tightening the grip around my tumbler, I drowned the memory with the last drop. Thankfully, the screen turned black, and applause filled the room. On cue, I walked over to Aria with a nod.

Time to put on the show.

She clinked her glass, and I got to her side, placing my palm on the small of her back.

"Thank you all for celebrating with us. It means the world to share our story with our little circle." She lifted her champagne glass, and the rest of the party followed. "Hear! Hear!"

Nala whisked her away, leaving my palm cold. For some reason, my eyes stayed glued to them as they walked to the bar.

I felt her before she opened her prying mouth.

"What happened with the two of you?" Sabrina with the mother of all questions.

"Shouldn't you ask your best friend that?" I scoffed, my eyes still on Aria, who was striding toward us, her long legs daring me to look.

"Like I haven't tried. The fact that she won't tell me only proves my initial thought… You did something!" she accused, and I snapped my gaze to meet her condescending one. I was about to retaliate when Aria's hand found mine, causing a flutter somewhere on the inside.

What's that about?

"I think we have done our part, don't you?" she whispered, leaning toward me. With her heels, she almost matched my height.

"I agree, I'll call the driver."

"Good, I'll say goodbye, and I'll meet you outside. I need some air."

"Fine."

"Fine."

About fifteen minutes of 'goodbyes' and 'congratulations on your engagement' later, I stepped outside to find one shivering Aria. I took off my jacket and threw it over her shoulders.

"You could have gotten in the car if you were cold." My tone came out more annoyed than intended. Aria let out a scoff, "I don't know what your sense of perception is, but I sure as hell don't see a car anywhere."

I took out my phone to call the driver again, Aria still shaking by my side. He pulled over before my thumb pressed the green icon. "I'm sorry, I went to gas up the tank," the driver said, opening the door for Aria.

"Put the heat on max," I hushed the order, and he nodded. Sliding into the back seat, I had to resist the urge to wrap my arms around Aria to warm her.

The entire drive home, all I could hear was Aria's teeth clattering while I was sweating like a pig. I didn't know she still had trouble with the cold.

"Cillian, look at this." I turned to look at Aria gliding over the frozen lake, making another pirouette. She loved ice skating and did it for fun; fell in love with it after watching

some 'Ice Princess' movie. We'd spent our winter holidays in Vermont, skiing, sledding, and throwing snowballs. It was all great fun, but watching Aria skate was the highlight of my day. The way she glowed with the widest of smiles, almost becoming one with the ice. In a blink, that figurative thought became a literal reality when she disappeared under the ice. It took us five minutes to locate where the undertow had taken her, two minutes to break the ice before dragging her out. It took my dad another two minutes to breathe life back into her. It took one look into her eyes to make my heart stop. It took her the entire day to stop shaking, cozied up by the fire, me never leaving her side, holding her tight.

When we arrived home, she was still shaking, so I turned on the fireplace and motioned for her to sit in front of it. Then, I grabbed a large blanket to cover her whole body. I sat on the floor next to her, loosening my tie.

"Do you want me to make you a cup of tea?"

"You don't have to act nice; nobody can see us. It will pass. It usually never lasts longer than an hour. You can go; I'll be okay."

I hated to think that this still happened to her after all these years. We were fifteen when she'd fallen in. She used to love Christmas; I mean, she still did, but she rarely played in the snow after that.

"Fine."

"Fine."

I never moved from the floor.

Unable to take the silence any longer, I muttered, "Do you want to use the sauna?"

My voice startled her, like she'd forgotten I was there.

"No, it's fine. You don't have to stay."

When I didn't move, she attempted to stand up, murmuring, "I'll go to my room." Her effort was stopped by her wobbling knees, and I jumped to my feet, holding out my arms. She refused my help, so without thinking, I swooped her up in my arms and carried her to her room. I laid her on the bed, then adjusted the thermostat, despite it being the cusp of summer.

I left her in her room, but I spent the next hour sitting on the floor with my head pinned to the door as I listened to her sobs, hating every single time I called her an Ice Queen. I had to fight every muscle in my body that wanted to stand up, barge in, and hold her tight. My hand started to spasm from the strength of my tight grip. After the sobs had stopped, I remained, staying for another half an hour just to be sure. When there was no sound to be heard, I retreated to the gym. Running outside usually relaxed me, but I didn't want to leave her alone, so I went on the treadmill. It was the first time I exercised without my earplugs in, but I needed the silence. I desperately needed there to be no sound.

When I reached the two-mile mark, I stepped down and took a quick shower. I got to her room and slowly cracked the door open enough to glance at her sleeping. My chest released a breath of relief, and only then did I head to my room.

Leaving my door ajar, I went to bed, never closing my eyes.

Chapter 22

Aria

I woke up feeling like I was in an igloo. I hated how the cold affected me. My whole body reacted to one gust of wind as if it were in a deep freezer.

Last night had been a living nightmare. With Cillian so close, and my body undecided between burning up and shaking with cold, I'd had trouble breathing. All I'd wanted was for him to hold me, like he used to.

He didn't.

I had to gather all my strength not to fall apart in front of him. But as soon as I'd gotten under the covers, I couldn't contain it any longer. It was the first time since Vermont that I'd spent the entire night shivering.

I had to go to the office today to work on damage control and the merger proposal. I got up, made myself a thermos of coffee, and called Daddy's assistant, Lisa, to let her know I'd be in in about thirty minutes.

Back in my room, I washed up and pulled on a power suit. I knew Cillian was leaving today, which meant I wouldn't see him for an entire week. And after last night, the separation couldn't have come at a better time.

The penthouse was quiet, and I instantly felt lonely, as if something were missing. I didn't want to admit to myself what it was. I knew, though…it was hard to deny.

Thankfully, I had my master's thesis to focus on, and I was determined to dig in and finish it by the wedding.

The wedding.

Fuck, now my mind went there. It was not supposed to, but it had, making me spiral in the middle of the kitchen.

Shaking it off, I took my thermos and drove my Bentley to the office. The moment I stepped into the building, people started congratulating me, and I smiled it all away. Passing Lisa with a wave, I went straight into my father's office.

"Peanut, you're here," he beamed at me, standing up to wrap me in his arms. I took his hug, relaxing into it.

"You did great last night," he whispered, planting a peck on top of my head.

"Yeah, I should switch my major to theatre," I deadpanned.

"Funny."

"They do stand-up comedy, too," I jested, noticing his eyebrows pushed together.

"Aria…"

My name, accompanied by that tone, dragging it out, was all the warning I needed to know he was not taking it.

"Fine, sorry. Anyway, I wanted to say hi before I dive in with the legal team."

"Okay. Give 'em hell," he prompted, sitting back down in his chair.

"You know it." Clicking my tongue, I pulled out the finger guns, backing away. I turned on my heel and went to the conference room, where everything was already set up. One employee was suing the company, which was without merit, but we still needed to devise a good strategy. It took us two hours, three coffee runs, and one jammed printer to get the nod of approval from our CEOs.

The rest of my days were much the same. I've worked in the office in the morning, typed my thesis during lunch, and spent as much time as I could with Sabrina and Nala in the evening. My nights were spent cuddled up in the screening room.

On Saturday night, nostalgia kicked in. Slumped in my seat, I turned on 'Boy Meets World'. It was a show both Cillian and I loved watching when we were kids. He would tell me that I was his Topanga and that we were destined to be together. My childish brain believed him, and so did my heart.

With the two of us, it was always us against the world. We never had a Shawn in the mix, never needed to fill any voids. We were more than enough for each other... until we weren't. During our high school era, he'd gained popularity as the jock and future prom king. His reputation rose, making all the girls crazy for him; I mean, why wouldn't they? He was the ultimate dream guy. Good-looking, athletic, charismatic...

When my boobs had finally kicked in, boys started to notice me more often. I'd gotten on the volleyball team and formed my circle of friends. We'd drifted... guess, that was when it all started to fall apart.

I held onto his words. He'd said we were meant for each other. That thought helped me cope while he'd dated the hottest girls. He'd been voted prom king and took Chrissy to the prom. She'd been crowned queen. I'd gone with Sebastian; he'd always been there, in the background.

Despite us getting close in high school, we didn't start dating until much later.

After a rumor had spread at school that Cillian deflowered Chrisy, I got drunk. I'd ended up at a beach party and almost lost my virginity to a random guy. I had started crying the moment he got me naked and fled, crushed, because I had always imagined my first time would be with him. And no matter how much I hated him after what he had done, my heart had always burned for him, despite my every protest.

I'd kept my mask on, a full-on performance just for him, one of the Ice Queen he'd so hurtfully named me—not knowing the sting's severity.

Now, my heart burned again, scared of my walls crumbling for the same person who'd put them up in the first place.

Worst part—my night ended with vivid images of my stupid, sexy fiancé, and I allowed it, thinking about him like that... like I always had.

"What are you doing?" I froze when Cillian started pulling off his shirt. With the rest of the family fast asleep, the two of us snuck out of our Vermont cottage into the guest house with the outdoor hot tub.

"Going in, wanna join?" He revealed a curious smirk, going from cute to straight-out cocky. His sixteen-year-old face lost the boyish charm but gained something far more deadly.

"Are you crazy? You'll get pneumonia."

"The water's hot, Aria." And there went his shirt, finding a place on the ground.

Despite it being dark, I couldn't help notice how his body had transformed from that of a little boy to almost that of a man.

He slid his shorts down, almost in slow motion, leaving him in nothing but a pair of white Calvin Kleins. He could seriously model for them.

My eyes drew downward to those dark, thick thighs and all the muscles surrounding them.

I shamelessly perused him, every inch of his glowing skin, the new muscles on his arms, ones that weren't there before. Basketball sure did him good. My gaze stopped at his long, stretched-out fingers, and I wanted them in my hair. My hormones were wild, spiraling all over the place, and I couldn't stop them. He noticed, letting it clear by biting his lower lip. I raked mine, and my tongue slid over where my teeth had just been. Our eyes locked, his twinkling in the moonlight... he looked hungry? And I had the strange urge to feed his every need.

And if I needed a hard smack in the face, I felt something warm soak my underwear. I could feel my cheeks burning with humiliation.

My period showed up!

Five days early!

Excellent!

That was the first time I'd started feeling different about my best friend. After that night, whenever I saw him, I would blush. It was a mixture of embarrassment and something else... it took me a while to realize it was attraction.

There were times I thought he'd felt it too, that he had the same desires... but soon I got an answer...woefully, it was not the one I'd wanted.

Chapter 23

Cillian

I'd barely slept during my time in New London. The base was too quiet, the smell too masculine. I would find myself trying to conjure up the floral scent of Chanel No. 5. It was the only way to get me to close my eyes and drift. The days had passed quickly as I focused on the young recruits. The boot camp was a ten-week program that transformed civilians into soldiers. I was in charge of the first phase, which involved intensive physical training. In my free time, I would hit the gym and hang out with other commanding officers while avoiding the heat.

The time had helped clear my head and gain a new perspective. I couldn't allow myself to get sucked into Aria's orbit anymore. We had a contract; this was business, and in a year, it would all be over.

On Sunday, I drove straight from camp to my parents' house for dinner with the family.

"I almost forgot what you looked like," my mother said the moment I stepped inside, gently smacking my cheek.

"It hasn't been that long," I pointed out, but she brushed it off with a "Oh, hush." If it were up to her, I would still be living with my parents. I advanced forward, searching for my sister.

"Where's Helen?" I asked as the dads emerged from the

hall.

"Bedroom," my father interjected. "She said she needed her strength for the wedding."

It made sense; she was growing an entire human being, after all.

Behind me, I could hear the sound of rattling keys, followed by my mother's loud gasp when the door swung open.

"Look at you, honey, you look beautiful as ever." Turning slightly, I watched her wrap Aria in a hug. She softened in my mother's arms, closing her eyes as she leaned in, muttering, "You're a bad liar, but I still love you."

I never understood why she snapped away a compliment with a joke. She was not a self-conscious person, quite the opposite…especially around me.

My father and Peter came to greet us. Aria hugged them, and I noticed the way she took in their scent, as if she were making it into a memory.

Peter cleared his throat, his serious expression matching my father's.

"Come on, kids, let's eat and talk!"

Talk?

Both Aria and I shared a look, the '*oh-oh' kind*.

With our dropped heads, we dragged our feet to their office. The desk in front of the large window took up most of the space, big enough to fit two large leather chairs. The surrounding walls were like a shrine, covered with articles of our family history and framed pictures of us growing up.

Our fathers took their seats, and Aria and I followed, taking the ones across the table. My mother chose to stand at my father's side, her hand on his shoulder. I swallowed a lump.

"So, as you know, you both have additions to your trust clauses," Peter directed. "And we need to discuss moving forward with them."

I released a breath at the same time Aria did hers, and I wanted to take her hand.

I knew better.

"I know the clause, Daddy, and I don't want it. It's bad enough that I have to live with Cillian in his place; I don't want to build a fake house for me to wither in."

Ouch.

Was living with me so bad? She was the one who'd come to me with the idea of turning it into a business opportunity; she was the one to make the first move. So why was she acting this way? It was a punch to the gut, and for the life of me, I couldn't figure out why it hurt so much.

"We could hire an architect and play it out like we're working on it to show you're upholding the clause. But that's as far as I am willing to take it," she disclosed, each word stabbing the knife deeper and deeper.

"Ok, that seems fair," Peter told her, his voice soft. I could see a bit of remorse and what could only be described as disappointment. Did he honestly want us to build a house together? Like the one we pictured so many moons ago?

"I wanna live in a house exactly like this one," Aria said, pointing her chin to our holiday home. She was skimming through her current magazine. "Except I want it to be blue."

She was lying on her stomach, propped on her elbows,

ankles crossed in the air.

"Where did that come from?"

"There's an article about Rihanna's estate." She turned the magazine to me, showing a large mansion plastered over both pages with the headline 'Inside Rihanna's $13.8M Beverly Hills mansion'.

"So, a large mansion got you thinking about this place?"

We both loved this house, but no one loved it more than her mother. After she'd passed away, we didn't come here as often as we had before. We'd bought the Martha's Vineyard estate to spend our summers there, but we came here every year for Thanksgiving.

"I love this place; it's my favorite. I want to live in a house exactly like this one, maybe with a bigger swimming pool."

"And paint it blue?"

"Is that even a question?"

I chuckled. If she could, she would paint the entire world blue.

"And what about me?"

"You want a say in my house?"

"You mean our *house?"* I wiggled my brows.

She sat up on her heels, glaring at me, *"We're not living together."*

"Of course we are," I blustered, a little bit offended by her reaction.

"Hypothetically, what would you want in our house?"

Ignoring the hypothetical, I perked up, picturing an entire future with vivid images flashing through my mind.

I blurted the first thing that popped into my mind, *"A game room."*

"Naturally, what else?"

"A basketball court," I added.

"If it doesn't interfere with the bigger pool size, sure."

"Deal!"

"Deal!"

"That's it?"

"As long as I get to live with you, I really don't care!"

Her cheeks flushed, and she froze for a minute, thinking over the words. She chose to shake them off, taking them as a joke.

It wasn't one.

I laughed that naive boy's thoughts away, trying to get a read on Aria. She was cold, distant, but then I saw her leg jumping up and down under the table. My hand started to move to her knee, but I stopped it in time.

If she doesn't want to live with you, what makes you think she wants you to touch her?

A pang hit my chest, and I rubbed the ache with my palm. It didn't work, but I kept on rubbing.

My mother gave me a look, but I shook my head, letting her know not to mention my clause, especially not after Aria's reaction to hers. That one was going to stay buried, at least from the woman trying her best to avoid eye contact with me.

Chapter 24

Aria

Sing with me: In New York! Concrete jungle where dreams are made of…

Anyway, it was my bachelorette party week, with Sabrina, Nala, and me conquering the Big Apple, while I continued avoiding my fiancé. Mateo tagged along but stayed at his brother's place. Tyler had been transferred from Tennessee and was in the middle of a basketball camp or something with his new college team. We girls were staying at the Ritz suite overlooking Central Park.

Naturally, as soon as we got settled, my friends started discussing my situation, and both made strong points—none of which I agreed with. As was anticipated, they'd made a bet. Nala stated that Cillian and I would *'for real'* get together before Christmas, Sabrina said later. It was all fun, honestly—them joking about my misery…totally entertaining…surely not soul-crushing…

No… I was fine.

I'm fine!—Cue Ross's face and tone here, from the TV show 'Friends', for those who didn't get it (for those who did, let's be besties).

"Hey, at least you're safe from the one-bed trope."

"What the hell is that?"

"It's kind of self-explanatory, don't you think?" Nala

hinted, but chose to indulge me. "You know when two main characters share a room, and there's only one bed?"

I gawked at her, mortified.

"Don't worry. Since your family is in on the fakeness of your relationship, they'll probably never put you in the same room..." she trailed off, wiggling her perfect eyebrows.

Ok, so now they managed to put another irrational fear into my already over-swamped head. Could you even imagine it? Cillian and I sharing a room, a bed... Him naked...

Nope! We are not going there. Snap out of it!

When they'd finished their characterizations of our character development and the various predicted plot twists, they decided it was time to get into bachelorette mode. It officially began when Sabrina gave me my early wedding present.

If you had to guess what she gave me, well... what could I say?

Yes! It was a state-of-the-art bullet vibrator, to be exact, in sky blue. According to the note it came with, it was for external use only, made of silicone, and had three speeds and seven patterns. It lasted up to two hours and was waterproof.

I was embarrassed to admit that I had never used one before, let alone planned to use one in the future. Holding it in my hand, feeling like a marshmallow, I was tempted.

"I have last year's model, this one is not much different; it's softer though," she said, copping a feel of the fake pleasure maker.

"I use the clit suckers, find them more stimulating," Nala said with reddened cheeks, and Sabrina retorted with no trace of shame. "Mine is over-sensitive, seems to only react well to Mateo's tongue."

"Oh, Dionysus. TMI!" I covered my ears, and Sabrina shrugged.

"Sorry, it's not my fault that I am the only one in the room with a healthy sex life."

"Hey, just because you have the real thing at your disposal doesn't mean it's any healthier than what we've been doing," Nala went on the defensive, waving her finger between the two of us.

"You're right, as long as you're satisfied, it's good enough for me." Sab lifted her hands in surrender, then gave Nala a curious stare. "Anyway, how's it going with the guy you've been obsessing over?"

"You mean Mr. Gallegos?"

"He sounds like a Greek god."

That piqued my interest. I was a sucker for anything mythology-related.

"He looks like one," Nala said under her breath, not silent enough for us to miss it. The two of them continued talking while my head snapped from one horny girl to another.

"Do tell," Sabrina prodded, working her hair into a side braid.

"You're married." Nala feigned shock, dropping her jaw for emphasis.

"So? I can look at other men. It makes me appreciate my husband all the more."

"Fair point."

"Greek god… Continue, please."

"I think he's gay!" Nala couldn't hide her disappointment

when she said it.

"Why?" both Sabrina and I gasped.

"Do you know how many women come up to him, drooling—literally?"

Last month, some hotshot had bought up an entire VIP area at the Brick, where Nala worked. He spent every Friday and Saturday at the club, and Nala soon became obsessed.

"And he doesn't give them the time of day, doesn't even flinch when they grope him… and trust me, it's some heavy groping," Nala finished, cheeks still flushed.

"What's his first name again?"

"You really are bad with names?" I gibed at her, knowing it wouldn't faze her one bit.

"If I read them, I don't forget them, but if I hear them, they tend to evaporate."

"It's Daniel," Nala responded, and Sabrina started typing on her phone with one hand while holding her hair in the other.

Never lifting her sight from the screen, Sab hummed, "He doesn't have any online presence, not even a social media account. No Insta, no TikTok, no Facebook. That's alarming." She waved her disapproving hands, but then lifted one finger. "Wait, he has a LinkedIn account." Her jaw dropped, and I joined her side, and so did my jaw. He was yummy, all corporate in a suit, like a sexy boss.

"Girl, you have to tap that!" Sabrina practically ordered.

"I told you I think he's gay," Nala scoffed.

"No way is this man gay. Just look at him," I pointed out, showing her the picture Sabrina had zoomed in.

"She has been," Sabrina jumped in, tying up the braid

and dragging her fingers to check if everything was in place. Nala shook it off with a laugh.

"I can see it, him bending you over his desk," Sabrina added, making Nala choke on air. She coughed, and I tapped her back, but Sabrina just kept on going, "You, trying so hard not to scream so his workers don't hear you."

Okay, so maybe our little circle was a bit perverted, obsessed with men, and just a bit over the edge, but it was the best damn circle this girl could ever want.

I loved these two crazy witches with a capital B. They were the best part of me, aside from my family.

To make the most of it, I pulled out my phone, opened my party playlist, connected it to the room's ceiling speaker, and hit play. Then I went to my bag and took out two bottles of gin and tonic. It took them less than a minute to jump on the bed, full mixed glass in hand, to get the session started. The first song I chose was 'Turn Me On' by Kevin Little. I found it very appropriate. We danced, drank, sang, and had so much fun that my face was hurting from all the smiling.

I hadn't thought about what was waiting for me back in Boston… Not at all… not about the first wedding night, and certainly not seeing the stupid one-bed trope blinking at me like a neon fucking sign.

Damn Sabrina and Nala for putting stupid shit in my head, ones I couldn't seem to get rid of. And now Cillian was naked in our honeymoon suite, gliding under the covers… in our bed… Did I mention he was naked? His stupid muscles, abs, the deep V… Oh, the deep V, like an arrow screaming *'I have a deadly weapon down there, and I am not afraid to use it, and trust me, I know how to'*…

Stop!

I didn't...

Instead, I became very close to my little Blue Marshmallow, and yes, it was now its given name.

Chapter 25

Aria

On our last day, Nala and I ordered breakfast, while Sabrina took Mateo around the city. The whole week we had spent talking, taking advantage of the spa, and all the alcohol mixes known to mankind.

"You look like shit," Nala point-blanked, rolling in the room service tray.

"Rude much?"

"You don't need my fake appraisal."

"Maybe I do." I let out a sigh.

"What's wrong?" She stepped aside, giving me the space to walk between her and the tray. I tossed my body onto the couch, my mind not following.

Everything.

How was I supposed to answer that one?

My fake fiancée is making my life miserable just by breathing.

How did that sound? Any thoughts?

"I don't know, I guess it's nerves with the wedding closing in."

My best friend gave me a sympathetic look. "Aria, are you sure you want to go through with this?"

No.

"Yes," I answered instead. "I have no other choice."

"That's not really true. You look miserable."

I felt like it, but chose not to share it. Getting married was not my problem. Certain feelings resurfacing... now that was the biggest pain in my ass.

"How's the program going?"

I was deflecting, sure, but I knew art was Nala's one weakness.

She'd enrolled in an art seminar for summer break, which proved to be an excellent distraction for her. She was a magician with graphite, her hand a work of wonder. She mostly drew for herself, but once she'd shown me her sketchbook, I was mesmerized. Her primary focus was people's eyes, and I'd found my own looking back at me between the pages.

"It's amazing. I've never worked with a brush before, so it's new and different."

Usually, I would have to ask, more like beg, to see her work, but this time she handed over a big Aquablok—voluntarily. With each new sheet, my eyes widened with disbelief. I was no art enthusiast, far from an expert, and it was simply nature painted on a piece of paper, yet I couldn't stop looking—the colors, the strokes, the details. On the last page, I had to catch my breath. I was staring at Boston Harbor, the water looking as if it were moving, the moon reflecting in the current. It was like a split image: the water reflected the night, but the sky was bright, as if it were midday, the sun at its peak.

"Nala, this is amazing."

"Yeah?"

"Can I have it?"

"I was thinking of you when we got that assignment. I know it's your favorite place in the city."

You know how every person had their place to hide, think, soul-search, contemplate life... This old bench overlooking Boston Harbor was mine, the view looking back at me from the artwork I held in my hands.

"Sooo," I dragged, "is that a yes?"

"Of course, it's yours."

"Thank you!"

"You wanna talk about it?" She tilted her head, eyes soft, no edges, just concern.

"It feels like I was promoted to Shit Show Supervisor tasked to solve problems made by others, and I am tired of it."

"Did Cillian do anything?"

Yes. He got under my skin.

"No. I'm angrier at our dads. We had dinner on Sunday, and they mentioned our trust clauses. All the kids had their own choices to add."

I could see the way her shoulder fell.

"Mine was a dream house."

"Oh, Aria." Her whole face frowned, and her hands found mine, surrounding them with her warm fingers.

Shaking my head, I faltered, "It's stupid."

"Let it out anyway." Her tone, a mix of soft and commanding, was hard to deny. Gathering strength or whatever I needed to get deep into it all, I took a deep breath.

"A year ago, I was engaged to the guy I thought I was going to spend the rest of my life with, and they never brought up that clause." I swallowed. "Honestly, I forgot all about it. I made it up when I was thirteen."

Her grip tightened, and tears welled up. I tried to blink them away, but there was no stopping them. Everything flooded… my life with Sebastian, my life with Cillian, my mom, my future…

It all came like a tornado and turned into a tsunami.

"Daddy?"

"Yes, Peanut?"

"When Cillian and I get married, will you make me a dream house?"

"Of course I will," he snickered. "I will make you whatever you want."

We were sitting under my mom's favorite tree, the grass tickling my bare feet. The sun was up high, but we were shielded from the rays.

"I want a big castle with a tower like Rapunzel so Cillian can climb up to me every day." My dad laughed, working on my braid. He was getting better at it.

"What makes you think Cillian would climb to you every day?"

"He always does it on the monkey bars," I blurted.

"Monkey bars are easier."

"He would climb to the moon for me," I assured, determination clear in my tone.

He chuckled, and I snapped, "You don't think he would?"

"Oh, that boy would go to the end of the world for you."

"Then why are you laughing?"

"Because you're only thirteen," he emphasized the number, like I wasn't aware of my own age.

"So? I know what I want, and you always say to fight for what I set my heart on."

"Is that really your wish? To marry Cillian?"

"Of course, Daddy, who else would I marry? He's my best friend. Besides, we already got married, remember?"

That girl had no idea where life would take her, how she would lose her best friend, only to be forced to marry him. Except now, Cillian wouldn't even climb one flight of stairs for me.

"I'm sorry," I croaked, feeling the knot in my stomach tighten.

"Don't you dare. I told you to let it all out. I am here for you, you know that, right?"

I gave her a nod, and words seemed irrelevant to the moment. My tears were enough, speaking louder than any word could. I stayed on the couch for an hour, and we shifted the conversation to school, my thesis, and her seminar.

At the mention of the wedding, she pointed out that she didn't want to come, thinking she would slip when drunk. When I pressed her more about it, she revealed that she loved love too much to be a part of the charade. Although she was supportive, she couldn't stand watching me get 'fake married.' Especially after today. And I loved her too much to deny her. She did promise me she would be at the real one. I didn't have the heart to tell her that it felt like it wasn't in the cards for me.

I gave her an invitation anyway, and I saw the look in her eye, the one telling me that for me, she would attend.

I hugged her and looked at the art she gave me.

The deep blue abyss hypnotized me into a state of calm, as if the water itself were reassuring me that everything would be all right, that even the troubled waters could attain some serenity. And for the first time, I didn't feel like drowning, but rather floating on the surface.

Chapter 26

Aria

Before I knew it, it was Wednesday night, and our flight to the Seychelles was tomorrow. We were taking our whole family with the company's private plane, including Sab and Marco, Cillian's best man. The only good thing about this whole charade was that at least the entire family knew the real story, so I didn't have to lie or pretend in front of them.

My nerves wouldn't allow me much sleep, so I snuck into the screening room and turned on 'Sabrina, the Teenage Witch'. I consistently binged shows I already knew by heart, making them my comfort. This show, in particular, knew how to take me back to my teenage years and reminded me not to grow up in a non-literal way. There were a few people who accepted me with all of my quirkiness, and I could count them all on the fingers of one hand. I cherished the fact that I allowed my inner child to live vicariously through me, unlike some people. But I was okay with that, with who I was, and that was what mattered the most.

"Why do you always have to do that?" Sebastian gave me his default disapproving look as I danced in the cereal aisle.

"Because it makes me happy and I love the song," I pumped my chest to the beat and continued to sing along to Lizzo's 'It's About Damn Time' playing out of the speaker at

Whole Foods.

He lifted his head with frustration. "I'll go get the wine; meet you at the register."

I grabbed a box of Cocoa Pops and headed in his direction, putting it in the basket that Sebastian was holding.

"Why did you get this one?" I pointed at the wine labeled Pinot Noir.

"It's wine, it's red, it was on the top shelf..."

It was also my least favorite.

There were many moments when I'd watched my self-esteem go up in flames. Many thoughts raced through my mind. Yet, as I remembered standing behind Sebastian at the cash register, feeling like nothing, the doubts resurfaced.

So many questions haunted me, and it ate me up inside. Truth be told, it wasn't the question that bothered me; it was the answer—or, better yet, the lack thereof. I couldn't imagine who I would be if I were happy. The concept of happiness was a distant dream, a puzzle I couldn't solve, and it weighed heavily on my mind. I hid it well, though.

I never allowed my guard to falter, never revealed my vulnerabilities. I had made that mistake once, and it had cost me dearly.

"You have three options: first is a total mastectomy, where we surgically remove one or both breasts completely; the second option is a prophylactic mastectomy, which is a preventive surgery aimed to remove all breast tissue that could potentially develop into breast cancer, and your third option is a lumpectomy. That requires waiting for the tumor to

appear, then we would remove the small volume of breast tissue containing the cancer, including the surrounding margin of tissue, but the breast would be conserved."

Sebastian suddenly let go of my hand, but all I could do was stare at the test stating that I was a carrier for BRCA1. I held back my tears as the doctor advised me to take my time to think about it.

That day, I'd cried like I hadn't since I was seventeen. All I'd wanted was to be held, reassured that everything would be okay. Instead, I got silence and distance. Sebastian hadn't slept in our bed that night, nor the night after that. Thinking about it now, that was probably the pin in our timeline where the drift had started to work itself up. He had seen the tears, knew the fears, but had chosen not to acknowledge them. So I'd buried it all and added another mask to my arsenal of protection.

A loud thud woke me up. The screen was still playing, and by the looks of it, a lot of episodes had been missed. I stood up, but was immediately pulled down thanks to a hell of a back pain. Sleeping in a seated position would do that to a person. With a great deal of effort, I made my way to the noise coming from the kitchen. I froze when I laid my eyes on Cillian, shirtless, working the coffee machine.

My throat went dry.

I cleared it.

He turned around.

Those green eyes pierced through me.

"What are you doing? We leave in fifteen."

Shit.

I checked the time on my phone—triple shit.

I bolted to my room without saying a word. Thank Dionysus, I'd packed yesterday; otherwise I'd be screwed. I worked fast, going straight for the shower. Multi-tasking, I brushed my teeth while scrubbing my skin. By the time I got dressed, I realized I would have no time to make coffee. I frowned, knowing the one on the plane would probably suck.

Guess I'll have to suffer through it.

Rolling my suitcase, I closed my door and walked to the kitchen. Cillian was leaning on the island, ankles crossed, naked chest covered with a plain white t-shirt. His attention was on his phone, finger scrolling. I hadn't seen him since the dinner at his parents'. Something pinged in the pit of my stomach. A growing kind of ping. What the hell was that?

You missed him.

Emma, what the hell are you getting at?

While the voices in my head bickered, my eyes zeroed in on two thermos cups next to him. I cleared my throat, and his eyes snapped to me.

"Finally. Ready?"

I nodded.

He opened the door for me, and I walked past him, swallowing a lump that was starting to form in my throat.

We got into the elevator, and I tried my best not to look at him. He had a duffel draped over his shoulder, his hands busy holding the two cups.

"Here." He handed me the blue one, and I froze. Cocking a brow, he grunted, "Don't read too much into it."

Tell that to my overthinking.

I hesitated, but ultimately accepted his offering without any commentary. I took a long sip, closing my eyes so my taste buds could get the whole experience. I moaned. He made it exactly how I liked it, with a double shot of vanilla creamer.

In the foyer, Pierre took our bags and carried them to the town car, which was already waiting out front. He opened the door for us, and I slid inside first. Cillian followed. Before Pierre shut the door, he gave us a wide smile and a loud "Good luck!"

We are definitely going to need it.

The drive was long and silent. Neither of us moved, not even to drink the coffee.

Was he as nervous as I am?

It was only when the car stopped on the side of the large plane that we both let out a breath. I stepped out first, watching the driver hand my suitcase to one of the stewards. Climbing the stairs, I felt instant relief when I heard cute little voices gushing. Lana and Karl jumped on me as soon as I stepped inside. I squeezed them tight and gave the rest of the family hugs and kisses before I made myself comfortable for the seventeen-hour flight ahead.

My little rascals curled up to me, and Sabrina read her book across from me. Our parents sat on the other side of the aisle, ready to doze off. Macro and Cillian were at the far end of the plane with their personal stewardess-slash-fan club. The long-legged brunette brought them two glasses of whiskey, and they engaged in a game of chess.

As soon as we rose above the clouds, most people were asleep. Sabrina tossed her book on the empty seat next to her with an exasperated breath.

"What?"

"The stupid scene made me miss Mateo."

I stared at her, wondering what that felt like. I couldn't remember a time when something would make me miss Sebastian whenever we were apart.

"How does that work? Do you play out the scenes as soon as you read them or…?" I didn't know how to finish that question. Frankly, I wasn't even sure why I'd asked it in the first place.

They spoke about their sexual life openly, without any shame, and with so much love. She had a thing for smut and wanted to try every sex scene from any book she'd read, and her husband made all her dreams come true.

And then there was me; all I wanted was for someone to look at me like I was their everything.

"You know what? Never mind…"

"How about a game of Rummy?" Sabrina suggested, turning to the guys who were awake as well. When they nodded, I carefully lifted Lana's head from my lap and placed a cushion under it. We sat across from the man, and Sabrina started shuffling the cards. Marco was a quiet person, and for some reason, Sabrina's presence somehow got him to act even more like his usual robotic-like self.

I ordered us a round of drinks, and we dove into the cards.

"Don't you dare lie right now! Admit you were cheating,

and I will spare your ego," I whispered-yelled in the middle of our fourth game.

Cillian miscalculated the opening points by one point, and I caught the mistake immediately.

"I made a fucking mistake; I took it back. What's the big deal?"

"Come on, Aria, give him a break," Marco insisted, but I wouldn't budge.

"He's a cheater," I argued, pointing my finger at him, making it look like he was guilty of something far worse than simple math.

What the hell was wrong with me? My tone was so over the top, and I knew I was overreacting. It was a stupid game, for crying out loud. Perhaps I was reflecting, or something in that realm.

"I added wrong; I didn't cheat." Cillian's eyes glared at me, virtually begging to let it go. It was Sabrina's hand on my knee that hadn't stopped jumping, that finally calmed me down.

"Fine."

"Fine."

The rest of the flight went without any significant hitches. We played more cards, slept, ate, and sixteen and a half hours later, we landed in paradise.

Chapter 27

Cillian

The manager greeted us when we pulled into the circular driveway of The Coral. The sight was a breathtaking masterpiece, surpassing even the picture Aria had shown me.

"Will you take us swimming, Auntie?" Karl pulled Aria's hand, and she squatted down to meet his excited gaze.

"I thought you'd never ask. Let's get changed and meet up in 15 minutes. How does that sound?" She poked his nose delicately with the tip of her finger, and he giggled at the contact. My nephew jumped up, mischief splattered all over his cute little face. For a four-year-old, he was a bit smaller than his peers, unlike Lana, who was six and tall enough to be ten.

"Yeeeeeeeej," they both screamed and hopped while Aria covered her ears for protection, grinning.

At the front desk, we exchanged the room keys and parted for our rooms, in awe of the beauty surrounding us.

Twenty minutes later, we were situated on the beach. The waiter brought us complimentary champagne and set the flutes on the table of our cabana. I took mine and saw Aria's face light up. I knew that expression very well; she had an idea.

"Sorry to bother you, but it just came to me." She grazed my arm, and my chest tightened when she started to untie her kimono; whether to the contact or to what was coming, I wasn't sure.

"Nala works with a mixologist who excels at creating new cocktails. We could ask her to craft a signature 'Coral' cocktail as a complimentary welcome drink."

With our stake in the hotel, she'd already devised an expansion plan, a marketing budget, and had set up the place with a personal party planner.

"Damn, that's pretty good," Marco jumped in just as her kimono slid down and revealed a simple blue bikini with a floral design covering her most delicate parts. There was nothing special about it, but it made my heart skip a beat.

"I agree, it's a great idea." I nodded, calming my breath.

"Aaaaaaaa," Aria shrieked when Karl squirted water on her back from a water gun.

"Oh, I'm gonna get ya!" And off they went, running towards the water, making my heart stop beating altogether.

I couldn't take my eyes off the sight of Aria spinning my little nephew on the beach. They toppled over and went with it, rolling in the sand. A chuckle escaped me, and an elbow nudged me right in the ribs. I turned to find Marco grinning at me.

"What?"

"Are you catching feelings for your future wife?"

Catching? No. My feelings had been playing ping-pong for over a decade, but I wasn't gonna let that one out. I shook my head instead. The prick tsked, and all I wanted to do was punch the amusement from his face, but a certain laugh made me snap in the direction of the water. Aria was in a splash fight, with both Karl and Lana turning against her. She'd always been amazing with them, with my whole family, for that matter, except with me. For some reason, I was enemy number one.

"Watch yourself," Marco warned, "you're getting awfully obvious."

I chose to ignore him, if only for a couple more minutes. It was impossible not to be drawn into Aria's allure. She had that aura about her, like it was screaming, *'look at me and make sure you enjoy the view'*.

I couldn't help but notice Aria entertaining the kids so Helen could rest. My sister was not four months pregnant with their third, and Joseph, her husband, was a seaman. He was tied to the sea more than he was to the land. He'd be arriving later for the rehearsal dinner. I took the vacant lounge chair next to her. "How are you feeling?"

From the corner of my eye, I saw Aria and the kids starting to build sandcastles.

"Swollen," Helen heaved, shielding her eyes from the sun with one hand. "You nervous?"

"Nope," I popped the P. Nervous was not part of my DNA, but there was some fluttering on occasion when thinking about tomorrow.

"So no cold feet?"

"I don't have much of a choice now, do I?"

"You always have a choice, little brother; this one just happens to be a simple one."

"What's that supposed to mean?"

She winked at me, smiled, and left me hanging, covering

her face with a towel.

I tossed my head back into the chair, losing all train of thought, more bothered than I would like to admit. As I was staring at the clear sky, a jet of water came straight at me so fast I had no time to react.

I groaned, but it turned into a chuckle when I saw Aria running right at me.

"And you call yourself a marine. I am disappointed." Her voice was prominent with taunt, and I leaned right into it.

"I was ambushed, so it's not fair."

"Excuses, excuses," she sassed, tossing me a big water gun.

"Come on, the kids made up a whole obstacle course." She nudged her head behind her, and I followed, noticing impromptu cover stations made of sand. I took the gun and grinned at the weight of it. I cocked a brow in warning, and Aria opened her mouth to protest, but I was faster, pumping it before I squirted it right in that beautiful face of hers.

"Hey, not the face, not the face."

"Afraid I'll ruin your makeup," I mocked, getting closer and aiming lower.

"Who wears makeup to the beach?" She gawked at me.

I took her in, and sure enough, there was no trace of makeup in sight. She turned serious, then let out a loud whistle. With that, two little rascals came to each side. I got attacked, water covering me from head to toe, my laugh unstoppable.

Thought out of the norm, our rehearsal dinner ended on an irregular, yet higher note. Dinner was fantastic; we talked, had fun, and joked around the table. The guests were to arrive early tomorrow morning, so this was our last mellow night before the big show.

"So..." Sabrina stood up, champagne glass in hand. "I know this is not a typical wedding, but I wanted to take the time to appreciate the woman that is Aria, who orchestrated this whole thing."

All eyes turned to the woman of the hour, following the echoes of clapping hands. She was stunning, as always. Her hair was up in a tight bun, with one exotic flower tucked in. She was wearing a simple floral maxi dress, but still exuded the same fearless beauty that we all admired.

"We all know that she's got the brains and the looks; now she'll be getting some fake muscle in the mix." All eyes darted to me, chuckles accompanying. Sabrina continued, "I know I haven't known Aria as much as you, Cillian..." She raised her glass in my direction. "But I know that this woman deserves everything good in this world. So fake or not, I expect you to take care of her."

Aria choked, her head focused on her plate.

"Just remember, I know how to use my heel in all the right places, so be afraid... Be very afraid." Sabrina placed two fingers in front of her eyes, then turned them to me with a death glare. "I'm watching you!" The unexpected turn of the toast left us all intrigued and amused.

I playfully lifted my hands in surrender and gave her a look that I hoped she could interpret, saying, *'I will always take care of her'.*

Chapter 28

Cillian

The day of the wedding started like any other. I went for a quick run by the beach, got back, took a shower, and headed for the venue. All 850 of our distinguished guests had been checked in and accommodated.

In the groom's area, Marco and I eyed the wedding present from my brother, 'The Tales of the Macallan Volume 1,' alongside a Macallan '71, priced at around 160,000$.

Too bad I couldn't drink it.

Last year, after a corruption scandal, his case was retried, resulting in his freedom. And what had my big brother done next? He'd disappeared. None of us knew where he was, but we would get an occasional postcard. Guess my fake wedding wasn't a good enough reason for him to come out of hiding and see his family.

"You ready?" My best man placed a firm hand on my shoulder and gave it a tight squeeze.

"Ready as I'll ever be," I said with all the confidence to mask whatever was culminating in my stomach.

We stepped outside and walked to the beach, where the ceremony was taking place. White chairs were scattered across the sand, arranged along a silk-lined pathway that led to a flower-filled arch. I was impressed with how everything turned out, especially knowing Aria had managed to make it all happen on her own. She never ceased to amaze me.

I took my place under the arch and nodded to the officiant, offering a handshake. He accepted, and I turned around, nervously waiting. All eyes were on me, and I felt the bow tie around my neck tighten.

Soft string music started to play, and the focus went in the other direction. Lana walked out first in a beautiful blue-and-white dress, throwing petals into the air. She had flowers in her hair and the biggest smile on her face. Karl followed, carrying a small pillow with a blue velvet box on top. Nala walked down next, looking fierce in a long blue dress. I turned my attention to Marco, trying hard not to drool at the sight before him. From the get-go, he was captivated by Nala, and the two seemed to click instantly.

Then Sabrina appeared in a dress similar to the one Nala was wearing with her hair tied in a side braid.

The orchestra started playing the wedding march, cueing the guests to stand up and turn.

My body forgot how to function. I couldn't feel my heartbeat, and my lungs held my breath despite my protests.

She was a vision. There was no way a human could look like that. Aria started walking down the aisle with Peter by her side. She had her hair up in a tight bun, and her dress was breathtaking. It had flowers in blue, red, and yellowish colors, suiting her perfectly, making her hips and breasts stand out around her tight waist. She wore a delicate tiara without any flashy diamonds and a veil that fell over her back, trailing behind her as she walked down the path.

Her hands held mine while the officiant read out for us to

repeat our solemn promises. Neither of us hesitated during the *'I do's'*, something reassuring about that notion. When we were declared husband and wife, we sealed it with a kiss. Five seconds, a hard peck, no tongue. That was the plan outlined in the contract. The moment my lips touched hers, I forgot how to count. Not a single number popped into my head. Not one. Warmth filled me, but it vanished when some idiot started whistling. The kiss ended, and we both stared at each other in shock.

What the hell was that?

The crowd cheered and clapped as I took her hand and we headed down the path. We'd held hands a million times before; it was always a perfect fit. Today was no different. Her small, delicate palm morphed in mine, like it was the safest place for it to be. While the people went to the main hall, the photographers guided Aria and me to the beach.

That was the most excruciating thirty minutes of my life, and I was thankful it didn't last longer. Getting the green light from the guy behind the camera, we all went straight to the reception.

When the band called us out for our first dance, I stood up, my hand extended in invitation. Aria looked at it for a long breath, and I saw her throat bob before she clasped her palm over mine. We walked to the middle of the dance floor, closed in on each other, and locked eyes. I placed my hands on the side of her waist, and she followed by putting hers on my shoulders. My breath hitched at the contact. The band started playing the Weekend's 'Dancing in the Flames', except it was a slower version more appropriate for a slow dance.

I let out a soft chuckle. "Smart."

"Right, it's perfect, don't you think?"

Though the song would be considered a love song, I understood the innuendo.

"So that's how you imagine killing me, a car accident?"

"You have no idea," she grinned when I pulled her into a twirl.

"Does that mean there are more scenarios?" I pushed my hand into hers, and she pulled back, coming right back like a rubber band.

"Oh, I've got a whole playbook." She wiggled her brows.

As the song sped up for the chorus, I gave her a pointed look, squeezing her hand. Picking up what I was putting down, she allowed me to pull off a quick dip. Ever so slowly, she straightened up, coming face-to-face with my smirk.

"I didn't think I occupied so much of your thoughts."

"Don't get too excited; I simply like planning your murder."

"Whatever makes you sleep at night?"

"Well, you six feet under will do just fine."

I chuckled, the sound making both of us snap to the realization we were dancing, all over the podium in perfect sync. Her feet followed mine with each step, each turn. The music stopped, replaced by a loud echo of claps. The Maid of Honor and the Best Man joined us on the dance floor as the next song started to play. We had already arranged to switch partners mid-song to end our suffering as soon as possible, but now I hated the plan. Sabrina shimmied over to me, and I stared as Aria went right into Marco's awaiting arms.

"Stop staring," Sabrina snarked, "people will think you're jealous of your Best Man." There was far too much amusement in her tone. I squeezed her hand, and she let out a knowing laugh.

Changing the subject, I stared at Aria's best friend, one brow raised like she was already ready for it. "What have you been up to?"

"Kicking law school's ass, and we moved into Aria's place."

Sabrina must see my surprise because she shook her head, one side of her mouth lifting. "Don't worry, it's only until the charade is over; in the meantime, we'll find something for the two of us."

Something about Aria keeping her place unsettled me, even though it made sense. This arrangement was for a year, and we both knew that meant she'd eventually move out. So, why the hell was I feeling empty all of a sudden?

The band asked the dance floor to be cleared for my parents as 'The Way You Look Tonight' started playing. It was the song of their first dance. We turned all the attention to them as fireworks spread across the sky, marking out the number 35.

My parents strode to the middle of the floor, swaying in each other's arms, love radiating out of them. Their relationship was one to aspire to. There was so much passion in each interaction; even when they fought, you could feel the love booming. Everything they did, they did together and for each other. Thirty-five years of a blissful, happy marriage behind them, and hopefully, so much more ahead.

I choked when my father closed in to her ear, whispering something that brought a twinkle to my mother's eyes.

"This was a good idea," I whispered to Aria, who was staring at their interaction, like everybody around us.

"I know, they're perfect."

Yeah, they are.

When the song faded out, my parents came right to us; Mama all teary-eyed, pulling both of us in for a hug.

"You didn't have to do this," Mama whispered between us, and Aria shrugged.

"People deserve to see real love today," she said, and it made my heart sink so low it formed a hole in the ground.

The reception was nice, people danced, ate, and congratulated us. A surprisingly large number of people shared that they had always known we would end up together. Once upon a time, I'd shared that sentiment. I'd never imagined it would be forced upon me.

The rest of the night went surprisingly easily. Both of us roamed the crowd separately, stealing each other's glances between handshakes.

At the end, we said our goodbyes and headed to Majorca.

Chapter 29

Aria

Waking up to the smell of the sea and sand should be illegal. The plane had just landed, and a car was waiting to take us to our destination.

The drive was quick and silent, and when we pulled to a stop, the door swung open, a hand already waiting for me. The heat, mixed with humidity, hit the moment I stepped out. We walked to the front desk, where Cillian took over, greeting every member by name. The tall man with a mustache, wearing a name tag that read 'Juan,' handed us our keys. I couldn't help but notice the guy handing Cillian two different sets, while I only got one. Why that little exchange caused a knot to tighten in my chest was beyond me, but there I was, losing oxygen.

The bellboy grabbed our bags, and we followed him through a paved pathway surrounded by palm trees. Our accommodation was a villa with two separate bedrooms—per my request.

After Cillian got the staff to sign NDAs, I went to my room and ordered room service. I had a private, small terrace all to myself, calling out to me, and as I waited for my coffee to arrive, I took in the view.

It was a breathtaking resort, the greenery mixed with the quiet chirping sounds giving it an almost desert-island feel. All the promised tranquility was shattered when the main building cut my line of sight like an eyesore. The hotel and casino stuck out like a sore thumb with all that glass, rising six floors. Lifting my hand, I squinted my eyes so that my open palm could cover it up and get me back to enjoying this little secluded piece of heaven. By the looks of it, all the villas were identical in appearance, at least on the outside, designed to impress. Each had a concealed path leading to a small private beach.

Ours had a high ceiling, sleek lines, and so much light coming in that I wanted to hug the blackout curtains with appreciation.

One big downer for me, personally, was the lack of a TV. The brochure did say this place was an electronic-detox paradise, but this girl still had some dreams left in her. But alas, I came here to escape—or to hide.

One thing's for sure—I'll make the best of it.

My first day went something like this:

—a whole lot of tanning

—coffee break

—walking along the shore

—lunch alone on the terrace

—coffee break

——trying to read a book that Nala made me take with me

Despite there being a whole series, my former best friend just happened to give me the one with a plot suspiciously similar to my life. Barely three chapters in, I closed it shut with a disturbing force of rage.

On a more positive note, I hadn't seen Cillian all day. It

didn't stop my mind from overthinking about all the fun activities he was probably experiencing. That stupid extra key flashed through my mind, mocking me. All those women gawking at him when we'd arrived, biting their lips.

We get it, ok... He's hot.

He was also taken, i.e., married—to me. That didn't seem to faze any of them, and frankly, why would it?! I was no threat.

Damn it!

Swallowing one last lump, I bobbed my head and decided to take the higher road. The sun started to set, and the sight took my breath away. There was this serenity about it, almost as if it were taking control of my lungs, making me breathe easily. When the last speck of light disappeared behind the horizon, I grabbed my longer kimono and went for a long walk with the night as my companion. My feet took me to the enormous pool in the shape of an infinity sign. The flickering lights, combined with the moonlight, cast beautiful reflections in the water. The resort was at half capacity, but surprisingly, the pool was on the sparse side.

I walked to the interconnected part, dropped my kimono on an unoccupied lounge, and dipped my toes in the water. It was warm, so I jumped in with ease. I swam an entire lap—if it could be called that, given the shape—but I was proud of myself nonetheless. I knew it was time to get out when my fingertips started to get all wrinkly.

Outside, the brisk air prickled my skin, and I grabbed a towel from a stack for guests to use and dried my slightly shivering body.

Eyeing all the cushions, I wrapped myself in my kimono

and settled into the lounger, enjoying the stars. I couldn't remember the last time I had seen so many sparkling up there. When I was younger, I was obsessed with the sky. I made up names for stars and created my own constellations. Cillian had always been right there with me, memorizing all the names as if they were something essential.

My view was obstructed by a shadowy figure with a British accent, "Pardon me. Do you speak English by any chance?"

As a matter of fact, I speak four languages: German, Spanish, French, and English.

"Yes," was all I said, pulling myself up into a half-sitting position.

"Oh, thank the heavens," he sighed in relief, then, as the British would say, nattered, "I don't know how I would have done this without you understanding me."

"Done what exactly?" He probably couldn't see it, but I could feel my eyebrows furrowing.

"Well, talk to you." His voice got softer, but it only multiplied the lump in my throat.

"Oh, I am sure you can find several people here who can speak English."

"That is not what I meant..." he exasperated. "My apologies. I wanted to talk to you specifically, but I was frightened you didn't speak English."

"Oh, I see."

Shit. How do I get out of this?

"Do you mind if I join you?" He took a step closer, and I started to panic.

"Her husband sure would."

Chills. Damn freaking chills crawled over, overwhelming me from my head to my toes at the mere sound of his voice.

"Oh, I am sorry, I thought..." He had no chance to finish before Cillian snapped, "Well, you thought wrong. Now leave before you lose the very thing that produced such thoughts."

The shadowy figure practically ran away. His departure relaxed me, but then I remembered what had happened.

"Not even a day here and my wife is already stirring up trouble."

Why did a shiver go through me? It wasn't even that cold for Merlot's sake.

"I was going to handle it, so thank you for robbing me of that opportunity," I snarked, crossing my arms over my chest.

"Yeah, I'm sure you were," he scoffed, and my whole body stiffened.

"What's that supposed to mean?"

"Oh, come on, he's the spitting image of Sebastian? Isn't that your type?" he scolded, ignorant of the fact that I didn't even get a chance to look at the guy.

"First of all, I only saw a shadow, and second of all, you know nothing about my type." I stood up and brushed past him, only to freeze when he sneered, "According to your track record, it's a pretentious douche." That got me to turn around and shove my middle finger right in his face. Of all the ways I saw my first wedding night going, this was not one of them. I stormed off, straight to my room, and shut the door with a rage that threatened to consume me.

Stupid Cillian!

Stupid tuxedo that fit him like a sexy glove. Stupid tie, loose around his neck, two buttons of his shirt undone, leaving me wondering who had the pleasure of untangling them.

Stupid! Stupid! Stupid!

Chapter 30

Aria

My second day in paradise, a place of unparalleled beauty, surpassed the first. I immersed myself in the enchanting allure of Palma by first paying a visit to the aquarium, where I greeted the familiar faces of Dory and Nemo. Then I marveled at the grandeur of the most exquisite cathedral. The day reached its pinnacle with a trip to Bellver Castle, a 14th-century Gothic-style masterpiece perched atop a hill. The view from the summit was nothing short of awe-inspiring. I stretched out my hands, closed my eyes, and savored the sensation of gentle breezes caressing my face. I wanted to go to this beautiful cave, but the tour was booked, so I signed up for one the day after tomorrow. After strolling down the old city and taking in the history, I found a charming little bistro by the coast offering a mesmerizing view.

As I enjoyed a delightful lunch and a glass of red, I found myself lost in a whirlwind of emotions. Something about the movement of the water always made me think about life—how everything could change in an instant, how mine got flipped upside down…

My phone dinged with a notification from my Robinhood app. Before the wedding, we'd fixed all the hiccups for the W&B group. I quickly checked the stocks and smiled. They were still rising.

I took in the vitamin D when an older couple approached me asking if I would take their picture. With a smile, I stood up, taking a dozen for good measure before I handed the man back his camera. They were probably in their late fifties and looked so in love. Their eyes sparkled with a shared history, and I couldn't help but feel a pinch of envy. I slumped down in my chair, thinking if I would ever have that kind of love, someone who would look at me with so much adoration despite the wrinkles on my face. I laughed off the image of an older version of me, all alone, with movies stacked instead of cats. Not being a pet person, I didn't find it that hard to picture myself as a creepy DVD lady. Cillian would probably be the Hugh Hefner of Boston, and with that, my lunch threatened to emerge.

My goodness, why was I doing this to myself?

Why did I care what he was doing or what he would be doing in the future?

Because once upon a time, you pictured him in yours—my inner Emma yelled at me.

I took another breath after a long day of walking and smiled at the nice time I had, then called the driver to take me back.

On the way to my room, I stopped by the reception to check if I had any messages, but the woman behind the desk gave me a strange look. I couldn't help but feel a twinge of discomfort at her gaze.

"I am sorry, Mrs. Wright."

Oh Dionysus, that sounds so wrong.

"For what?"

"For staring. It's just that you are so beautiful."

I brushed it off with a wave of my hand. "You don't have to lie, but thank you anyway."

She opened her mouth to say something back, but I focused on the two women behind her whispering in Spanish. I could hear them, and thanks to my polyglot tendencies, I understood every word.

"¿Qué ve él en ella?" (What does he see in her?) said the one with her back turned to me. "Maldita sea," (Damned her) joined the other with a death stare pointed in my direction.

What was their problem?

I turned my attention to the redhead behind the counter, politely smiling at me with kind eyes. I decided I liked her.

"Do you have any messages for me?"

"No, señora."

Her soft voice got my lips to curve up, but my mouth pulled together when I felt the gawking two sets of eyes still pointed at me, sending chills down my spine. Confrontation with unimportant people was my jam. I lived for good banter.

"Would you mind getting me in on whatever that is?" I lifted my hand, fingers stretched out, and waved a circle, covering the two gossip girls.

The one in front of me, Leila, according to her name tag, froze, gulped, and her face turned red.

"If I can be blunt?" she got closer, leaning over the counter. I mirrored her actions.

"Please do."

"They're all checking the woman who stole Mr. Wright."

"Stole? What does that mean?"

She averted her gaze to the ground, and the gesture spoke volumes.

All the comebacks I had at the ready at all times puffed out of my head, and the all-familiar knot tightened in my chest. I felt defeated for some reason.

"Thank you, Leila. Have a nice evening," I murmured, trying my best to act like this whole scene hadn't gutted me. It was the one thing I was good at, after all. So, refusing to let it break me, with my head held high, maintaining the confidence facade, I strutted out of there. My pride was intact, but on the inside, a storm of sensations raged.

Each new step got heavier, especially when it all hit me at once.

The looks, the other key, the NDA's.

To my surprise, a wave of sadness and a hint of envy washed over me. This was quickly overshadowed by self-anger, fueled by the realization that I had suggested this resort. I was the one who proposed to partner with the very place he used for his pleasures. The feeling of betrayal was overwhelming.

Wait! What?

That didn't make any sense... why would I feel betrayed? This was an arranged marriage of convenience, with a fake relationship thrown in.

Ooof. That was a tongue twister.

Now I felt sick. Guess dinner was off the table. Great.

With that settled, I sought solace at the beach, hoping the rhythmic waves would soothe my turbulent emotions.

With my feet digging deep and the water playing with my ankles, I lay back on the cold sand, allowing my mind to take me back to a better time and place...

"What is it with you and the sky?" Cillian asked as we both stared into the night. We snuck out onto the roof, fluffy blankets under us keeping us warm.

"I don't know," I shrugged, trying to count as many clusters as I could. When I lost track, it was with a sigh. "I keep on hoping that one night there will be a star, different from all the others, and that it will speak to me, with my mom's voice."

Tears gathered in the corners of my eyes at the thought, but I swallowed them away before turning to face my best friend's profile.

"Do you think she's in heaven?" I croaked, a sob trying to break through.

"No doubt about it. She was an angel on earth, so I know she's rocking her kind heart with the rest of the good ones," Cillian attested. His green eyes met mine, and his tone was sincere.

Growing up, Cillian had this superpower... He'd always know exactly what to say; at least he did before Judgment Day.

Chapter 31

Aria

Day three was orchestrated, with paparazzi tipped off to capture fake candid photos of the happy newlyweds.

What was another day of pretending to love my husband? No biggie, right? I could do it…

Maybe, if I said it a couple more times, I would actually believe it.

After some heavy back and forth picking up the perfect place for some pretend PDA, we'd decided on the main beach.

My outfit of the day was my favorite floral bikini with the cups perking up the twins just right. Lying on the lounger under the bamboo beach umbrella, I held my Mojito, painting a perfect picture of a loving wife.

Gag.

Cillian had gone for a swim a while ago, leaving me alone with the sun, but I didn't mind it. I knew we had to play nice today, so the less time we spent together, the better.

You know those Bawatch scenes… when the male actors emerge from the water, shaking it off in slow motion with their hands running through their hair? That was happening now, in full slow-mo. Okay, that last part might've been in my head…

Thanks to my shades, I could stare without being

obvious.

Cillian was approaching, half-naked, glowing in the sun, water dripping over his toned body. I had to restrain my tongue from slipping out. The bastard had unholy thoughts, specifically licking every moving drop. The gawking women around me were no help either. For some stupid reason, I slid my shades on top of my head. The closer he got, the more my throat tightened. He was closing the distance, full stride, heading straight for me, fire in his eyes with hunger, the kind unrelated to any food.

Three steps...

Two steps...

One...

Oh my...

He placed his knee between my legs and snaked his way over me, locking both arms on each side of my waist. My body went rigid, my chest the only part moving. His lips found my ear, and goosebumps sprang out the second I felt his breath. It was shattered with a whisper, "Smile, wifey, camera is in the bushes."

Show.

That was all for show. Right... that made sense, the only sense. My breath hitched, our eyes met—mine scanning his for any sign of something, anything proving me wrong.

He moved away, took a towel, and ruffled his hair with it, giving me a wink. His dark skin glistened in the sun, every single muscle on display. The flexing of his biceps caused a lump to form in my throat, affecting the dryness of my mouth.

"I need to get rid of the salt," he muttered, straddling there like a freaking statue.

"And you think I needed to know that because?" I dragged the last word.

"If someone comes to my beautiful wife and asks her where her loving husband is, I would want her to know the answer. We wouldn't want to start rumors now, would we?"

I scoffed, adding an eye roll into the mix, if only to calm the flutter one particular word caused in my stomach. *Beautiful.* Show or not, it provoked a reaction.

"Oh, for Merlot's sake!"

The bastard snickered, "Back to that phase?"

"Yup," I popped the P. "As long as it gets on your nerves."

The mentioned phase had started at the same time my obsession with wine grew. I was so in love with it that it infiltrated my vocabulary—mostly to replace the curse words, but that was beside the point. While we were still friends, Cillian had found it endearing. Hades, on the other hand, would scoff and roll his eyes just like he was doing right now.

"Good luck with that," he quipped back, tossing the towel and turning on his heel.

And like the crazy girl I was, I watched him walk away.

"Wow, you're one lucky woman."

I turned around at the sound of a delicate voice with an exotic accent. A gorgeous strawberry-blonde woman in her early forties was sitting on a wooden chair staring right at me. It wasn't her staring that sent a chill down my spine... No, it was the look. The same look Sabrina gave me whenever her filter went off, which was pretty much all the time.

"I bet he is a beast in bed."

Yup. Called it!

I choked; unfortunately, so did the waitress, setting down

my drink next to me. I didn't even notice her approach. I took in her flushed cheeks, fidgeting hands, obviously doing her best to avoid eye contact. Unlike me, that girl probably knew the answer to the question posed by the woman behind me. That hypothesis got me to my feet and away from her so fast I practically turned into the Road Runner.

Today was not the day for me to act like this. Today was the day I was supposed to show the world how happy I was, in love, and all that accompanying bullshit.

Jealousy was the last thing I needed to feel, and yet, it was impossible to rid myself of it. My eyes found a bathroom, and I beelined for it, locking the door behind me when I entered. The mirrored image of me needed a slap in the face; I needed a punch or two as well.

I washed my face and looked up again, but this time, instead of focusing on the mirror, I zeroed in on the small flyer next to it. The answer to all my problems was right there, flashing before me. Paper in hand, I walked back to retrieve my phone, finding Cillian occupying my lounger, his head facing the other direction. Turning on the stealth mode, I carefully plucked my phone out of my bag and scanned the QR code. There were a couple of free slots, the first one in about an hour. I could last that long without spiraling. So I booked it and went for a swim, leaving my husband with his admirers.

Since I wanted to be dry for the upcoming adventure, I got out and sat in the wooden chair next to a passed-out Cillian. Biting my nails, I watched the minutes tick by. My nerves didn't usually take me so far, but today was an exception. I watched the horizon, the clear water before me, and the sand colliding with the sea. When I saw a boat drawing nearer, I got up and started walking to the shore, determined to avoid my company.

Three young men were on the boat, all locals by the looks of them. One, wearing a bandana around his head, jumped off and came to me, hand stretched out to greet. I took it with a smile.

"You Aria?" The R rolled off his tongue.

"Yeah, that's me."

"Great. Since you already signed the waiver online, I'll go right into giving you a quick rundown."

"Sounds good," I said as he guided me on board, where the other guys were waiting to help me climb on.

"I'm Fernando," Bandana revealed.

Of course you are.

He got in front of me, his eyes giving me a once-over, and I smirked. He was my age—maybe a year younger—obviously cute. He pointed behind him to the two men, one bold and younger, possibly even underage, and the other with highlights in his shoulder-length hair.

"That's Mario." The bold one waved. "And Leo." The other one gave me a chin-nod salute.

"Nice to meet you, I'm Aria," I greeted with a wave.

"First time?" Leo asked, giving me a picture-perfect smile.

"Yeah," I replied, trying to hide my nerves.

Mario questioned next with a slight grin. "Scared?"

"Not really; but it will come, I'm sure."

Fernando explained every step while putting the life jacket on me, carefully tightening each strap.

"Does that feel good?"

I nodded, and he continued walking me through it all as the boat started to move away from shore.

Usually, when I was overstressed, I would get in my car and drive. The best stress reliever was the wind in my hair on the road. Since I had no fast vehicle at my disposal, I got the next best thing. And when Fernando released the rope, all the anxiety and everything that had been consuming me disappeared. It was exactly what I needed—a moment to forget, stop feeling, stop hurting.

Oh my Merlot.

I screamed, but not out of fear. It was a mix of freedom and adrenaline that made me let go of everything that was crushing my lungs. I was breathing fully and flying. No! I was soaring. The water beneath me, waves forming from the boat's motor, the parachute behind me making a flopping sound... It was a new kind of rush, and I welcomed it wholeheartedly. I was paragliding over the Mediterranean Sea, my lungs breathing the fresh air, and my mind blank...

Liberating—no other way to describe it.

Chapter 32

Cillian

I must've dozed off on the beach due to another sleepless night in paradise, because I woke up next to an empty chair, with no sign of Aria. Running fingers through my hair, I sat up, facing the water, trying to find any trace of blonde, but came up empty. It was when I heard a familiar laugh that the tight grip around my lungs loosened.

The ease lasted for a short moment before anger took over at the sight of her, happy, on a boat with three guys gawking at her.

My feet stomped over the sand, fists forming on reflex. When I reached the water, her eyes snapped to me. The three boys froze, their stares widening. Meanwhile, Aria looked peaceful, glowing even. There was a twinkle in her eyes, an expression I hadn't seen in so long that I had forgotten what it looked like.

"Had fun, *honey*?" I gibed, pulling out a fake smile, all the while scanning the setting—she was in a life jacket, a parachute rolled up on the deck.

"I sure did, hubby," she singsonged.

One of the guys stepped in front of her and began loosening the straps that held the life jacket in place. Her eyes never left mine while the idiot groped her, right in front of me. I felt my Adam's apple bob, and then she smirked, like this reaction was exactly what she was going for.

The blond Julio extended his hand to help her down, but with one pointed look—courtesy of yours truly—he withdrew. She got to the edge of the boat, grinning at me while she bent down and placed her hands on my shoulder. Mine flew to take her waist, swooping her into the water.

"Thanks, guys," she chirped over her shoulder. I watched them wave back at her, with a side of drool. Aria, per her usual, was utterly oblivious to it. Her eyes met mine, my hand still on her waist, hers still on my shoulders. The moment stretched while we stayed like that, before her hands slowly glided down, grazing my skin on the descent. We had a part to play today—I knew that—so why did I shiver at her touch?

Her hands stopped at my wrists, head tilting, taunting in challenge.

I was in so much trouble... Sweet, sweet trouble.

My eyes went to her breasts, her chest rising and falling, and my dick jerked at the sight. It was so fucking obvious, and I feared she'd notice it. My suspicions were confirmed when she opened her mouth enough for me to see her tongue grazing the tips of her teeth, causing another jerking movement in my swim shorts. Her grip tightened around my wrists, and just as I was about to pull her closer, she removed my hands, leaving me in the shallows. I watched her ass sway with each step, letting me know she knew I'd be watching. She never turned back to check, though.

I couldn't keep my eyes away. Not when she dried herself, not when she gathered all her things, and not when she sashayed in the direction of our cabin. There was a strong need—a desire—to follow her, to see if she was putting on a show for the cameras or trying to ruse me. I chose the deep water instead, swimming in the other direction, far away from the temptation.

When I got back to our cabana an hour later, a note was waiting for me, taped to my bedroom door.

> Dinner at eight at the Reef.
> Wear something nice for
> the cameras, Hubby!
> -A

In my head, I could hear the tone of the message so clearly that it made me snicker. The two of us had been communicating mostly through Post-its, but this was the first one that put a smile on my face.

To pass the time, I went to the gym. After a long workout, I showered and got ready for dinner with my wife. I hadn't seen Aria all afternoon, and I didn't hear her in the room while I was getting ready, so I texted her to say I'd meet her at the restaurant.

Arriving early, a first for me, I took a seat at the bar before ordering my drink. Somewhere around my third sip, the room went quiet. The guy tending the bar froze, his brows flaring. The waiter, on his way to the kitchen, had the same reaction, as did a man eating dinner with a woman across from him.

Every bone in my body knew what, or better yet, who was the reason behind all the awestruckness.

This place was high-end, with all the patrons wearing designer suits and over-the-top cocktail dresses. But I knew my wife better than I wanted to admit. I knew the real meaning behind the note, and although we needed to put on a show, I knew she never wanted the act to change who we were. So with my dark jeans and my white polo shirt on, I finally turned around to meet the woman who could stun a man wearing blue sneakers. Aria joined me at the bar, her hair up in a ponytail, with natural makeup accentuating her matte, dark pink lips. She chose to torture me with bare legs to her knees, the rest covered by a short sundress matching the color of her lipstick. The bartender handed her a glass of pure vodka, and she gulped it in one quick motion.

"Shall we?" She straightened up, her hand waiting for mine in between us. Without a second thought, I took her invitation, and we followed the hostess to our table. For a better view, Aria reserved one on the outside terrace, giving the paparazzi the best angle.

We both ordered the fish special with the bottle of white recommended by our server.

"Did you look over my proposal?"

She'd asked this question every single day, and I gave her the same false answer. I'd read her binder a month ago, one detailing a private poker tournament for wealthy amateurs. It was a great idea, but one I didn't want to discuss, especially not with her.

It took me too long to answer because she was now aggravated, pouring her second glass of wine.

Our dinner came soon after, taking all the focus. Halfway through the meal, she set down her fork and knife and clasped her hands.

"How about a game?"

"How 'bout no?"

"Oh, come on, hubby, we need to make it look like we're having a good time. I mean, if you're not up for it..." she trailed off, doing that thing with one shoulder meeting her cheek.

Oh, she was good, knew how to get me every time.

"Two lies, one truth?" I challenged with a smirk.

"Fine."

"Fine."

"I'll go first." She wiggled in her seat so she could straighten up some more, like she was turning it into a full-on battle of wits. "I stole a pack of gum from a 7-Eleven on my eleventh birthday. My current song on repeat is Eminem's 'Shake That', and I am bored to death right now."

Guess we were playing one lie, one truth, and one opposite.

"I can't believe you stole a pack of gum. You little thief," I ribbed, giving her a shake of the head.

And there went the eye-roll.

"My turn," I started, "I cheated on a history exam. I threw away your Britney CD. And you look way too sexy to be bored."

She tried to ignore the last part, but I saw the faint blush creep up her neck.

"I knew you took it!" She pointed a finger at me, a death glare trying to hide her crimson cheeks, failing miserably.

"You had the same song on a loop the entire day."

I hadn't taken her CD; she knew it, I knew it... the whole family knew it; yet, she continued to accuse me, if only to keep up a fight.

"I hate you." She put up one finger. "I'm not wearing any underwear." She put up another one. "And right about now you're sporting a hard-on." She bit on her lower lip, lifting a third finger. She was changing the rules on me, trying to win another game I didn't realize we were playing.

I took her hand and dragged it under the table, proving one point. The small table was covered with a white cloth, so no one could see what was happening underneath it. Our chairs were pushed close, knees brushing. Her hand stayed pressed over my pants while my fingers deliberately grazed her thighs in the direction of the forbidden zone. The sensation of her soft, warm skin was too much. Her hand never left my manhood, only pressing harder the closer I got to the motherland.

"All three points proven."

"You have only proven two," she snarled, one eyebrow rising in challenge.

"Sorry, *honey*, your wet pussy seems to disagree with you," I hoarsened.

Her cheeks went full blush, and for a moment, I thought she was daring me to keep going. Fuck, I was sure of it. So I let my fingers roam, her legs slowly parting.

A waitress chose that exact moment to refill our glasses, and Aria stiffened at the sight of her. Her eyes went dark, her hand snapped away from my crotch, mine left hanging when she pulled her chair away.

She turned from a confident vixen into a puddle of shame in less than a second, her eyes never leaving the girl pouring the wine into my glass.

She stayed silent until she had cleaned her plate.

"I'm gonna go to bed. I have a headache."

Lie.

Still, I let her go. I dried my glass, thanked the staff, and went to entertain the last point.

Chapter 33

Aria

It was the twelfth of never, the sky fell, Hell froze over, and a flock of pings was flying around here somewhere... All because I wanted to fuck my husband. Ok, I knew pigs didn't go in flocks, but I wanted to prove a point. That point being that for a whole minute, an entirety of sixty seconds, I had the intention of jumping Cillian's bones.

To my dismay, likely his too, faith had intervened in the form of the same waitress from the beach, the one who reacted at the mention of Cillian being a beast in bed. Sooooo... The moment had passed... I had choked and run away. Big surprise there...

Although a part of me wished, maybe even hoped, that he would follow me, it never happened. After waiting around in our cabin, I gave up on the possibility and went for a walk. My steps took me to the beach. The waves tickled my feet while I sat there and stared into the darkness.

I wanted my husband—sexually. Without any emotions, he won't get those from me. Never again. For a moment, I thought he wanted me, too, but when he didn't show up, I figured he'd gone and used the other key.

Thinking about it now, it was for the best. The situation was complicated enough without sex being dragged in, no matter how tempting it was.

I only wish I had brought Sabrina's gift with me. Why on earth had I thought it would be inappropriate to bring a toy when my husband was enjoying the real deal was beyond me, but I guess I had more common sense.

I found myself exactly where I needed to be. The water didn't ask questions. It just existed, relentless and calm, pushing itself toward my toes, then pulling away again. I sat there, barefoot in the cool sand, my knees drawn up to my chest, fingers tracing absent patterns near my ankles. The night fell silent, except for the hush of the tide and an occasional call of a bird overhead. It was the kind of quiet that made me feel like the world had stepped back to give me space to think—or to fall apart.

I tilted my head back and stared at the sky. My heart ached with a hollow I couldn't name, and frankly, I didn't want to try. It was easier to blame the sea breeze for the shiver that ran through me. This marriage was supposed to be a simple business transaction, strategic and very much pretend. A neat lie wrapped in expensive rings and signed papers. I agreed for our parents' sake because it made sense, and feelings weren't supposed to be part of it. However, here I was, alone on a beach, chest tight with something that definitely wasn't pretend.

The sound of his laugh, the real laugh, not the polite, practiced chuckle he wore with his suit, but the real one, knocked something loose in me. The sound had curled around my ribs and stayed there, lingering. Only to be replaced by female laughter. It shouldn't matter, but it did. I hugged myself and watched the moonlight turn the water to silver. I sighed and leaned back on my elbows, letting the sand cling to my skin. The wedding ring caught the moonlight and flashed, mocking me.

"What are you two doing?"

"We're coloring our wedding invitations," I answered my mother, not bothering to look up from my paper, where I had drawn two stick figures of Cillian and me.

"I see," my mother hummed, her head coming between us. Cillian had the same pose as me, his stomach on the grass, ankles crossed, and moving in the air.

"And when's the big day?"

"Tomorrow," Cillian answered this time, swapping his green marker for a blue one.

"But tomorrow is Aria's birthday,"

"Yeah, that's her wish," Cillian said unbothered, and I stuck out my tongue at him. He snapped his teeth, making the biting motion that made me giggle.

"Is that really how you want to spend your big ten?" My mother pulled out that serious tone, the one reserved for all the big talks. I gave her an enthusiastic head bob, and she kissed my forehead, then the top of Cillian's head.

When tomorrow came, I forgot about my big day, ran past all the presents, and went straight to the backyard. My jaw dropped when I saw Cillian. He did something to his hair that made it all shiny, as if he had washed it in grease or something. But I didn't care.

"Hi, future Mr. Wright, you look ravishing."

"What does that mean?"

"I have no idea, but it sounds cool." He smiled at my shrug, and my lips curved upward. It was impossible not to

smile at him.

"You ready?" he asked, popping his elbows so I could loop my arm around them.

"More than ready."

How sure of herself was that little girl... Her trust had never been broken before, all the faith in the world paving her way. So innocent, unaware of all the heartbreak she would face.

Chapter 34

Cillian

I got to my room after taking everyone on the table. I was ready to go to bed when I saw a speck of blonde shining in the moonlight down by the beach. She was sitting on the sand close enough for the water to wash over her toes. She stayed like that for an entire hour while I stood there at my window watching her look at the sea.

I thought she'd be in her room, covering her lie of having a headache, but she went somewhere. And I needed to know more. The prick that had the audacity to approach her the other night popped into my head, and my body reacted by clenching my fists. This had nothing to do with pride or ego; it was simply a matter of her. No one on this earth deserved her, was good enough for her, myself included.

In my quick chat with Rafael, the manager, I found out she'd spent all day yesterday sightseeing. She also had a driver booked for tomorrow morning to take her into town. To say I couldn't think straight the entire night would be an understatement.

What if she meets someone? What if she falls in love and moves here, away from all of us? Away from me.

That just won't do. A plan formed in my head rather quickly, so I took out my phone from my back pocket and dialed. Rafael answered mid-first ring, "Si, senor?" I hated it when he played formal, but I guess he was still pissed off that I took all his money.

"Find out my wife's exact plans for tomorrow and add me to all of them."

Five minutes later, I got a confirmation text saying he had taken care of everything.

I could barely sleep over the excitement, but I managed to get a couple of good hours. I woke up and got ready to explore the caves with my wife.

When I arrived at the front desk, I immediately saw her standing over the counter, talking to one of the younger receptionists. They were laughing and being friendly. Aria never had trouble making friends, something I could never comprehend, given her often cold demeanor. That said, maybe I was the only recipient of her coldness. She was wearing a yellow sundress with puffy sleeves loose around her shoulders, a large bag hanging over her left one. Her hair was hidden behind a sun hat with a bow, matching her sky blue Converse. She was relaxed in her interaction with Laila, but when she noticed two other workers approaching, her whole body tensed.

"Mr. and Mrs. Wright?"

Damn, that sounded good.

The driver called for us, and she turned, stunned.

"What do you think you're doing?" she perplexed, striding to me, crossed arms with narrow eyes.

"Exploring the caves," I quipped, "what are you doing?"

"Funny, now tell me the truth."

Usually, her acting all hot and bothered had a different

effect on me with a side of disgust, but now it was in the line of cute meets sexy.

"I did. I signed up for the tour."

"No, you didn't!" It came out almost like a command, and her stern look only intensified it.

"Did too," I echoed, not backing down. All eyes were on us, but I didn't give a rat's ass. Let them see the fire in her eyes, hell, even I couldn't control my glare.

"Well, do it tomorrow; today's my day," she muttered as one strap of her bag slipped down her arm. She quickly pulled it in place without untangling her arms, her ocean blues tearing through me.

There was that spark, loud, but somehow different. It didn't come with the typical animosity; it was filled with friskiness, something I hadn't seen or felt in far too long.

"Why would I do that? It's already booked. What's the big deal?"

Her nostrils flared, her aggravation making me grin, even though I wanted to giggle like a schoolgirl.

"Fine," she said in defeat, her arms falling to her sides.

"Fine."

On the inside, I was pumping my fist and jumping; on the outside, I kept it cool.

"You look beautiful, by the way."

"Oh, come on, say it like you mean it."

I always do.

The caves turned out to be interesting, but Aria's face, enjoying every detail of every rock formation, was the thing that caught all of my attention. The tour started with a concert followed by a boat ride across Lake Martel. Aria, being a walk lover she was, decided to take the path we'd crossed with the boat just in case she missed something. Her whole face was filled with an unstoppable awe. The way she admired her surroundings, taking everything in, the lights reflecting in her eyes and hair, made it hard for me to catch my breath. When the tour ended, there was a crack in my better judgment, and I slipped. "Do you want to grab lunch?"

Her eyes narrowed at the question.

"Rule number 5," she reminded, getting me riled up. Aria wasn't a stickler for the rules, so what was it about this one that made her such a disciplinarian?

"Do you see all the people around us?" I snarked, making a point by turning my head to the crowd.

"Fair point. I thought it'd be nice to grab a picnic. I read there are several areas on the cliff."

Liking the idea, I nodded. "Should we grab something from the cafeteria and find a nice spot?"

It took her longer than necessary to consider it. And for the life of me, I couldn't figure out why it made me nervous.

"Fine."

"Fine."

At 'Cuevas del Drach' cafeteria, we grabbed whatever looked good, and Aria snatched a map so that she could navigate us to the picnic area. There were still a few free tables, despite the overcrowded lookout. I found one right under a set of trees, shielding the area from the burning sun.

"This looks like a—" I stopped when I didn't find her next to me. Panic struck, and I wanted to punch myself for not even noticing she'd wandered off. Scanning mode on, I sighed in relief when I spotted her by the edge, taking a blanket from her bag before laying it on the ground. Of course, she'd pick the point with the best view. I slowly walked toward her, watching her head snap in every direction. She was searching for me. When I came into her line of sight, I swear, her lips curved an inch upward. Smiling, I moved in closer just as she turned her back to me and parked her perky ass on the blanket. I took a seat next to her and began to unpack everything we had bought, spreading it over the blanket. She took out a bottle of wine, but then put it right back in her bag.

"What's wrong?"

"I only brought one glass."

I started laughing uncontrollably.

"Would you mind getting me in on the joke?"

"Nothing. You being thoughtful threw me off."

She pushed me on the shoulder, knocking me off balance, but I recovered quickly.

"My apologies, it won't happen again."

She took out one bocadillo and started devouring it. I joined her with my chicken escalope. Enjoying the fresh air, the trees that provided shade around us, and the sun rays that brushed through the branches, we ate in silence, but it was far from awkward. Simple, yet perfect.

When we finished eating, we cleaned up and threw away any trash in the bin. Then, she stepped to the edge of the cliff, spreading out her arms.

Fuck.

The sight of her like that, free and careless, always did a number on me. She had done the same thing when we were kids. Every time we were on a boat, she would spread out her arms like they were wings, eyes closed, enjoying the wind. Back then, she'd never tied up her hair, and it would sway in the wind. These days, her hair was tamed, just like her personality.

And as if some higher power heard my thoughts, the wind blew her hat away, freeing her pearl strands to fly. She didn't even flinch, didn't turn to see where her hat went; she stayed in the moment, and I never wanted it to be over.

On the drive back to the hotel, I noticed her wiggling in the seat; it was impossible not to.

"Out with it." My words froze her still.

"You might want to pay more attention to your fan club; they seem to believe that I am the one occupying all of it."

She smiled awkwardly, tucking a strand of her hair behind her ear.

"Go on," I prompted, "I am going to require some more details."

"The staff kept looking at me all weird, so I asked one of them what it was, and her look pretty much said it all."

She played with her fingers in her lap. When nervous, she had a specific order of things: shaking her knee, fidgeting if seated, and the same with her fingers. The last one happened only when she was extremely nervous, which was a rarity.

"So maybe use the key more often or whatever."

She started shaking her head, shutting her eyes, face cringing, mumbling to herself the word *Merlot* over and over again. She thought I hated it when she did that, but in all honesty, I found it cute.

"I'm sooooo sorry, that was way out of line and totally none of my business. I just..." she trailed off, her leg bouncing again. "Forget I said anything."

Too late.

When we arrived at the resort, she let herself out of the car before even the driver had a chance to be a gentleman.

Typical.

I took her hand and started pulling her along.

"What are you doing?" She put up resistance, but it was pointless.

"Follow my lead," I said, not bothering to look at her. Then I raised my hand, shouting, "Rafael?"

"Si senjor Wright e senjora Wright?"

Aria looked at both of us in confusion.

"Put my wife on the list."

The girl behind Rafael started coughing dramatically.

I draped my arm over Aria's shoulder, feeding on her surprise.

"But sir?"

"I said, put my wife on the list," I dragged each word out, knowing the tone of my voice would do the trick.

After some heavy typing, he handed her a black key card, looking dazed.

"Gracias." I tilted my head slightly, scanning the area. "You, miss?" I snapped at the woman behind the manager. When she looked up at me, I commanded, "My wife needs a dress! Call Monique to bring some choices for her."

"Yes, sir."

Aria looked at me, confusion eating her up, but the question '*Who the F is Monique?*' came to the forefront.

We walked away together, and as soon as we were out of prying eyes, Aria pushed my arm away.

"What the Merlot do you think you're doing?"

"I don't think I understand." I frowned and bit my lower lip, adding to the fire I knew was starting inside her.

She shoved me off with both her hands, and a loud chuckle escaped me.

"I am not interested in any kinky things you've got going on in that room. You do whatever you want to do; just leave me out of it."

"Pick a dress and use the key; it's room number one."

"No!"

Stubborn woman.

Why the hell did she have to make everything so difficult? I had to fight the urge to wrap my fingers around her neck and squeeze.

"Pick a dress and use the key," I said through gritted teeth this time.

"Fuck you," she snapped, that fire in her eyes doing something to me.

"Pick a fucking dress and use the fucking key." My tone was harsh and firm, but her eyes remained deadly.

"Fine," she grumbled at my triumph.

"Fine."

She stormed off with steam coming out of her ears, the sight igniting my insides.

Chapter 35

Aria

You stupid, stupid woman! No! Child!

I know, Emma; I know.

I found myself berating the patheticness I had displayed earlier, a wave of self-doubt washing over me.

What was I thinking?

To be fair, the *'WTF is he doing with a woman like that'* looks pointed at me, got all the insecurities to play with my head. Cillian was every girl's dream, even if his muscles were an eyesore, and his dark skin hugged his physique. Plus, his thick lashes made his green eyes even more striking. Everything about him was perfect, down to his slightly crooked (barely noticeable) nose. He got elbowed during one of his high school games, and the thing never healed properly. Let's not forget the deep, husky voice that added to the mystery of my husband. Sure, it made my skin crawl, but I bet it got all the girls wet.

Don't get me wrong, I had no problems with my appearance... my body was fit, I had a nice set of legs, and an impressively tight ass thanks to my excessive hip thrusts workout. But none of that satiated that little voice in my head telling me I was not enough while also being too much.

While I was in the shower, I heard a knock on the door. I turned the water off to be sure I'd heard that right when another one followed. It soon stopped, telling me Cillian must have opened for whoever it was.

Turning the warm spread back on, I took my time, pampering my scalp with a thorough scrub. All rinsed off, I stepped outside onto the soft little mat, dried myself, then covered my body with the complimentary robe. It felt like I was wrapped in a cloud, and I made a mental note to ask what fabric softener they used here. Using another towel, I made a makeshift turban for my damp hair and exited the bathroom.

My bare feet were sticking to the marble floor as I made my way toward my room. I had to go through the common area, and I froze in place when I found Cillian and a woman resembling Naomi Campbell in the middle of a conversation. Clearing my throat, I made my presence known, and they both snapped their attention to me. The woman spoke first, "Hello, Mrs. Wright, my name is Monique." Fuck me, even her voice was angelic. As I closed in, she continued, "I brought you some dresses; all are in your size." There was no harsh tone, no condescension, no mean appraisal, just a nice woman looking at me with a drop-dead gorgeous smile.

"Thank you, Monique, it's nice to meet you, and it's Aria, please," I said, extending my hand, biting my tongue not to say I hated being called by my new last name.

After she gracefully shook my hand, I touched the sparkling dresses. The fabrics slid between my fingers, soft and daring. I pushed aside my nerves and doubts about what lay behind that door. The key had been burning a hole in my bag the entire day. But I wasn't going to turn down a chance to get all dolled up on account of my fears.

"These are beautiful," I praised, my fingers lingering on the red Versace dress. She gave me a knowing smile.

I took a black dress that was more on the conservative side; a safer choice. Cillian jerked it out of my hand and set it back on the rack, then pulled out the dress I'd secretly been eyeing. On full display, I could see how high up the thigh slit went, and I swallowed. It was beautiful, but I couldn't do it justice.

"This one."

"No, that one is too…" I tried to find the words, but failed.

"Perfect for you." He had a threatening glare, and his dominating tone was impossible to ignore.

"The Medusa is an excellent choice," Monique approved, adding a wink for my eyes only, and once again, I found myself settling on a dress based on its name. What could I say? I was a sucker for Greek mythology.

"Fine."

"Fine."

With a simple 'thank you' and an accompanying smile directed at Monique, I headed to my room, red dress in hand. I hung it on the bathroom door and used the wall-mounted hairdryer to dry my hair. Feeling bold, I used my flat iron to curl it, then tied it into a low ponytail, leaving some of my shorter strands to frame my face.

It took me more than usual to do my makeup. I went with a subtle look but made my eyes the focal point.

The dress was easy to maneuver, so I didn't need any help zipping it up. Dressed to impress, I stood before a long mirror by the bed. I focused on the strap. Medusa's head was engraved on the hardware that held the fabric together. My eyes downshifted, and I cursed at my negligence. I've packed for the beach and sightseeing, not a black-tie affair. Meaning, I had no heels. I even left the ones I wore at the wedding for Sabrina to take home. I was about to tell Cillian I couldn't go. There was no way I'd wear that dress without the right shoes. Just then, I almost tripped over a box outside my door. To my surprise, the box contained the most beautiful pair of shoes: the black leather Azia Jimmy Choo in my size. There was no time to question anything at that point; all I wanted was to slip my feet into them. Suffice it to say, my feet went straight to heaven. This unexpected gesture and the added confidence boost set my mindset for the evening ahead.

As I strode to the common area, the sound of my heels on the marble floor caught Cillian's attention. He stood up, and I couldn't help but admire him in his black tux with dark gray lapels covering a white shirt. His own perusal was blatant, burning through every inch that his gaze covered.

"Like I said, perfect."

I lost all words with that sentence; he stole every letter, including the punctuation marks.

"Shall we?" He made a triangle with his arms, inviting my hand through it.

We walked in silence; the pounding of my heart was almost perceptible.

He purposely walked us past the front desk, women's gasps straightening my spine with aplomb.

When we stopped in front of a black door, I focused on the golden number one staring at me. I tried and failed to swallow a lump in my throat. It refused to go away, almost as if mocking me. Cillian nudged me, motioning with his head in the direction of the card slot. In one quick swoop, I unlocked the door, and it opened automatically, revealing a Monte Carlo setup. Roulette, poker, and craps tables were spread out throughout the entire room.

The interior was a designer's dream, with crystal chandeliers hanging from the ceiling above each table. The black walls displayed various pieces of art, giving it a sophisticated look. There were around thirty people, all dressed to perfection; the scale was tipped with the overflow of XY chromosomes, and that statistic made me gulp.

It got quiet, at least in my head, when all eyes snapped to us. Unbothered by the attention, Cillian led us through the room, shaking hands and nodding at people. He was a natural, and I swear I'd hear him growl a couple of times when some of the men's gazes drifted to my cleavage.

We reached another black door, and my mind went into a spiral. I started imagining all the things that could await me on the other side. But my curiosity got the best of me, and I gave Cillian an assuring look. He opened the door with his card, and I held my breath. It was surely not what I had expected. The back room consisted of one poker table, with five people already seated and three empty seats. In the corner, there was a bar and a pretty mixologist behind it.

We took the two empty seats next to each other.

"Everyone, this is Aria, my wife."

The way he said 'wife' was not supposed to make me blush. But thankfully, the make-up concealed the natural one.

They all politely introduced themselves, and I welcomed each of them with a smile. On my right was Dominik, a famous Australian rugby player (never heard of him); on his right was Rafael, the staff manager; and next to him was Federico, the owner of this fine establishment. Diagonal across from me was Philip, who spoke out in a familiar British accent, "I believe we have already met." He turned my hand from the shake and closed his lips to my skin, all the while looking sideways at Cillian, whose jaw clenched with irritation. That left us with Gabriel, the wolf from Wall Street, who was sitting between Cillian and Philip.

A second later, a beautiful, red-haired woman wearing a black pantsuit and a red tie entered, taking the remaining seat right between Rafael and Frederico.

She started dealing the cards, and one glided right in front of me. I turned to Cillian and whispered.

"I'm playing?"

"Yes."

"Are you sure?" I tilted my head.

He mimicked my tilt but still nodded to confirm.

A devilish smile lit up my face because little did he know I was damn good at poker.

The social dynamics at the table were palpable, with each person exuding a unique energy. The tension was high, and the anticipation of the game was thrilling.

After a couple of hands, I pretty much knew everything there was to know about each person. Rafael smoked a Cuban cigar, and every time he bluffed, he would hold it with his teeth instead of his mouth. Frederico did a barely noticeable eye twitch; Philip was just plain dumb, and Gabriel touched his collar when he was nervous. Cillian wasn't that hard to read since I knew all his tricks. Dominik was tough to crack at first, but eventually he revealed a neck tick.

By the end of the night, I had taken all of their chips. In the meantime, we'd tossed some funny comments and bickered here and there, but all in all, it turned out to be a positively enjoyable night.

Feeling parched, I stood up and approached the bar, read the mixologist's name—Caria—and asked for a glass of vodka. When she handed it to me, she leaned over and whispered, "You are my new idol!"

"Thank you," I chirped and took a sip, grinning at the fact that I outsmarted a table full of pretentious men.

"You know that you are the first woman, aside from the dealer and me, to enter this room?"

I turned to look around, taking a second longer, lingering on Cillian.

"That makes no sense."

"Trust me, every woman here hates you because they have been wanting to get into Mr. Wright's pants for the past 3 years, but none were successful, and now he's here with you." She pointed at me and motioned with her hand up and down. "Every woman here wants to be you. They want to kill you, but they want to be you."

I repeated that sentence far too many times in my head before I smiled at her.

"Thank you for your candor. I couldn't really figure out the looks and whispers, so it is good to know."

Wrapping my head around it seemed impossible. You mean to tell me that for three years, women had tried to be with him, and he'd never... No, that was impossible. Cillian was a player, a womanizer, and all that. I knew it, I saw it...

In tabloids..

No, it made no sense, and I was gonna leave it at that. I shook it off and pushed up my box of chips, which the dealer had neatly stacked.

"Where do I leave these?" I asked Caria, who answered with another glass of vodka.

"You can cash them at the exit."

"Cash them? They're real?" I squealed, and I was not proud of it. It caught me off guard.

"Yeah! What did you think they were, Monopoly chips?"

"Kinda." I grabbed a bunch of the blue ones and gave them to her.

"Oh no, that's too much." She slid them back, and I grabbed her hand.

"Trust me, it's not enough. You made my night."

And she did by spiking up my confidence.

When I turned around, I was ambushed by Philip, who blocked my way. "Well, that sure was unexpected."

"What exactly, the fact that I was good, or the fact that you were bad?"

I heard Cillian's muffled laugh from across the room. That gave me a little boost before I quipped, "Now, if you'll excuse me, I have anywhere else to be."

Caria tried to hide her laugh with a cough as I walked toward my husband.

"Wanna get out of here?" Cillian did the triangle again, and I looped my arm around his.

"I thought you'd never ask."

We walked around the usual path and ended up at the beach. I took off my shoes and jumped into the sand.

"How'd you do it?"

I turned to face him, narrowing my eyes.

"I don't know what you're talking about." I twirled around, my head still buzzing from all the rush.

"Come on, tell me."

That tone, husky and assertive, sent shivers up my spine. I closed in on him, lifting my head just as he dropped his.

"I don't play the cards; I play the men," I confessed, batting my lashes.

Looking him right in the eyes, vodka making me lighter on my feet and tongue, I slurred, "Don't think I didn't notice you fold three times when you had the upper hand."

One of his eyebrows went up, and he took a step in my direction, swallowing a breath. We were standing close, too close, and I was tipsy enough and tempted to get rid of the remaining distance.

Realization hit me, panic rose, and I pulled back, going straight into the water to cool off. I splashed it around with my feet while I watched Cillian walk away to the villa, a heaviness pressing on my chest.

Chapter 36

Cillian

I had almost kissed my wife.

There we were, a mere breath apart, both lingering under the moonlight, her eyes blocking my windpipe. My adrenaline was pumping with a new kind of high—the anticipation palpable. Leaving it up to her was a mistake because the kiss never came. And before I could take matters into my own hands, she pulled back, leaving me feeling hollow.

It had taken everything in me to walk away, but it had to be done. Once again, I'd misread the situation, thinking she wanted me back—the story of my life—standing on the sidelines, hoping that one day she would feel the same.

Shutting my bedroom door behind me, I smacked my forehead on the surface, feeling seventeen all over again. My judgment had been clouded, but no more. I won't allow myself to go through all that heartbreak again. No matter how good she looked or smelled.

This entire night had been pure torture, which was saying something, considering I had undergone rigorous SERE training. Nothing in this world could have prepared me for seeing her in that dress. My chest would tighten every time she took a deep breath, exposing her cleavage. All the attention she'd gotten from the heeding men wasn't helpful either. And then she'd gone on making me laugh by brushing off that British pompous ass. I swear my dick had saluted her from the inside of my pants when she walked over to me, oozing with confidence.

It was an image that had been playing on a loop in my head, half the night, my hand wrapped around my shaft, her signature scent taking over the orbit.

After a miserable hour of sleep, I got up and packed. Our flight was in the afternoon, but I needed something to distract me.

Finished with the final check of my room, I went to the common area to do a quick sweep when something caught my eye. There, on the table next to the armchair, was a large gift basket. Only one person I knew was obsessed with those, so I went straight for it with a smile. It had bags of candy, limited-edition chocolates, a bottle of Aria's favorite red, my favorite whiskey, and three magazines, all perfectly wrapped in cellophane. A card tied on top stared at me, getting me aggravated by the written words.

Hope you two are having fun.
We do want more grandchildren!
Wink! Wink!
Love Mom & Dad!

Tearing through the wrapping, I eyed the magazines, each with a different picture of our wedding on the cover.

The photo shoot had taken place immediately after the 'I do's'. They'd set us up at the beach, a large swing covered in flowers of different colors and sizes as our prop. We'd taken a couple of shots with both of us sitting on it, looking into each other's eyes with a loving gaze, per the photographer's request. The cover showed me in front of Aria. My hands were outstretched, having just pushed the swing. She laughed with her mouth open, nose scrunched, and eyes fixed on mine.

Breathtaking.

I remembered thinking it back then, at that exact moment.

The more I looked at myself, my expression, mesmerized by her, the more I tried to deny it. To whom? I wasn't even sure. Any outsider would look at the photo and think about how in love that man was, staring at his wife. You could pick up on the admiration, even if all you got was a glimpse of my profile. But it was clear as day, the way my eyes glowed, the way I stared at her like I was a lost boy who discovered Neverland…as if she were some long-lost treasure. It was as if no matter how hard I tried, I couldn't escape her pull, her gravity.

I decided to go to the gym to work out some of my frustration, and Aria went for a last swim, according to the post-it she had left taped on my bedroom door.

With the honeymoon officially over, we went to check ourselves out. The staff still eyed Aria, but with more respect.

"It was nice meeting you, Mrs. Wright. We hope to see you again soon," Rafael bubbled, overdoing it with the pleasantries.

"I doubt that, but thank you," Aria snarked, not giving him the time of day.

Ouch.

She waved at the others and audaciously walked to the car, swaying her hips with each step.

Now that's the Aria we know and hate. Good girl.

"By the way, I left the chips on my bed with a note," she said in the middle of our drive.

"What does it say?"

She pointed a look, something equivalent to *'wouldn't you wanna know'.*

I gave her my best puppy-dog eyes to soften that pretend mean mug she had going on. Her eyes rolled, and I knew she was about to indulge me.

"It sounds better in Spanish, but goes something like…" She paused for dramatic purposes, I was sure. "To be shared equally within the staff of the Admiral, maybe it will teach you something about hospitality."

"I approve."

She scoffed, "No one asked for your permission. The only reason I told you is so you don't get blindsided if they call you up or something."

"Noted."

"Fine."

"Fine."

The rest of the drive and the plane ride were silent. She had her headphones on and looked out the window the entire time.

Guess we were both ignoring the elephant on the plane.

Aria was barely breathing, gulping down my mother's roast. The entire table was staring at her. You would think she'd starved herself the entire honeymoon by the way she was demolishing her plate.

We went straight from the airport to my parents' place, where our entire family welcomed us with open, expectant arms. Thankfully, Aria took care of the souvenirs, securing a keepsake for every member. Per Lana's request, they were handed out before we sat down for dinner.

When the table was all cleared, my mother and Helen joined Aria on the couch, where she showed them all the photos she had taken.

We, men, went into my father's study to smoke a Montecristo. The two of them darted looks at me, playing with their brows like they were expecting me to spill some major secret. Their bubble got burst by a simple head shake. I didn't know what was worse, our fathers forcing us into a fake marriage, or them wanting it to be a real one.

Karl stormed in, the door swinging open.

"Uncle Cillian, is Aria our real aunt now that you're married?"

My heart, my stomach, everything in me sank.

"She was always your real aunt," was all I could muster to say.

"Yeah, but now it's artificial?"

That sounds about right.

"You mean official, little bug," my father corrected.

"Official," he said the word slowly, making sure every syllable was precise.

Thankfully, Lana called out for her brother, and he darted out, forgetting all about the question he had left lingering in the air.

The three of us remaining shared a look, with Peter's a bit more perceptive, as if he could read the turmoil from within. He placed a firm grip on my shoulder, grounding me. "Are you okay, son?"

I managed a nod and straightened my posture—no point in overthinking. A knock on the door interrupted the moment, and the door swung open again, revealing a yawning Aria.

"Can we go? I need to get into the time zone."

I chuckled, 'cuz—same.

"Sure."

"Wait, kids…" Peter mumbled, looking nervous for some reason, something I'm not sure I've ever witnessed before. "Thank you. I know the sacrifice you had to make, and I want you to know that we appreciate it."

"Oh, don't worry. I'll find a way to make you pay, with interest," Aria deadpanned.

"Funny. Cillian said the same thing," my father ratted me out.

Aria turned to face me, head tilted to the side. She looked tired, with dark circles under her deep blues, ever the breathtaking.

"Come on, let's go. The driver's outside," I said, holding the door open for her. She said goodbye to everyone, taking extra long to hug the kids before we got into the car.

On our drive home, her phone rang, and I could hear the scream on the other end.

"You're back?"

"Holy Merlot."

A short pause.

"Great, I'll be right over. Margaritas?"

And here I was thinking she was tired.

She hung up, setting her phone in the cup holder between us.

"That was Nala; she got back from her seminar, so if you could tell the driver to drop me off at her place, I'll unpack tomorrow. Sorry. I'll probably spend the night there."

I gave her a nod, not bothering to look at her.

Forget one step forward, two steps back... We were on another level, from going in circles to going backward. Messed up as ever.

Chapter 37

Aria

"Sooooo," Nala dragged the moment her door swung open, "How was the honeymoon?"

Terrible, thrilling, hot; pick your poison.

I was too tired for this.

"Fine," I sighed, my shoulders heavy. The head was heavier, but I was fully ignoring that one.

"Well, well, well." Sabrina stood up from the couch, theatrics at play.

"I am begging you, BFF to BFFs…" I trailed off. Because what the hell was I begging for? For them not to ask or enter interrogation mode? Well, since I needed to let it out, it was probably the latter.

Tired be damned. I needed this more than I needed sleep.

"You know what? Fuck it!"

I slumped on the couch, lifting my ankles on the coffee table, and got comfortable for the therapy session. Sabrina sat on her heels next to me, and Nala dragged a chair by my feet, both of them wide-eyed and ready.

You know that famous scene from Hamilton where the guy raps out his life story while the others bob their heads. Well, that's how this whole thing went down. It took me five minutes to get all the bullet points out, and their jaws dropped.

"So you're telling me that you had a PG-13 kind of a honeymoon?" Sabrina gawked at me.

"I am telling you, my honeymoon would be approved by the Amish."

"Uuuff." Nala's whole face wrinkled when she abruptly stood up, disappeared into her room, and came back a minute later, holding a drawer. Yes, a drawer. Slowly, she sat down and extended her hands to me.

"I think you need this more than I do."

I stretched my neck, taking a peek at her offering. My eyes instantly started to water, and I had to suck in my lips—hard. Her curiosity winning over, Sabrina stood up, only to drop on her ass, hitting the floor with a thud. Snorts were involved, with some laughing mixed in, along with heavy hyperventilation. It took us too long to get all demure and shit, but we managed—barely.

"Nala, you've been holding out on us," Sabrina marveled.
Understatement of the century.

You see, my friends, Nala just showed us a drawer filled with toys—different shapes and sizes, a rainbow of colors, very, very realistic looking, adult toys.

I choked on nothing, and the closeted dildo collector wasn't even blushing.

"OMG!" Sabrina shrieked. "Where did you get this one? It's like a mock-up of the real thing; I mean, look at the vein." She turned it around as if it were on display. "How did they do that?"

"It's 3D printed," Nala explained.

"Ooooo, I likey."

"I love the bonding experience, I do," I interrupted the love fest, "but I came here for your help."

The future lawyer was too blinded by the found treasure to bother looking at me when she asked, "And what exactly does that help entail? Harsh truth, or rose colored glasses?"

"Is there a middle?"

"Sure. It's called suck it up."

"Hey," I whined.

Sabrina sighed. "Look, if you're gonna be in denial, then we can't do much here. However, when you do decide to confront the feelings and admit them to yourself, then you'll get us with open arms and ears and no filter whatsoever."

To make a point, the courtroom wonder hit an imaginary gavel, accompanied by the sound of a thwack. Nala bobbed her head in approval, and me? I just sat there—mute.

My head started spinning, like a Tilt-a-Whirl ride at full speed. Flashes of a boy with green eyes made my insides crumble...all the promises broken...the heartbreak. Everything was right there. It finished off with the almost kiss at the beach, and that was when my heart burst, and tears tried to break free. But I wouldn't let them.

He hurt you.

And that was all it took to get the mask back on.

"I guess you chose door number one?"

I nodded.

"Alcohol it is. Bring 'em out, Bartender," she commanded, and Nala jumped to her feet, running to her fridge. Two Margarita pitchers were placed on the small table. I didn't even bother getting myself a glass—I went for the whole thing—and gulped, and gulped, and gulped until everything in me went numb.

Chapter 38

Aria

Today was Marco's birthday, and he was kind enough to invite me. Cillian drove us, saying he wouldn't be drinking much since he had a seminar early in the morning. I didn't even hide my excitement when he told me it would last three days. I loved having his place to myself.

After a brief escape to Mallorca, we found ourselves back in the familiar routine, each of us avoiding the other. The resort's beauty had a disarming effect on us, or at least that was what I made myself believe. The armor was back on, leading to a week spent on my thesis, inspired by the wedding and honeymoon that had turned into a business venture.

The party took place at a bar near the Base, called 'The Eagle'. I remembered seeing it when I'd dropped off Cillian once.

The place was stacked with US Navy paraphernalia and photos of men in uniforms. Above the bar on the wall, three golden plates were spread out, each bearing a different motto. The first one on the bottom right said Semper Fortis (meaning Always Courageous), and the one on the bottom left said Non sibi sed patriae (Not for self, but for the country). It was easy to translate, thanks to my average knowledge of

Latin. I didn't know why, but the language fascinated me, alongside Greek mythology, both of my unnecessary electives. My eyes took a bit longer to focus on the one in the middle. It was a bit larger and had an eagle silhouette engraved above the words stating *'Forged by the sea'*.

"Aria," the sound of my name made me turn, and I saw Marco walking toward me.

"Hi," I beamed at him. "Happy Birthday!" I exclaimed, pulling him into a hug.

"Thank you for coming," he smiled with his blue eyes. Out of Cillian's friends, Marco was the nicest one. He had a good heart, though it wasn't easily noticeable in his stiff demeanor. Throughout the time I've known him, I've never seen him relaxed. Even now, in a bar on his birthday, his back was straight, his shoulders raised to the sides, making his whole frame rectangular.

"Thank you for inviting me."

I met Marco last Christmas when Cillian had brought him to our family dinner, feeling guilty that he had no one to spend it with. Marco didn't get along well with his parents, so he became a regular at our family gatherings.

The bar was overcrowded with testosterone, with the exception of a couple of girlfriends and wives. The five of them were sitting at a corner table and invited me with a wave of their hands. I smiled and waved back, making my way to them.

"Hi, I'm Jessica; I'm Criss's wife."

"Hi, I'm Aria, I'm..." Before I could finish, she interrupted me, "Oh, we know. We postponed our book discussion on our monthly book club night to talk about you."

Fabulous, more book girlies.

"That's a weird thing to confess to a stranger, but I'm down."

"Oh, don't worry, none of it was bad, quite the opposite. We needed a smart Blondie to complete the circle."

That sounded about right, considering all the women had dark hair, with the exception of one who had ginger hair. They all introduced themselves and welcomed me with warm hugs. It felt all sorts of weird but nice at the same time.

"We love Cillian, but that man is hard to tame, and you, my new friend, have managed to do the impossible. Hats off!"

They all mimicked the action. I bowed in response to the gesture but remained reserved.

"Oh, I don't know about that."

"Don't even. He is one lucky guy." The unexpected praise caught me off guard, stirring a mix of emotions I didn't have time to face.

"Aria?" Another call of my name made me turn. "I thought that was you." The sight of Dave, an old high school friend, took me aback. We had been close before he left for college, and frankly, this was the last place I'd expect to see him.

"Wow, Davey, what are you doing here?"

"I'm a man of the sea now."

Color me surprised. Davey used to be such a klutz, so much so that he'd barely passed P.E.

"I have trouble believing that."

"Oh, you would, but I've changed."

I took him in; he'd gotten taller, more muscular, and was sporting a nicely trimmed beard. He still had that boyish charm about him that even the shiny bald head of his couldn't hide.

"Yeah, you look like it." I shook my head. "Sorry, that came out wrong."

"Hey, anything coming from you is more than welcome."

Was he actually flirting with me? No, that made no sense. I snickered anyway.

"Do you want to grab a drink at the bar and catch up?"

"I would love that." I turned to the table, "Ladies, I'll be right back." I waved and followed him to the bar.

Our conversation covered everything that had happened since we last saw each other. It was comfortable and easy. I've caught myself laughing more than I had in a while.

"We need to go! Now," Cillian's groggy voice startled me.

"Is everything okay?" Dave's face filled with worry.

"What makes you think you deserve to know that answer?" Cillian got in his face. "Do we have a problem?" His words were slurred, making me think he had one too many.

I stepped between them, facing Cillian. "Come on, let's go." My voice almost got caught in my throat. I tried to drag him away, but his body was too hard to move.

"Please," I pleaded, and our eyes met, softening his stance.

Facing Dave, I bemoaned, "I'm so sorry, I'll get your number from Marco." He smiled back awkwardly and waved while Cillian growled over his shoulder. When we got outside, I called for a taxi, figuring it was for the best, knowing Cillian would never let me drive his car. While we were waiting for our ride, the drunken idiot walked around in circles, mumbling to himself. His hands were glued to the back of his head, and his nostrils flared in overload. The SOB was wasted.

I got him into the car before I gave the driver the address with a hundred-dollar bill, just to relax his face staring at the fool next to me.

During the drive, Cillian kept cursing and mumbling gibberish through gritted teeth. But his body language was what worried me most. He looked... angry? Clenched fists, every muscle tense, and the veins on his neck all popped out.

What happened to get him like this?

The cab pulled up in front of Cillian's building, and I thanked the driver, barely able to get Cillian out. Pierre helped me get him upstairs, his body too heavy for me to carry by myself. I expressed my gratitude and dragged Cillian inside, throwing him onto the couch, the easiest place to clean.

"You should take a shower," I murmured.

When he didn't move, I turned on my heel, went to the pantry, grabbed a bucket, and then brought it to his side. He hadn't moved an inch, his eyes closed shut, body relaxed. All except the fists.

I went to the kitchen to grab him a glass of water, and when I turned around, I bumped into his chest. I took off my heels so the tip of my head was in line with his chin. Slowly raising my head, I was met by his glossy eyes. I hated how green they were, with little specks of gold in the corners. The stench of alcohol hit my nostrils, and my nerves started to play around.

What the hell is he doing?

But the question never slipped from my mouth because he caught my chin between his fingers, demanding attention. His other hand found purchase next to my head.

He inhaled. I swallowed.

"Cill…"

There was no warning, no notice before his lips met mine in a hard press.

My chest tightened, tears gathered in my eyes, and my heart burst with despair. It took everything in me to push him away. He stumbled, then our eyes met, mine filled with tears, his filled with rage.

I blinked.

His door slammed shut. And I was left alone with my thoughts, and the vanilla taste lingering on my tongue.

I stood there, looking at my bare feet glued to the floor while my tears joined their sides.

Did that actually happen?

Did he seriously need to be drunk to kiss me? Was it so appalling that he had to be intoxicated?

Just when I thought he couldn't hurt me any more than he already had, he proved me wrong… But then again, Cillian always was an overachiever.

Chapter 39

Cillian

I couldn't get the image of Aria's disgusted face out of my head. Not throughout the entire sleepless night. Not during my drive to Quincy, and certainly not sitting through the first day's presentation. I'd hoped a three-day seminar on new statutes and regulations at NOSC (Navy Operational Support Center) would get my mind out of the gutter, but so far, there had been zero success.

I'd crossed a line. I knew that. Getting drunk and forcing myself on her was the last thing I wanted. Seeing her all smiley with that oddly familiar guy, something in me had snapped. I couldn't understand why it had bothered me so much. She had every right to talk to whoever she wanted to, and yet, the sight burned my eyes. The urge to punch him in the face was strong, but then her hands were on me, fogging up my brain. To make matters worse, she'd taken care of me, turning all gentle and worried.

Than... I'd kissed her. I never expected her to recoil in revulsion, lower lip hanging, eyebrows pulled down, eyes shut, as if it were painful to look at me. Every waking hour, that image stuck with me. Mocking me.

On day two, our section unit got called to duty after a notice of a vessel obstructing the path of a U.S. ship. Thanks to that endeavor, I was able to head home a day early.

The drive back was lonely, soundless, with all the ways I should apologize crossing my mind. By the time I pulled into the garage, the sun had already set, and my plan to grovel was all laid out.

As soon as the elevator door dinged open, my eardrums were hit. By the sound of it, that loud music was coming from the penthouse. Anxiety spiked with each step, the noise intensifying.

Was she having a party?

Or worse?

I unlocked the door and entered, shouting out her name in vain. Not even I could hear my voice over the music. Following the sound, my heart kept pounding, only for it to stop beating when I reached the kitchen.

There she was, dancing, screaming her heart out. The island was covered with flour, a milk carton placed next to three little bowls. I swallowed, drinking her in. She was wearing an oversized white shirt that fell over one shoulder, leaving it exposed. My eyes followed the lines of the fabric covering a set of pink boxers down her long, naked legs, all the way to her feet hidden in fluffy slippers. On my tiptoes, I pulled back to hide behind the wall, watching her in astonishment.

While whisking the eggs, she moved her hips in circular motions, her head bobbing. When the beat of the song switched, she slid to the right, then to the left, doing twirls in the middle. She put the bowl down and started jumping from one foot to the other, making her hair, tied in a messy bun, loosen with each hop. The blue scrunchie fell to the floor, letting her strands go wild, grazing her back. My breath hitched when her delicate fingers started playing with it, pulling it up high. She released the locks as she lowered herself into a squat, turning her hips on the descent. I wouldn't classify her movements as sensual, but my dick would strongly disagree. I've never heard this song, so I tried to catch some lyrics and memorize them for research purposes, but the vision before me wouldn't let me, demanding all my attention.   Goofy, free, sexy, and so unbelievably happy... How could I possibly know that since she was facing the opposite direction, you ask? Well, despite my ears bleeding, I could hear her smile so clearly—feel it was more like it.

God, I had missed this old Aria. I wasn't even aware that I longed for that time, for the version of her I thought was gone, lost... Alas, it was still there; she'd just locked it away.

Realization hit.

She only locks it away from you.

She'd done it again; took me back. Suddenly, I was seventeen, ignored and rejected by the one person who meant the world to me.

"Do you want to call Cillian to join us?" Sabrina and Aria walked through the hall, passing my room.

"No way in hell."

"Why? You two are always attached to each other."

"I am above that, and so over it." There was a lot of bite in her tone, and it sent all the wrong shivers down my spine.

"Oh, look at you, coming to your caliber finally; welcome to the club, Biatch."

The words and attitude made my entire breakfast rise, feeling the eggs rise to my mouth, tasting them raw.

Shaking the recollection away, I backed away, making sure not to make a single sound. With an ache in my chest, I drove to the nearest hotel and booked a room.

My bag in hand, I headed straight to the bar. The guy behind it placed a coaster in front of me and kept wiping a glass with a white cloth, waiting for my order.

"Give me your best top-shelf Whiskey," I said in a harsh tone. A tumbler filled with ice appeared, and he filled it with amber liquor.

I scoffed when I zeroed in on the label—Old Forester.

Even the whiskey was mocking you.

"Leave the bottle," I grumbled.

He cocked a brow, but did what I asked. My endgame was washing the thoughts away, but the whiskey had other plans—every new sip piling on the memories.

"You two sit down and shut up!"

My father brought us to his study, and Peter strode to his side, both of them giving us their disapproving looks.

"You broke your mother's favorite vase," my father fumed. It was rare to witness him so angry.

"I'm sorry, but it was all his fault," Aria yelled, pointing a finger at me.

"My fault?" I turned to face her, my hand hitting the center of my chest. "You're the one who knocked it over with your excessive hand-waving."

"You provoked the hand to do the waving!" Her hands

243

started flying again, replaying the exact moment leading up to the crash.

"That's enough," my father snapped, not hiding his wrath, and the two of us stiffened.

"We are very disappointed in you two," Peter chimed in. "You are acting like children," he sighed. Couldn't they see that she was being unreasonable and irrational?

"It's just that..." she started deflecting, but my father intercepted her thoughts.

"I don't care, as long as you are under the same roof, our roof; there will be no fighting."

"Then don't expect me to be under the same roof with him," she seethed, crossing her arms over her chest.

The mere thought of not seeing her froze me on the spot. As much as I hated her, I needed her.

"You don't mean that, Peanut."

"Oh, but I do." For a second there, I thought there was a crack in her voice, but her next words were loud and clear. "From now on, count me out of everything. We'll do shared custody or something. I don't even want to breathe the same air as him."

"Behold the Ice Queen." I gestured with my hands, like I was presenting her to the court.

"Fuck you!" She blew her middle finger in my direction.

"Language," Peter bellowed, but she remained indifferent.

"Sorry. I meant Merlot you!" Her tone was a reminder of the distance between us that I couldn't bridge. She shrugged and then stood up. "I mean it. I don't want or have to put up with him. You will see me only when he is not around. I don't care at this point what either of you thinks," she deadpanned, *storming out, leaving us bewildered.*

I poured and gulped a glass down like it was a straight-out shot. The flashbacks were getting more intense with each new downpour.

"I have some news." Aria pulled up her left hand, something very new sparkling on it. "Sebastian asked me to marry him."

The moment stretched, silence all around, during which we took turns looking at each other, leaving Aria confused by our lack of words.

"Don't congratulate me all at once," she muttered through a fake smile.

My mother stood up first. "Congrats, honey, we are happy for you."

My heart sank, and I felt all eyes on me.

"I still haven't said yes," she uttered. "I'm thinking about it."

"Then why are you wearing the ring?" Helen asked the question in my head.

"Sebastian said to try it out, to get a feel for it, but…" she trailed off, and my mother took her hand, taking a better look.

"It's nice," Helen interjected, then added, "It's a bit tight, isn't it?"

The idiot couldn't even get the right size, not to mention the ring itself being all wrong for her. It was gold, for fuck's sake—she hated gold.

Maybe the new high and mighty Aria didn't.

"I am sorry, sir, but the bar closes in five minutes," the bartender said, bringing me back to my new reality. I looked at my clock but couldn't see the numbers, so I stood up, paid my bill, and retreated to my room. I slumped on the bed, turning on the air conditioner, comforted by the frigid air that reminded me of her.

Chapter 40

Cillian

Late Thursday night, after avoiding my wife/occasional roommate long enough, it was time to face my demons. Head groggy, hand visibly shaking, I reached for the knob.

Get it together, man!

I registered sounds coming from the screening room the moment I opened the front door. Dragging my feet, bag draped over my shoulder, I walked past, going straight to my room. A soft voice stopped me. "You're back." The execution came with reservations, as if she regretted speaking out, all the while seeming like she was maybe, just maybe, waiting for me…

"Yeah, I'm gonna turn in. I'm beat."

That was a stretch. Walking dead over here. I hadn't slept in… Fuck, come to think of it, I hadn't slept adequately since Aria had moved in.

"Ok, good night."

When I didn't move, she paused the screen and cocked a brow, expectant.

Was there a reason my feet were glued to the same spot? Probably, but I had no clue what it was.

Think! Think!

"I'm gonna buy tickets for the flight to Martha's Vineyard;

what seat do you want?"

Nice save.

We never used our private jet for local flights.

"It's a two-hour drive," she scolded, crossing her arms over her chest. Looking comfortable, cozy, in fluffy pajamas, a messy bun on top of her head, she nudged her glasses to the bridge of her nose. The woman had perfect vision but wore glasses whenever facing a screen. I'd used to mock the shit out of her for it, calling her ridiculous. But now... That would be the last word I'd use to describe her.

"And it's a 30-minute flight," I rebutted, not sure if she was trying to pick up a fight for sport, or if there was an actual point in this. With Aria, it was probably the former.

"Yeah, not really."

"Care to elaborate?"

"It's a twenty-minute drive to the airport with no traffic. You need at least five minutes to find parking. Then, it takes about ten minutes to get to the gate. Checking in and going through security can take around thirty minutes. Boarding adds another fifteen minutes. Plus, the same awaits when you land," she said, grabbing a chip and tossing it into her mouth. Crunching, she mumbled, "By the time you get in the air, I'll be relaxing by the fire, sipping on my wine."

"Smart-ass!"

"Oh, come on, say it like you mean it." She bit another chip.

"You make a good point. Mind if I tag along?"

She shrugged, without mulling it over. "It's your funeral!"

"Every interaction with you sure is."

I left her to her screen and turned in.

"Mmmmm," I mumbled, turning onto my back, my hand grazing my naked chest. Eyes wide open, I sniffed, blinked, then sniffed some more. A familiar smell instantly got me on my feet, practically running to the source, where I found Aria pouring coffee into a thermos, her back to me. My eyes snapped to the tray on the countertop, steam evaporating through the air. I heard, or maybe read it somewhere, that scents are correlated with memories. It was my first time experiencing it.

"Aria, why are you crying?" My mother rushed to her side. I took a step back, hiding behind the door to eavesdrop.

"I ruined it all," she sobbed, "I wanted to do something nice for his birthday and make his favorite, but I ruined them all."

It was my 11th birthday, and she wanted to do something special… for me? I had no knowledge of this, as evidenced by the tempo of my racing heart. Turning full-on ninja, I peeked through the small crack, watching as my mother wiped Aria's tears away.

"Oh, honey, it's okay. It takes practice."

When that didn't do the trick, Mom took her chin, demanding attention. "Look at me, sweetie."

My best friend in the world obliged, lifting those ocean eyes filled with regret.

"Let's try it again, shall we?"

I remembered hiding all afternoon, peeping while my mother worked with Aria in the kitchen, both of them covered in flour and laughing. Her laughs were a rarity at that time, so I took in each one she let out.

"These are the best cookies I have ever tasted!" I exclaimed, then turned my puppy eyes to my mom. "Sorry."

"I agree," My mother cackled, pinching my cheek. Oddly enough, that always got me to blush.

"Woo-hoo!" Aria crowed, taking another bite. Then she noticed me looking at her, and she simpered.

As Aria's best friend, I would do anything to hear her laugh, even lie if necessary (don't worry, I only dealt with white lies), but in this situation, lying wasn't necessary. Her cookies actually were the best I've ever tasted. Something was different about them, something I couldn't quite map out… They tasted like… her.

She looked up at me, those blue eyes going wide when they noticed my stuffed mouth.

"It wasn't in the recipe, but I added chunks of vanilla chocolate…" She hesitated for a beat, but then nodded her head like she was assuring herself to continue. "You know, to add a bit of me into the mix."

I knew she was joking, trying to play it off, but I knew better.

That was one of my favorite birthdays and the start of a new tradition. It had been eight years since she last baked me cookies.

"Wow, those look amazing," I raved, my hand outstretched midair.

As expected, it got smacked away.

"Thanks, I've gotten better over the years."

In more ways than one.

I opened my mouth to tell her off, but she interrupted, "I was thinking we leave in half an hour to avoid the morning rush."

"I won't object to that."

Something was off. She was being suspiciously nice. Even the smack was tamed. And when she handed me a cup of coffee, I swear my knees buckled. There were serious doubts in my head, mainly about whether the coffee had been poisoned. I took a sip anyway—death by coffee, not the worst way to go...

It was when I was offered one vanilla chocolate chip cookie, my all-time favorite, that true panic struck. Yup, I was gonna die today.

Tell my family I love them.

Reluctantly, I took the cookie, eyeing it as if it were a ticking bomb.

"I didn't poison it, Hades," she intoned, grinning at me. My brain failed me with its lack of retort. I didn't believe her for a minute.

"We haven't gotten the money yet, remember?"

When I still couldn't move, or talk, or do anything at this point, she snatched the thing out of my hand and took a large bite. "There. Happy?" she quipped with a mouthful.

"No," I spat, but the rest was winged, "you ate half my

cookie."

"It was one bite, you big baby," she huffed, grabbing another one and tossing it to me. Like the ex-pro I was, I caught it with a smirk.

Twenty minutes later, we were riding the elevator down, each of us with a suitcase in hand. We entered the garage we now shared, and she opened the trunk of her Aston Martin, setting her bag down.

"What makes you think we are taking your car?"

"Because it was my idea to drive there, plus I want to be the one doing the actual driving—the sole point of this whole thing." Her hands were flying around, like it was self-explanatory.

"Don't worry, you'll drive, but it'll be my car."

I took my key out of my pocket and pressed the button that sounded the click, unlocking it.

Aria's jaw dropped. "Are you serious?"

Making her stunned was my favorite sport.

"You would seriously let me drive your baby?" Her eyes narrowed in assessment. The baby she was referring to was my golden Bentley Bacalar. Only twelve were produced, and I owned one of them. It was also Aria's dream car.

"What? I am tired as fuck and in no mood to drive. Plus, it goes with your hair."

"It goes with my everything. But seriously, you trust me with it?"

I don't think I have ever heard the word seriously spoken so much in a span of one minute.

"I've seen you drive." I handed her the keys, adding, "I kind of like the idea of being the passenger princess."

"Swear on Merlot!"

I rolled my eyes, got our bags in the trunk, and slid into my seat.

Now, I could lie and say that Aria taking the wheel wasn't something worthy of the big screen… I could also lie and say that her smile had never been so bright. But my poker face would easily give me away. So we'll leave it at that.

"I presume you have earplugs or headphones."

I nodded confusedly, taking a pair out of my pants pocket.

"Good, use them. I suggest setting the volume to the max." She gave me a slight smirk and started the ignition, taking a deep breath. Her eyes filled with fire as a devilish smile spread across her mouth. After connecting her phone to the car via Bluetooth, she exited the garage while I made myself comfortable, filling my eardrums with plastic. Relaxed, I closed my eyes with the intention of using the drive for much-needed rest, except my eyes had an agenda all of their own. They cracked open just enough to see her without getting caught, my phone muted.

It didn't take long to figure out she was taking the longer route, and as much as I hated the idea, the drive turned out to be—interesting.

She sang her lungs out to every song, dancing in her seat. Leave it to Aria Nicol Brooks to make a simple car seat into a whole fucking dance floor. She bobbed her head to the sides, swirled her shoulders, and never stopped smiling.

Her playlist was, let's say, colorful, for lack of a better word. She rapped to Fort Minor, Eminem, and NF, screamed to Angels & Airwaves, Guns 'n' Roses, and the new Linkin Park. Then bubbled Britney Spears, Taylor Swift, and Sabrina

Carpenter.

When it came to her driving, fucking Lewis Hamilton had nothing on her; she was Hamilton of the state side road. One hand on the wheel, the other on the gear stick, that was, when it wasn't in the air, flowing. Her foot on the gas made itself as comfortable as it could. I remembered when we'd both gotten our learner's permits, the excitement in her eyes when our dads took us on our first drive.

"I don't want to drive an automatic. I want to learn how to drive a stick."

"Why? This is easier." My father was already frustrated, and this was only our first driving lesson.

"Exactly. I want to learn what is harder first so that everything else gets easier, not the other way around."

I kind of liked her logic.

"You are only complicating everything," Peter jumped in. I shook my head at them. They didn't get it, they didn't get her.

"I think it's because she wants to drive a Formula 1 car one day, and they only come in stick mode," I declared, winking at her. She gave me her signature scold/smirk look I've been prone to my entire life. "Not the only reason, and I don't need you to speak for me, but thank you for your support." Then, she winked back.

Aria had a thing about driving and cars in general; she'd once told me that she felt freest while driving, that she felt like herself. I hadn't fully understood it then, but I sure did now.

Chapter 41

Aria

There were many reasons why I loved Martha's Vineyard. It held most of my best memories, and it was my mother's favorite place. It's where we spread out her ashes, right behind the house under her favorite tree. The same tree under which we'd spent hours reading her favorite sonnets while she combed my hair. Every time I was there, I would get out a blanket and sit under it, catching her up. Even in the spike of winter, I would do so, and it was only there, when I was with her in my mind, that I wouldn't shiver. The love for this place, the memories it held, and the connection it provided all filled me with a deep sense of nostalgia.

Everyone knew of this one endeavor and respected it, allowing it to be the first thing I did before greeting everyone. This year was no different. As soon as we pulled up to the driveway, Cillian had taken our luggage and gone inside without me, and I beelined out back with my bag draped over my shoulder.

"Hi, Mom. I miss you so much," I started, spreading out the blanket and making myself comfortable. "I wish you were here, but I know you're in a better place. My only hope is that you're not disappointed in me, with the person I've become—this weak version I try my best to diminish."

Hugging myself, I kept going, "It's so hard, Mom; all I do

is fall over and over again… and it hurts…"

Sniffling, I played with my wedding ring, rotating it with my thumb.

"My head knows better, but it's my stupid heart that has trouble remembering, and I've been reckless with it. I need your guidance now more than ever because I don't know how to handle my feelings. I am fighting not to surrender, and I am losing every ounce of strength."

Tears streamed down my face, my voice choking with emotion. "I can't take another heartbreak, Mom… I just can't," I bawled, hiding my face in my palms, letting it all out. Tears—I was used to; meltdowns—my best friends at this point…and yet it never got easier.

I stood up, dried my eyes, and took a long breath.

"Anyway, I miss you, I love you." I looked up at the sky, the clouds moving ever so slowly, and for some reason, I smiled. "I'll leave you to it; say hi to Gam."

Giving her a wave, I picked up my stuff and headed inside.

The moment I opened the door, Lana and Karl crashed into me. "Hi, you little buggers," I yelped, squeezing them tight. "I'm feeling a little hungry; I might just eat you up!" And so I did, making them cry out with laughter while I tickled them with my mouth, making chewing noises.

"Oh, honey, it's so good to see you." Loren showed up out of nowhere, opening her arms for me. She held me for a second longer, knowing I needed it. "Happy Thanksgiving," I said softly, planting a peck on her warm cheek.

She returned the kiss. "I've missed you. Did you two have a good talk?"

"Yeah, we always do."

She cupped my cheeks and looked at me with pride, not saying a word, not needing to; her eyes said it all. Her love was evident in the little twinkle sparkling out, as her mouth joined in a smile.

"There's my Peanut." My dad practically ran, stretching out his arms, and I allowed myself to fall into his protective clasp. John followed, squishing the air out of me as per his usual. I glanced at Helen, so radiant with her bump, now quite big for only five months. Her eyes had the same shade of green as her brother's, but the shape of her eyes was more like Loren's, unlike Cillian, who took most of his father's features. Her dark brown, long, kinky hair (the expression she'd taught me when we were kids) fell down her back while she smiled at herself, apologizing for wearing pajamas.

"Don't you dare," I told her as I copped a feel of my future nephew. "You don't dress to impress; you dress for comfort."

The sigh of relief and gratitude escaped her face, and I felt a little kick that made my heart stop.

"Well, hello there, little one." My facial muscles started to hurt from the tension of my smile, the smile I couldn't seem to shake off.

The familiar sounds, comforting smells, and loving faces all contributed to an overwhelming sense of warmth and belonging. It had been so long since I last felt at ease in this place. Too damn long.

"I am thankful for all of you. You are the family that I never knew I needed, but so desperately wanted," I said before passing the baton to Cillian, sitting on my left. "I am

thankful for basketball, my height, my looks, my family, and for the best friend a guy could ask for." He turned to face me, *his eyes confirming the statement. It made me lose myself in his forest greens. Our eyes were a manifestation of sea meets land, each wave coming in stronger, closer, marking its territory.*

Tears pricked my eyes at the memory of that last Thanksgiving with us on speaking terms. I only wish I had appreciated it more. Not even a planner such as myself could have predicted a betrayal coming.

We headed down the hall before we all separated. The men took their positions in front of the TV, preparing for the game, and the ladies retreated to the kitchen. Lana and Karl sprinted by me, going straight into their uncle's lap. I lingered for a beat, my eyes unable to look away at how they snuggled into his broad chest. Cillian had always been great with kids, and I hated that once upon a time, I'd imagined little versions of us running around the house.

Sighing, I turned on my heel and jumped into the conversation regarding morning sickness. Helen mentioned that Joe was considering coming home permanently, how he missed them, and that he couldn't stand to be apart anymore. Her face lit up at the mere mention of his name, and I couldn't help but wonder if I'd ever be so lucky.

They'd married young, and she'd gotten pregnant soon after their vows. Despite their young age, they were mature enough to take that step and make it work. At nineteen, she'd brought Lana into this world while her husband had been somewhere in the middle of the ocean. Loren and I had helped her as much as we could in the beginning, but truth be told, she didn't need it. I've always admired her strength. They raised two of my favorite little humans into the kindest, most vibrant, full-of-life beings, and I loved them even more for it. She was the sister I never had, and even though our lives took different paths, every time we saw each other, it was as if no time or distance had passed between us. That was our family, albeit somewhat dysfunctional.

I heard Cillian yelling at the TV, followed by my dad cursing, and I checked the score. Damn, the Cowboys were losing, and it was going to set off a whole mood.

"Don't worry, guys, Lance and Lamb got this!" I usually sat with them when I was younger, but that changed after the fatal day. I loved watching sports, especially basketball, but football was their thing. Wanting to be part of the inner circle, I'd learned everything there was to know, falling in love with it in the process.

"I'm sure McCarthy will switch on to shotgun formation any second now," I pointed out, eyeing my dad's proud gaze. Cillian smirked, "Smart-ass."

"Oh, come on, say it like you mean it."

We both smiled without breaking eye contact, and something warm hugged my chest. It felt nice, like old times.

Loren called us over, prompting us to rush to the table. When we sat down for dinner, for the first time in forever, it felt like home. We all said our thanks, saying the same word over and over—family.

My eyes couldn't be tamed; they kept stealing moments shared with him. Now a bit darkened but still showing the golden specks around his pupils, Cillian's eyes froze on mine, piercing through me. My chest burned at the mere gaze that intensified with each breath. I didn't like the feeling, but I couldn't stop my blood vessels from flowing with the flames throughout my whole body. Whatever this was, it was trying to shatter all the shackles that held my feelings in subjugation.

I excused myself and left the table, mumbling something about having a headache before turning to my room and locking the door behind me.

Chapter 42

Aria

A notification on my phone interrupted my spiraling thoughts with a link from Sab. A dab of my finger revealed a photo of Cillian stepping out of a building, a bag draped over his shoulder, the headline under it turning the room to sub-zero.

'Trouble in paradise. The prodigal son was seen leaving a Boston hotel only a month after his 'I do's to the Mine heiress. Guess it's one eruption-less marriage.'

It would be funny if my lungs weren't so busy trying to cease the hyperventilation. The complete opposite of a laugh escaped my mouth as I continued reading. Noting the date, I paused, rubbing my eyes as if my vision had mixed up the numbers. It didn't. Right there, in black and white, plain bold font, mocked me. It was the time he was supposed to be in Quincy.

My heart felt that all-too-familiar ping.

Why was it hurting? Aching, tearing me apart?

Earth-shattering, walls around me closing in, I placed a pillow on my knees and mumbled my screams into it. Tears erratically fell down the side of my face, the pain taking charge, making me lose myself in its familiarity. A knock sounded on my door, but I ignored it, unable to face whoever was producing it.

"Aria?" His voice, so soft, sent an impulse right through my spine.

I didn't respond; the sobs wouldn't let me.

"Open the door."

I tightened my grip around my knees, bringing them to my chest, crushing the heart-shaped pillow in between.

"Please, I won't go away until you open this door."

Knowing he meant it, I took a good minute to gather whatever was left of me, calming down every part and drying out my tears. I gave myself a nod of assurance and headed to the door. With a shaky hand, I twisted the knob and swung the door open. His green eyes, full of lies, hit me like a knife to the chest.

"What's wrong?" He looked sincerely worried, but I knew better.

"What's wrong is that I was stupid," I blustered, taking a shaky breath. "Thankfully, I have come to my senses. I'm adding a new addendum. I never want to see your face!" I seethed in cold anger, sure my face was full-on red.

"What's your damage?"

Thump Thump
Thump Thump
Thump Thump
Beeeeeeeeeeeeeep

There went my heart, smashing into a gazillion pieces.
What's your damage?

If there was one word in this whole universe that had the power to shatter me, it was the word *'damage'* in any form, tense, or gender. But the word coming out of Cillian's mouth… now, that had the power to open the ground from underneath and swallow me whole.

If I could go back to the old days, somewhere right before it all started to fall apart, I would go to that exact moment, the one that broke me, and cover the ears of a hopeful girl to preserve her innocence. But instead, all I got was the memory replaying, suffocating me.

"Are you free Saturday? Maybe we could go watch a movie?" Tony ran from the water straight to me, droplets dripping from his hair, hypnotizing me. He was the only guy on the basketball team with longer hair, the length stopping right at the tip of his ear. His lower lip got caught between his teeth, waiting for my answer. He seemed nervous, which only fed my anxiety, and that thing was already high due to the 'mandatory' dress code—i.e., swimwear. It'd taken me forever to find a bikini that hid the scar and kept my boobs at bay at the same time. But even with the right fit, I still felt self-conscious, wondering if others could see it.

"Sure, who else is coming?"

"Uhm…" He scratched the back of his head, looking everywhere but at me. When his complexion turned pale, I began to worry. "Are you okay?"

"Yeah..just…I." His voice turned low, the smile he was giving me—awkward.

"A couple of guys on the team," Jake jumped in, literally, wrapping one hand around my neck, the other around Tony's,

pushing us closer. Being in with the team came with the territory of being Cillian's best friend, plus I've never missed a game, earning extra points.

"Any girls?"

"You're the first we asked," Tony replied, the cute puppy dog eyes gleaming, and then there were the dimples. They not only formed with his smile, but with each word, and it would make any girl's knees weak. Well, almost any.

"Do you have any preferences? For the movie, I mean…" He handed me his phone, a new contact tab at the ready. I spoke while typing in my number. "I like all genres, so whatever you guys pick, I'm good."

I gave the phone back and waved with a wink, trying to act all cool as I walked away.

"Can't wait," he shouted back, but I never turned, too busy wondering if Cillian was one of the guys going. Spotting Sabrina cozied up by the fire, I took a seat next to her on the sand, scanning the Nantucket beach. My breath hitched when I spotted him, talking to Tony, laughing. I could hear the sound of it so clearly… it was engraved in every fiber of my being.

An elbow jabbed my ribs, and I turned to face Sabrina. She had that all-knowing look about her I hated, but secretly loved. Confessing that I saw Cillian as more than just a friend was a mistake, but it happened—as did the feelings, despite my efforts to suppress them as hard as I could.

Swallowing a lump, I stood up, intending to get closer when I heard Tony ask my best friend about me. Cillian's words stopped me in my tracks—"You don't want her, trust me, she's all kinds of damaged!"

It was the first time I realized that heartbreak had a sound.

A shiver brought me back to reality. Tears welled up, and panic struck.

Shit!

You are not going to cry in front of Cillian fucking Wright.

I clenched my fists and made my eyes suck all the tears back.

"You're right. I'm sorry," I faltered, slamming the door in his face before locking it twice for good measure. Tears unleashed, and at this point, it was impossible to stop the flow. I wanted to scream at the top of my lungs, but barely suppressed it, knowing others occupied the house, children included. I pulled myself into the tightest of hugs and rocked forward and backward on my bed. It was amusing how I had so many rooms, each holding a memory of me crying—the same person being the culprit in each one.

Needing to escape, I stood up, thankful I hadn't unpacked when we got here, making my exit strategy quicker. This house was too much for me to handle. This place was my one safe haven, and he took that from me. He took the safety of it, the calm, the very soul.

I grabbed a framed photo from my nightstand, wiping my tears to get a better look. I was in the middle, around seven or eight, Cillian's arm around me, Mario on the other side, blowing a raspberry, and Helen lying on the grass beneath us. I took the frame and smashed it against the wall. The glass broke into a dozen pieces, imitating my heart.

It clicked then and there... My broken ticker wasn't mine

to begin with. It had always belonged to him; he consumed it whole and was free to discard it, stomp on it...and he was freaking good at it. And there I was, thinking it would be safe with him. It was about damn time that my stupid heart caught up to my brain, closing the door on him forever.

Chapter 43

Cillian

Were my eyes playing tricks on me, or did I actually witness tears forming in Aria's eyes? The last time I'd seen her all red and puffy was the last time she spoke to me with any passion. The night was forever mapped in my memory—when we went from everything to nothing, ironically, with a door slam in my face.

Noticing Aria leaving, I ran after her, shouting her name. Not once did she stop to turn, and I knew for a fact she'd heard me. Picking up my speed, going full sprint, I managed to catch her before she reached her room. The tears were the first thing I saw, and my arms opened so fast, expecting her warmth. Only, she didn't lean onto my chest like countless times before—quite the opposite, actually—she stepped back, face red, eyes swollen.

"What happened?"

Did someone hurt her? Did Tony say something mean? We never should've come to this bonfire.

"Leave me alone, Cillian," she seethed.

"Aria, come—" I never got to finish because Sabrina swooped in, pushed me away, and walked Aria straight inside, my nose almost getting hit by the door. Not bothering

to knock, I pressed the knob but felt resistance when I tried to push it open. They had locked it. Loud music came from the other side, muffling the banging of my knuckles.

After what seemed like forever, the door swung open, revealing two dolled-up friends, not holding off the glam. All too naturally, my eyes took in Aria, her tight dress barely reaching her mid-thigh, her hair pulled up in a sleek bun.

"Where are you going?"

God, I sounded like a protective brother, and that was the last thing I wanted.

"Out," Aria barked without a single glance my way. A lump got stuck in my throat at the coldness in her tone.

"Can I come?"

And now I sounded desperate. Maybe I was.

The laugh that escaped my best friend could only be described as that of a witch. "No. I don't want to be seen with you," rasped Aria as she grazed my shoulder and walked away.

What was that supposed to mean?

The confusion from that memory matched my own right about now.

This was ridiculous. It made no sense. Why would I care if she had tears in her eyes? Why should I care about the look on her stupid, beautiful face?

I didn't care. I didn't care.

Fuck

I lifted my hand to knock, only to turn and go to my room. Intended to sit on the bed, I stopped with my ass mid-air and walked back to her door, raising my hand. It quickly dropped down, followed by my head.

Don't be a fucking pussy. Suck it up!

With a full-on sense of determination, I knocked.

"Go away!" she yelled through the door, and I knocked harder.

"I mean it, go the fuck away." Even though there was a barrier, the crack in her voice was loud. This time, I hammered.

Three loud pounds were enough for the door to swing open, revealing a puffy face, the same one from when we were seventeen, only more mature now. "What do you want?"

"Are you okay?" I lowered my voice, trying to get a good read on her.

"Don't act like you care, Hades. It doesn't suit you. I mean it, leave me alone," she scowled, trying to slam the door, but a simple slide of my foot stopped it.

Guess we're back to the nickname. I didn't like it.

"I know you; you never cry unless it's something big. So tell me." According to the flaring nostrils, my words seemed to aggravate her more.

"That's funny, you thinking that you know me," she snarled through her tears, crossing her arms over her chest.

I leaned on the frame, raising my voice an octave, trying my best to prove a point she was blind to see or hear. "It's me, Aria. I've known you since we were babies."

"You don't know me; you never did! Now move your foot, or I'll break it!"

"I know you better than you think. And the foot stays." I was practically shouting at this point, my frustration catching up.

"If you really knew me, you would... ugh," she screamed with a grunt, her hands pulling her hair.

"I would what?" I demanded as she passed by me and headed to the stairs, dragging her suitcase behind her.

"Aria," I shouted, stretching out to grab her arm, but she turned before I could reach her.

"Don't even think about touching me!"

The look on her face struck me like an arrow, and not a sharp one.

"If I really knew you, I would what?" I took a step closer, and she raised her hand, motioning for me to stop. I didn't want to feed her anger, so I obliged.

"You would know how much I hate that word, and you would never, *ever* use it!"

Three slow tears fell down her face before she turned on her heel. I stood there in silence, focusing on the sounds I knew were coming. The slamming of the door first, followed by the ignition, and then a screech of tires.

You would know how much I hate that word, and you would never, ever use it.

Hated what word?

Replay, reverse the conversation, replay it.

What word?

Then the image of her face going pale flashed through my mind.

What's your damage?

And it hit me.

I was standing right by the fire, but I might as well have been in an igloo. Tony was talking to Aria, putting a smile on her beautiful face. He handed her his phone, and she typed on it.

What the fuck does she think she's doing, giving her number to another guy?

A guy like Tony. He was a fucking jock. What was I saying? So was I. We were on the same fucking basketball team.

Oh shit. He's walking toward me, and so is Jake.

"I can't believe you finally found your balls and asked her out," Jake whisper-yelled, "then choked and said it's a group thing."

"Thanks for the save, man." Tony patted Jake's shoulder when they reached me. "I'm thinking, everybody cancels at the last minute, so Aria and I make it a date."

The hell you are!

Tony nodded his chin. "Hey, you and Aria are close. What's she like?"

Think, Think.

What lie would scare a guy like Tony away? Aria was perfect, so only a nicely placed lie would work. But what?

Lightbulb alert!

"You don't want her; trust me, she is all kinds of damaged!"

Just like that, the last eight years unraveled in a single second. She'd overheard a lie, believed it, and I had never made the connection. It was soon after she'd had her surgery. A ball had hit her chest during P.E., and the pain was so intense that they had rushed her to the hospital. They had found a lump, and with the family medical history, a certain scare filled every single one of us. It was benign, but she'd insisted on a removal. They'd taken a chunk of her right breast, and with it, a piece of her self-confidence. And then she'd heard the word 'damaged' coming out of my stupid, ignorant mouth.

All this time, I've thought she had stopped liking me, that society had morphed her into this ice queen who believed she was better than everybody. But it was me; I was the reason for the winter that had lasted eight years too long.

I was the one who'd hurt her…

You're the one who broke her.

My mother came to my side. "Son, what did you do?"

"I broke her," was the last thing I said before I fell apart. Actual tears slid down the sides of my face, the words echoing around us.

I broke her.

I hated myself, hated how clueless I'd been, not realizing it sooner. I could have spared both of us; I could have saved the years we've spent hating and hurting each other.

My mother grazed my hair while I cried like a baby in her arms. "It's okay, honey, you can still fix it."

Could I? Was there any chance of unbreaking? There was nothing I wanted more than to pick up all the pieces and glue them together.

"Cillian." My mother pulled my chin to look up at her. "Go, explain, use your words, use your eyes that have always been filled with love for her. Let her see and feel it all."

Her soft words spoke directly to my heart, forcing my feet to spring into action.

Chapter 44

Aria

The drive calmed me down enough to reduce the urge to smash something or someone. I parked in the garage and decided to walk around the block to clear my thoughts further, leaving all my stuff, sans the keycard, in my dad's Mustang. I sure as hell wasn't going to take Cillian's car, or it might have ended up in a ditch somewhere. And that would be a disservice to the car lovers community.

The streets were deserted and quiet. Only the rustling leaves broke the silence. Not a single car passed as I turned the corner. I looked up at the sky, hoping for an answer I knew I'd never find. Tears reemerged, clouding my vision while my idiotic heart kept on pounding. The bastard was being way too loud, so much so that you'd think it was trying to tell me something. 'Run' would be my guess.

My state of mind wasn't ready to face Pierre, so I walked past the main entrance and back to the garage. I used the elevator up to the penthouse inhabited by a lie.

I kicked off my shoes and went straight to Cillian's custom bar, in desperate need of a fix. Bitter and borderline malevolent, I opted for the black box set on display, one I'd gotten him for his sixteenth birthday. We were both obsessed with the Godfather movies as kids. Since I was a minor, my dad had ordered the personalized gift box. It had a 'The

Godfather Cocktail' bottle and two tumblers—one had Cillian's name engraved, and the other had mine. We were supposed to open it together when we'd turned twenty-one. That never happened.

I found it poetic, so I poured myself a glass of amber liquid. The smoky smell hit me as the sweet flavor swam over my tongue. My throat burned when I swallowed, and the sensation followed all the way down.

The rest got guzzled down fast, not giving me a chance to revel in the potency. Somewhere in the middle of my third glass, my throat started to tighten. I tried to stand up, but it felt like a chore, as if my feet didn't belong to me.

Wrapping my hand around my throat, I pressed my fingertips to feel it swell up.

This can't be happening... I was careful... I am always careful.

My lungs hurt with each new intake of air, not reaching their intended destination.

My EpiPen... where is it?

In my bag.

I left my bag in the car.

Oh my Dionysus, I'm gonna die.

I tried to scream, but nothing came out. Spots obscured my vision, my legs gave out from under me, and I collapsed.

Shit.

My butt was too skinny to soften the blow.

Great!

We can add that to the pain mix.

I can't breathe.

Everything burned, and I felt myself slipping into

nothingness.

I'm never again gonna feel the safety of my father's arms... hug my friends, my family... hear the innocent laughter of Lana and Karl...

I won't meet my new nephew...

Cillian, I'll never get the chance to tell him I love him...

I am going to die.

"Aria, are you okay?"

I would know that voice anywhere.

Cillian.

I opened my mouth to speak, but nothing came out, not even a breath.

"Oh, fuck. Aria, look at me."

His voice sounded shaky, or maybe it was just me.

Complete and utter silence; obscurity.

Someone is touching me; it's nice and warm.

I could feel my eyes rolling to the back of my head.

Darkness is taking over, pulling me in.

"Breathe, Baby, breathe for me, please."

Who the fuck is Baby?

I'm going to be sick.

He brought someone here...

I opened my eyes to a pair of greens. Were those tears? I was going crazy.

My heart hurts; it burns.

Tears, so many tears.

"Did you drink this? Shit. Where's your EPI?"

He's gone. He left me. I am going to die.

Fade to black...

The last thing I expected after I'd sped home, disregarding every speed limit, was to find Aria passed out on the floor. I had rushed to her so fast, tapping her cheek, shouting her name, only for her to go limp and unresponsive.

Then, I saw the glass of amber liquid, and full-on panic struck.

I put her in a half-sitting position and ran to my room, my phone between my ear and shoulder.

"911, what's your emergency?" a woman answered just as I opened the drawer in my nightstand.

"My wife is allergic to nuts, and she had a glass, maybe more, of Amaretto, and she's unconscious," I informed, grabbing the EPI, then bolted back to Aria.

Nerves kicking in, I winced and repeated the mantra Peter had taught me when we were five, "Blue to the sky, orange to the thigh…" Exposing her mid-thigh, thankful she was in a dress, I pushed the thing in, holding for three seconds before tossing it aside.

"Did you inject epinephrine?"

"Yes, in her thigh." I nodded vigorously, knowing the woman couldn't see it.

"Good, now monitor her breathing."

"Ok."

I gave them our address and focused on her breaths, my thumb on the pulse line of her wrist, taking note.

Her eyes were open, but all I could see was white, no ocean blue, no aquamarine—just plain white.

Oh God, please don't leave me.

I can't live without her.

"Breathe, Aria, please, please," I choked when her chest stopped moving.

I parted her lips and gave her my breath, offering my life in exchange.

She closed her eyes and then opened them to reveal the one color that made my heart skip a beat—blue.

"That's it, Baby, breathe."

"Sir, is she conscious?" I heard the woman through the speaker, but all I could focus on was Aria in my arms, coming to.

"That's it," I encouraged, cupping her cheek.

"Am I in heaven?" Aria mumbled, and I had to fight off a chuckle.

"Look at me!"

It took her a beat before she obliged, seeming vivid as she lifted her eyes to meet mine. They widened when she whispered, "Cillian?"

"Yes," I breathed, a wave of relief washing over me. "You're ok."

Thank God.

My heart resurrected when I saw her chest rising and falling.

"It's ok, you're ok," I crooned, pulling her into a hug.

"Sir, is she conscious?" the friendly and very patient woman asked, and I got my phone to my ear. "Yes, yes, the EPI worked, she's coming to."

"Paramedics are in the elevator."

The tension in my shoulder lessened at her words. I ordered, "Tell them to come right in. I can't leave her; the door is open."

Not a minute later, two paramedics rushed in, tending to Aria with impressive speed.

"Miss?"

The female paramedic flashed the flashlight in Aria's eyes, and she squinted with a growl.

"Miss?"

"Who's there?" Her voice was strained, but she managed to open her eyes so that the EMT could examine her. After some checks, the ginger guy turned to face me. "We're taking her to the hospital; she was in anaphylactic shock."

"I'm coming with you," I insisted, and both of them nodded, placing Aria on a gurney. Holding her hand, I followed them to the ambulance when Aria lost consciousness.

Chapter 45

Cillian

It turned out to be the longest night of my life. She was lying in a hospital bed, looking fragile, something I never thought was possible. Nala rushed in, Sabrina on her heels, both with a worried expression. I called everyone while I rode in the ambulance with Aria to Mass General. Since her friends lived in the city, it made sense that they arrived before the family, though technically, they were family as well.

"Is she okay?" her friends whisper-shouted in unison.

I nodded. "She needs to rest and regain her strength." I stood up to greet both of them, and they closed in on me, hugging me. "Thank you for calling us," Nala gasped.

Her unexpected kindness caught me off guard. Despite our limited interactions, I had assumed she harbored resentment toward me. But her gentle hazel eyes revealed no such feelings, only a deep sense of empathy.

"You look pale. When was the last time you ate?" Sabrina asked, her concern palpable.

I thought back to our dinner, unsure if I had even taken a single bite of the food.

"I don't remember," I answered, and she turned to Mateo, whom I noticed standing by the door. "Hi, man, sorry."

"No worries. I'll go grab something for you to eat, be right back," he said before pushing off the frame and disappearing.

I sat back down and wrapped Aria's cold hand in mine, warming it.

"That video of you two as kids..." I turned to face Nala's kind eyes. "It's like I was watching a different version of Aria."

You were.

"You were," Sabrina chimed in with my thoughts. "Back then, she was more of a sunshine than you are."

Nala gasped, her hand flying to the center of her chest. "What? Impossible."

"Trust me, Aria was the happiest person on the planet. She used to dance all the time, sing off-tune on the street, in a store, without a care in the world..." Sabrina trailed off while I nodded, knowing the exact pinpoint when it all took a turn.

"What happened?" Nala asked with general concern, and Sabrina answered with a pointed look—the blaming kind.

"My big stupid mouth happened," I interjected, my voice cracking. "I broke her."

"Oh, Cill, no!" Sabrina blustered. "Sebastian did that; he dimmed her light. You were the one who kept it from fading completely," Sabrina assured with firmness, almost making me believe her words... almost. "Whatever happened between the two of you at that bonfire had nothing to do with it. Sure, she turned cold, but it was a front. She put on this facade so you wouldn't see how much she truly cared."

Dropping my head with a shake, I squeezed Aria's hand tighter.

Why is it still cold?

Nala cleared her throat, making me lift my head to look up. "I don't know your past or how you were before. But when she talks about you with a concerning level of hate, her eyes tell a different story."

I swallowed a lump, only for a bigger one to appear.

"When we were planning the engagement party details, every time you were mentioned, she had to add, and this is a direct quote, 'I am going to kill him, bring him back and kill him all over again,' end quote." A laugh escaped me with the image. I could picture it perfectly. Her hair in that tight, perfect bun, hands crossed over her chest, foot tapping in annoyance, one brow arched, pursed lips. My fingers went to my mouth. So far, our lips had brushed three times, and not once was it right. Not once was it real. My right fist clenched.

"She was all like, his name has the word Kill in it or something like that... but you see..." Nala took a breath, leaving me in suspense. "It's the fire in her eyes when she talks shit about you that speaks volumes."

My breath hitched, and I was sure my heart skipped a couple of beats.

"She never stopped being your person, Cillian," Sabrina spoke next, a sincere look on her face. "She is going to kill me for this, but you deserve to know."

I looked at Sabrina, not liking where it was going.

"When you got hurt and were in a coma, I had no idea. I noticed Aria was distant, so I did what I do best..."

"You pried!" I blurted just as she said the same. We both chuckled, and I choked on the memory of waking up in the hospital room, no Aria in sight.

"She was like a zombie, crying so much. Then she revealed what happened, how they wouldn't allow her in because she wasn't family, and how she snuck in every night, never leaving your side…"

She was there?

How?

Nobody ever said anything. But then again, I've never asked, just assumed she didn't care. But she did, and I had been blind to it all. Aria hated hospitals, hated me even more, and still, she'd never left my side.

God, the time wasted hating her when I could have been… I shook my thoughts away and focused on her breathing. Mateo emerged and handed me a tray with a bowl of soup, mashed potatoes, and turkey. I looked at them, feeling the luck we had in the friends department. Marco took that moment to knock on the open door, proving my inner point. He took a glance at a sleeping Aria, then shifted his gaze to me, giving me a concerned look. Nala stood from her chair and moved to the far one in the corner, freeing a spot for him. He took it without a single word, but the little flare in his eyes was impossible to miss.

I wasn't hungry, so I had to force the food down my throat, knowing I needed the strength. As soon as I finished eating, our family burst in.

"How is she?"

"What happened?"

"Is she okay?"

I couldn't say who asked what, so I just stood up, lifted my hand, and that was that; they all stopped talking. I explained everything that had happened, told them they were keeping her overnight for observations, and that she would be back to her feisty self by sunrise.

My mother came to my side, her hand grabbing mine with

a tight squeeze. "Are you okay?"

"I will be when she wakes up."

She mumbled something under her breath, then I lifted my head to meet her gaze. "Why didn't you tell me that she was by my side?"

The look on my mother's face made me know I didn't need to clarify the time or the place. The guilt in her eyes said it all. "I'm sorry, but Aria made me promise not to tell you."

I should feel angry or jealous that my mother chose Aria over me, but I couldn't blame her. I would've done the same thing. When it came to Aria, it was impossible not to give in.

The nurse came into the room and told us that only two people were allowed inside. Everybody nodded, and without any discussion, it was down to Peter and me.

I took my seat next to Aria, taking her hand in mine, while Peter did the same with her other, taking a seat on the opposite side of the bed.

"Thank you," he said, his eyes never leaving his daughter."

"For what?"

"Don't play dumb with me, son; I know you were there, and I know what you did."

"I made you a promise," I stated, and he turned to face me with full glee.

"You and I damn well know that it has nothing to do with the promise you made me, but thank you anyway. You know I love you?"

"I do." I nodded. This sentimental shit was not Peter's forte, nor was it mine, but the situation called for it. "I love you too."

He stared at me for a moment, waiting for more. I almost said, 'and I love your daughter,' but something told me he already knew that.

Chapter 46

Aria

Thirteen hours of sleep, and I still managed to wake up tired as fuck. My chest hurt, and every muscle surrounding it. When I opened my eyes, it was dark, with the only light coming from the one over my head. I saw Nala in the chair, snoring on my left, then I turned to the dark brown, almost black curls next to my hand. Marco was in the corner, the only one awake, his eyes locked on Nala. My fingers moved slightly, and Cillian lunged up, locking eyes with mine.

"Hi."

One soft word, two simple letters, his voice, and my heart exploded. He whispered to Nala, stopping her loud snoring. Her eyes flew open, and an instant smile illuminated her face. "Hey, Blondie." She leaned in for a soft kiss on my cheek. "How are you feeling?"

Confused.

Heartbroken.

Hurt.

I chose to give them the ultimate shoulder shrug.

Marco raised his chin in a nod, and I smiled at him, not needing words to show my gratitude.

"I'm a bit tired, but nothing a better mattress won't fix."

A soft laugh escaped their mouths, one louder over the others, hitting the center of my chest.

The nurse came in, and after I passed all the checks, I was given the green light. While Cillian took care of all the release paperwork, Nala hugged me goodbye.

"I'll drive you home," I heard Marco tell her after they both waved at me.

I was rolled out of the hospital in a wheelchair, despite every protest. It took one pointed look from Cillian for me to cave.

The drive to his place was silent, not even a background noise from the radio filling it. And when I stepped over the threshold, the urge to run took over.

"I'm going to sleep now."

"Can we talk?" His words were so soft, so needed, but I couldn't face them… face him.

"No!" I yelled out, my mind set on escaping to the comfort of my room.

"Aria, please," he pleaded, the gentleness in his voice stopping me in my tracks.

"I can't," I whispered, too weak to fight all the urges.

There was physical pain in my chest, but it didn't overpower the pressure I felt from his mere presence—the all-consuming kind.

"Look at me, Aria." My name, passing his lips, sounded like an entreaty of its own. I could feel his breath on the back of my neck. My whole body felt it too. My knees wobbled, and it had nothing to do with my fatigue.

Please go away.

I wanted to say it; I really did. But words failed me.

"I can't," I breathed, shutting my eyes, if only to numb all the pain.

"Yes, you can, just look at me, Aria. Please." Dionysus almighty, the way he said my name, as if it existed for his mouth and voice alone.

"If I look at you, I'll..." Tears emerged, and I started shaking my head. His hands took hold of my waist, and he turned me to face him. With my lids closed, I turned my head to the side, hearing the pounding of my heart.

"You'll what?"

I'll crumble, cave; I will lose this fight, surrender. Take your pick.

"Look. At. Me!" He placed his palm on the backside of my face, making his thumb graze my cheek, the rest of his fingers tightening around my neck.

"Baby, look at me!"

That word opened my eyes almost like a command.

"Who..." I sputtered, "Who is Baby?"

The scene replayed in my head, me on the floor dying, him calling someone Baby, it hurting more than the agony of my body's reaction to the almonds I'd later found out were the main ingredient of the drink.

There was confusion on his face, and for the life of me, I couldn't figure out why. Then he said the last words I'd ever expected—"You are."

"What?" I mumbled, taking a step back, my head shaking, mind spiraling. I lost my words, my thoughts, my mind went puff. I was the epitome of a blank.

He framed my face between his palms and lowered himself to reach my eye level, making my breaths short and shallow.

"Look at me, *really* look at me!" I did, my eyes so focused on his, switching from his left to his right. The look was new but so familiar. Like it had always been there, in the background... He held my gaze, allowing me to define his. When the wrinkles around his eyes relaxed, I stopped breathing altogether.

"Did you get it?"

My mind was working overtime trying to understand what I had to figure out here, and my body answered with an ache—no, with need.

It can't be.

There was something wrong with my vision because it couldn't possibly be true.

My shoulders fell at the sight of a curve rising into a full, wide grin.

And then his lips met mine.

Explosion, fireworks, tears, flames. I moaned when he pulled me in closer with his arms around my upper back. I parted my lips, and now our tongues were touching. I have died and gone to heaven. It was the only explanation. My wildest and only dream was playing out as my hand grabbed his hair to pull him closer. I thought it was hard to breathe after I tasted a nut, but kissing Cillian, there were no breaths to draw in. As if my body no longer needed the air, it only needed him. His hand slid to the small of my back, and the other met the side of my face. Then his palm rounded my waist, slowly drawing upward. The thought of the next possible stop for his hand placement startled me, and I pulled back.

Damaged
Damaged

Damaged

"Don't go there!"

Just like that? That's all it takes?

He interrupted the spiral, stopping it at its core.

"Focus on my eyes," he drawled, his tone tender, like a caress to my being. And when my eyes lifted to meet his, I was airborne.

Noticing the direction we were headed, I challenged, "Rule number four?

"Fuck the rules!"

"Fine."

"Fine."

He opened the door and laid me on his bed. The first time I was here, I didn't engage in looking around; my sole focus was on the bathroom, but now I couldn't help myself. His entire room was dark, with gray curtains and a black matte closet. But the walls… how didn't I notice them the first time? They were blue, sky blue. That was all I was able to see until my sight was stunned by his naked body over mine. How did he get undressed without me noticing? Then it hit me.

Holy shit! This is happening!

He leaned toward me for a deep kiss, laying his body on mine, barely pressing on. His mouth moved to my neck, and my whole body felt the movement of his tongue, making my skin ache, wanting more. He snaked down to where my shirt met my pants and began lifting the hem before pulling it off. Then his skilled fingers unbuttoned my pants and slid them down in one simple tug, together with my underwear. While his mouth was busy sucking my neck, his hand glided to my back, reaching for my bra clasp. Panic struck.

"The bra stays on," I gasped, frozen in the moment. He looked at me with reassurance and finished his initial intent, freeing my breasts. Biting his lower lip, he took in my completely naked body with appreciation. I noticed the moment his attention shifted to the scar. Before a lump could form in my throat, he bent down and traced kisses over the length, making me shatter in the most beautiful way. And when our eyes met, I felt my whole world crashing.

"What you heard was me being jealous."

"What?" I shivered, searching for the lie in my favorite shade of green.

"I didn't want you to go out with Tony, so I said it to scare him off. I didn't mean it. I am so fucking sorry that you had to hear that, and it hurts me that you took it to heart," he bewailed as tears blurred my vision.

I wanted to believe him so damn much, but the pain resurfaced, the pressure growing heavier by the second. The knot in my chest tightened, the memory making me feel small.

There was a beat of silence, the moment stretching to a point of no going back, while his eyes begged me to trust it—trust him.

And then, he spoke. "The fact that you believed it, when I held a torch for you for the better part of my life, when you were my... *are* my everything." The desperation in his tone was loud and clear, as was his torturous sigh. "I'll never forgive myself."

This right here... the confession, that look in his eyes, held all the power. I felt a piece of me lighten up, forming a base for something. His deep kiss that followed brought out another piece atop the base. His tongue on my hard nipple brought out another. And the orgasm his fingers produced at the end revealed my heart put together; all that was needed was the glue.

Chapter 47

Aria

My Dionysus, I never want to leave this bed.

Not because the mattress had the perfect firm-to-cloud ratio, not due to the silky sheets that felt so good around me, not even because I was too tired to move. It was the smell, combined with a naked Cillian snoring next to me. And yeah, even his snoring felt like a mating call.

I stretched out my arms, looking around for a clock or a phone, anything to tell me the time. The curtains were closed, making it seem like it was the middle of the night; then again, maybe it was. I zeroed in on his phone when I felt movement under the covers.

Propping on my elbows, I looked down to catch Cillian slowly slithering between my legs.

"What are you doing?"

"I have some built-up tension that needs to be resolved."

There was something about him between my thighs, on his knees, ready to worship, that brought out a temptress in me.

"Do you now?"

"Be a good girl we both know you are, and spread them for me!"

Swallowing a lump, I dropped my head back and moved

my legs to the side, opening my space for him to invade. He took a sharp breath before he introduced his tongue to my clit. My skin burned, desperately wanting to be peeled off with each lick and twirl. His finger started teasing the spot under it, gently pressing before he thrust it inside me.

I moaned out, "Please," not even sure what I was begging for.

He drew his eyes up, his tongue never leaving that place, pulsing for him. With one brow raised, he smirked.

Smug, perfect jerk.

I had my fair share of fingers, tongues, and cocks—but his, doing whatever it was doing—fuck me! It was a tool of the Greek gods; its sole purpose—my enormous pleasure. Another finger joined in, then another as the triplets rushed in two more times, making me coat his hand with my explosion. He parted my downstairs area and moved up with his tongue, never leaving my skin. He traced over my belly button, each rib, and my breasts. He kissed my scar, then continued to my neck, where he made a pit stop under my ear.

"I told you I had a lot of built-up tension I needed to resolve, but I wanted you to rest first." His words were like a gentle caress wrapped around confidence that was both alluring and intimidating. "Now, I'm planning on breaking you."

His hoarse voice added to the pool, no, make that a lake forming underneath me. He sucked the spot behind my ear as his hand played with my nipples. It was at this moment that I thanked the surgeon for sparing the nerves, allowing my nipples to react to his touch. His lips parted my neck, and he brought his captivating greens into view. He was so fucking beautiful it hurt to look at him—like he was the solar eclipse.

"What are you thinking about?"

"Honestly... How beautiful you are," I admitted, my confession coming out comfortably.

"I got nothing on you," he said it so effortlessly, so sweetly that it made me giggle. Then his lips drove into mine, our tongues dancing around each other, making me lose myself in him, in us. I tilted my head, giving him more access, and locked my legs around his waist, my voice breathy as I husked into his mouth, "I also have some built-up tension."

My words brought on a devilish one-sided curve on those panty-dropping lips of his. I zeroed in on the foil between his teeth, wondering how on earth he got it without my noticing, before he ripped it open. A skillful move of sliding a latex over a hardened shaft wasn't supposed to be hot...right?

"You all rested?" he asked, spreading my legs wider.

I nodded, arching my brows.

"Energy full?"

I gave him another nod, narrowing my eyes. I could go for coffee, but I kept that to myself.

"Good, 'cause I'm not going to be gentle, Baby."

Oh.

Oh.

"I don't like you calling me Baby," I faltered, not sure how to explain it... Luckily, Cillian read right through it.

"Too generic for you?"

One shy nod was all it took for his smirk (I hated loving) to appear.

"Fine, wife."

O fuck. I think I just came a little.

"Fine, husband."

He groaned, and I felt the tip of his cock pressing against my opening.

"Say that again," he growled.

"Husband," I enunciated in a raspy way, causing his eyes to flare.

Without any warning, he bottomed out in one deep thrust, hitting a place never reached before.

I've dreamed of this for the greater part of my life. I'd had literal wet dreams ever since I'd developed my hormones. There was always a part of me that wished he were my first. And damn my heart for now expecting him to be my last.

I drank him in, how the tension put every inch of his body on display. He could serve as a live doll for show-and-tell in biology class. He'd point out every muscle without needing dissection, providing a detailed outline of each.

Fuck me for missing this, for depriving myself of him inside of me for so damn long. The way we fit, like he was the yin to my yang, the tip to my iceberg. I cursed at every icy stare I gave him. Damn it all, because I finally saw it. I understood the love songs, the romance movies, the books, the sonnets—I recognized what it was that made people so crazy. And damn if I wasn't one of them. All wrapped in the madness that was him, filling me up. Crazy for the feel he gave me with one look, doomed for the way he got me undone.

He turned into a starved animal, our eyes locked while he throbbed in and out with a whole new kind of elation. One that made me scream uncontrollably, my pleasure bursting out through loud gasps, my climax so hard I practically erupted.

I only knew of vanilla sex, thought it was my preference.

Boy, was I wrong. It turned out that I liked it animalistic.

The headboard thumped, Morse-coding, spelling the words *'harder'*, *'more'*, and Cillian never stopped, hazed, hungry. He placed his hand between us, and when his hard thumb began circling my clit, it was like releasing a pin from a grenade. I didn't know it was possible, but there it was, rising from my core. Shouting his name, I reached nirvana, and I felt the warmth of his climax as he yelled out mine.

Chapter 48

Aria

You know how the knowledge that something was forbidden prompted a person to think about it more. That's what I'd been doing for the last couple of months. Specifically, the reason it was off-limits in the first place. It had been occupying most of my thoughts, right there at the top of Cillian's naked body. Now that I had seen it and touched it, the only thought that remained in my mind was the one regarding this room.

Why the hell didn't he want me in it?

And as if he read my mind, he rolled out of bed, leaving me naked and alone to gawk at his tight, hot ass while he went to the closet. He opened the black door, uncovering a rainbow of colored wrapping paper. Except it was not rolled up; instead, formed different shapes and sizes. I wiggled out of bed, getting closer to get a better look, and immediately started counting.

Nine presents, stacked on the shelves.

"One for each birthday we didn't spend together."

I gasped, then recounted. We spent eight years fighting, plus one for my birthday that was coming up next month.

He handed me the largest one in the bunch with the year 2015 written in his scrawling handwriting.

Right now, I had no objection, not even a question… I

tore the paper and laughed. In my hand, I held the original 'Clue' board game. He had destroyed the one we had in Vermont by throwing it in the fire after he had lost miserably, like a sore loser. The reminder warmed me through and through.

He then handed me the one with the year 2016.

"Am I going to open all of them now?"

"All except for one."

Right, I had to be patient for the last one.

The rest of the gifts were all personal, from a first edition of sonnets my mother had loved to the bracelet with a small blue heart that reminded him of me. Each gift so meticulously thought of, each gift just so... *me.* The one he got me for my twentieth, ten years after my mother had passed, was the one I appreciated the most. It was a heart-shaped silver locket with the letter N engraved on it. When opened, it revealed a picture of my mother on one side and of Cillian and me at age 5 on the other.

Seven gifts in, I hadn't even noticed we'd skipped one. He handed me a box with '2022' written on it. It felt light in my hands, and when I opened it, I understood why. It was empty. It all clicked rather quickly. During the eight-year gap, he was present only once, at a surprise party Sabrina had thrown without my knowledge. There was one gift among a pile that didn't come with a card.

"It was you? You gave me my favorite mug." The last part was not a question, but a fact. The mug was sitting in his kitchen cabinet. It was blue with black glitter writing on it saying: 'Sarcasm, because Avada Kedavra is illegal.'

I was a hardcore Potter girl, referring to the movies, not

the books—never having read a single one. But when it came to the movie franchises, it was my whole damn comfort zone, sometimes even my personality. Normal people watched 'Home Alone' or 'Santa Claus' for Christmas, but I would curl up in my blanket and binge 'Harry Potter'. It was and always would be my go-to Christmas movie.

He went from leaving me speechless to a babbling mess. I told him how much I loved each gift and ranted about how I couldn't believe they had been here all along.

"Was this the reason for rule No. 4?"

Though I knew the answer, I wanted to hear it from him.

"Yes."

Straight to the point; I liked it.

He grabbed the tip of my chin between his thumb and his pointer and lifted my head, grazing his thumb over my lower lip.

"What happened after dinner?"

A rush of fear overcame me as I remembered the article.

I hesitated, but his eyes were demanding, so I caved, extending my hand.

"Give me your phone."

He gave it without hesitation. "The code is 2742."

I tried to decipher the code, but the numbers made no sense. Before I could table it, Cillian snickered, "It's your name, you dummy."

I punched him in the chest at the insult that wasn't really an insult, but that was beside the point.

The screen unlocked when I entered the last digit, and I proceeded directly to the Google search bar. I clicked on the first article and turned the phone to him.

"Fuck."

"Yeah."

"So much for my rule num—" Before I could finish, his phone was snatched from my hand and tossed onto the bed.

"That was not. I was not... Shit." He turned his back to me, his hand scratching the back of his head. "This is going to sound so fucking weird."

He turned back, framed my face, and kissed my forehead. "I was in Quincy, but my section got called on assignment, and I didn't want to scare you, so I went to a hotel and slept the night." He placed his palm on the back of my neck.

"I would never..." he trailed off, his eyes widening. His pupils followed, engaging me in a look that could only be defined as begging for trust.

"When I read it, I couldn't think straight, and then you said the..." I gulped, a lump forming in my larynx.

"The word that shall not be named."

"Smart ass," I giggled, shoving him, but he didn't even flinch, almost as if he expected it. Knowing him, he probably did.

"Oh, come on, say it like you mean it."

"Hey, that's my line," I piped, digging my elbow into his stomach.

"I couldn't resist." He took a step closer, facing me, engaging my full attention. "I don't want that word to have a hold on you."

"I can't help it," I doubted, my nerves kicking in.

"Try."

Finding the tiny gold specks in his greens, I curved up a

smile before I rose on my fingertips and pressed my lips to his.

"Where did you get the EPI?"

His eyes widened at my question, and I don't think I ever saw Cillian looking scared. He swallowed, took a deep breath, and looked right at me. "When we first found out that you were allergic, I asked Peter to give me an extra one to keep with me at all times just in case."

My knees wobbled.

"Even when we hated each other, you had it?"

"Always. I switched it off every year before the expiration date…" he trailed off, averting his gaze. My chest tightened.

"Cillian, I…"

What does one say to that? Sorry for being stupid, blind, unforgiving… None of it had the power to change the past. So I stared at him, speechless, cursing on the inside, at the wrong perception I held over him for so many years.

One thing led to another, and after some heavy schmoozing, he was inside me again, without any barriers between us. There was no need for a discussion. All it took was a pointed look, my trust whispered, and his nod. I was on the pill, which he knew thanks to overhearing a conversation between Nala and me.

Honestly, I had never felt so alive as I did while our bodies connected. The way he moved, the speed, the pressure, it was pure torture, an elevating bliss. The vein in his neck popped out more with each thrust, and I focused on it, trying my best not to get too lost in him. The burning sensation spread through my bloodstream like wildfire when my eyes found his. He held all the power with his peer. I never knew that one look could be so influential to the soul. But there I was, consumed, captivated, and forever changed.

For the first time, I felt loved, appreciated, and happy. And just as I thought it couldn't get any better, his hand found my clit. The sensation of his fingertips circling got my whole body to arch, curving my spine to the breaking point. Encouraging his speed, I answered by pushing my hips closer, and then my toes curled, sending the current throughout every inch of me, shocking my nervous system. Still, he didn't stop, letting me ride it out. To my surprise, it somehow continued, evolving into a new wave that created the most delicious interference my world had ever known.

My scream was uncontrolled, uncensored, and loud enough to conceal his rapture. Despite it, I had the pleasure of feeling it... the way his ass-cheeks spasmed, eyes darkened, and mouth dropped. The way my insides warmed as he pumped his essence, filling me whole. His body crashed onto mine, his head digging deep between my neck and shoulder. I felt him getting softer, but he didn't pull out. Not until both our breaths steadied.

Chapter 49

Aria

A conversation started to prepare itself in my head while I lay on his chest, his hand drawing lines on my arm. His gentle voice blew it all away like you would blow out a cloud of smoke. "Don't overthink; just say it."

That got me to lift my head and look at him, the softness in his eyes so evident that I couldn't believe I had missed it before.

"About what Sabrina said…" I took a breath, trying to figure out where to start.

"You heard?"

I nodded, my throat tightening with remembrance of that time, the helpless feeling, the fear…

"When I got that call from your mother, my entire world crumbled."

I could hear the crack in Loren's voice as if she was telling me what had happened all over again.

"She didn't even finish before I was on my feet and running up the stairs from the office. You were still in surgery when I got to our family. Later, when the doctor said it was up to you, that's when I truly got scared. I thought that because you hated me so much, you wouldn't want to fight…" I shook my head, trying to laugh it off. "You finally found a way to get rid of me permanently, so I thought that was the reason you wouldn't wake up."

Tears started to fall, each revealing the image of him lying in that bed, barely breathing.

"I took your hand and held on to it so tight. All I kept thinking was that if I let go, so would you. You would leave us, leave me…" I choked through my sobs. "And the last thing you told me was how much you hated me."

And that was when I saw it, tears escaping from both of his eyes, trying to hide the golden little specks like a halo around his pupil.

"And still, I wouldn't let go. I would rather have you in my life hating me than live in a world without you in it. That's where my head was at."

He shook his head, like that act would make him understand it any better.

"Why did you coax them not to tell me?"

"You were always my biggest weakness, Cillian. And there was no way in hell I ever wanted you to know that. I couldn't allow you to have the upper hand on me, at least not consciously."

"Aria. Fuck," he gasped, then it felt like he went stagnant. And it was when I knew I'd fucked up.

"Let's back up. You said you ran from the office up the stairs?"

Shit.

"I meant down," I lied, knowing it would be pointless.

"No, you didn't," he countered, sitting up and turning to face me. I followed, dragging my knees to my chest and propping my chin on them.

Before I could even say a word, tears fell down my face,

and my chest tightened. The moment I'd dreaded, the thing that scared me the most, was about to happen. But at least I got to feel him, taste him. Even if just for a minute, it was worth it.

He peered at me patiently, while I gathered the strength I no longer had. I lost it all once before, and I couldn't allow my heart to go through it again.

"Aria?" He raised his voice enough to make it sound serious.

I took a deep breath.

"I was on the oncology floor." His eyes widened with worry.

"I got tested for the BRCA gene, and I was in the middle of a fight with Sebastian in the doctor's office when I got the call. So, without thinking, I ran out."

"Everything, Aria. I need you to tell me everything."

I looked at him, biting my inner cheek, full of dread. It would take about three minutes for me to explain everything. He would be gone in four. So I took one last look and inhaled.

"I couldn't stand not knowing, so I took the test, and it was…" I shook my head, correcting myself, "is, positive. The doctor gave me my options and left for me to discuss them with Sebastian. I wanted to do one thing, he wanted to do the other… That's it."

"No, it's not. I need all the details, Aria. All the options given."

I shook my head, not wanting this to end, as more tears welled in my eyes.

"Hey, hey, relax. We're just talking."

He grabbed my face between his hands to stop my

shaking. The warmth spread from his palms all the way to my core.

"No, we're not; we're ending!"

And we only just started.

I started to hyperventilate. I didn't even know how the breakdown happened. The memories rushed through my mind; every rejection, every word, every self-doubting thought burst out in the form of a full-blown meltdown.

Cillian grabbed me tightly, pulling me onto his lap, his hands locking around me.

"What are you talking about? We just fucking started."

His voice brought even more tears out to join the others. He held me tight until I somehow relaxed my breath, then he pushed my face in front of his, his eyes reaching deep. "I am here, I am not going anywhere, ever. Now, tell me!"

"You say that now, but when you hear the..." I couldn't even finish, averting my eyes.

"Was that what he did?" I looked back at him, his eyes filled with rage.

"The fucking bastard!" His jaw tightened, and he stood up, pacing. Both his fists were clenched at his sides. He mumbled a couple *fucks* before he squatted before me, dragging me to the end of the bed.

"This is not about him. This is about you. Now tell me what the options were?"

And so I did. I sucked it up, and I told him everything the doctor had shared, followed by everything Sebastian had said.

"I am going to kill him."

I looked at him, trying to understand his next move,

expecting the worst.

"Would you have done the full mastectomy if it weren't for him?"

"Yes," I blurted without a second's thought.

It was an easy answer.

He stood up again, his back all I could see before his fist found the wall next to the closet.

"Is it too late to do it now?"

When he turned to face me, I suppose he noticed my scared expression because the next thing he did was grab my hand and pull me to my feet.

"I know it's your body and your choice. But if there is a possibility to prevent you from," he swallowed the word, "then you should do everything you can to make that happen."

"But…"

"You are not your breasts."

I glared at him, unable to comprehend his statement. Vile rose in my throat, but I swallowed it all down. My lower lip trembled as he continued, "You are the smartest, strongest, most beautiful woman in the world, and your cup size has nothing to do with it."

There was a long beat of silence, both of us scanning each other's faces.

"I'm sure there are some reconstruction shit that can be done if you wanted to, but it should also be your decision, and yours alone."

He pulled my hand to his cheek, leaning into my touch. It felt so natural, familiar in some messed-up way.

"No matter what you decide, I will be there every step of the way, but don't decide for me or anyone other than for yourself."

At that point, I was visibly shaking; except this time, it was not out of fear.

"Promise me," he pleaded, and when I didn't say anything back, he grabbed my face, demanding, "Promise me!"

"I promise."

"Good girl," he muttered.

I pressed my thighs together because why the hell did those words make my pussy throb? His calloused palms still holding me, keeping me afloat, he cleared his throat. "Just know that I will worship your body no matter the choice you make. Now come to bed; you still have to rest."

We got under the covers, and I found my spot under his arm, locking him in with my leg.

I replayed the last ten minutes over and over again, each replay widening my smile. The ease, the simplicity, the lack of drama…it was new. He was listening to me, handing out an opinion but leaving the decision to me. I had never experienced anything like this, and it felt oddly satisfying.

This spot, which I now claimed under the safety of his arm, became my haven in a single instant. The rise and fall of his chest alongside the feel of his heartbeat were the only things I needed to lull me into a blissful sleep.

Chapter 50

Cillian

I couldn't sleep. I wouldn't allow myself to sleep, with Aria tucked in my arms, dreaming of something that eased the wrinkles on her forehead. I was afraid to close my eyes, as if the action would reveal that all of this was a dream, a mirage of some sort, and not the reality I desperately wanted it to be.

I gazed at her sleeping so peacefully and began to think about all she had gone through, masking it all so that it never showed on the surface. Then I remembered I was the person who made her put on the mask in the first place. I'd shattered a part of her, making it hide behind the icy facade, so it was fitting that she never showed her vulnerable side to me. She'd made it easy for me to hate her, but I never pitied her. And her plan worked. Even now, after everything she'd told me, after all the tears she'd shared, my image of her never changed - she was still a force. The fact that she went through it alone gutted me. But she won't be doing it alone anymore. I won't allow it. Now, she was mine to keep, mine to protect, and it was about damn time.

My mind turned to Sebastian, the bastard who let vanity take over instead of doing everything he could to keep her safe.

A strand of hair slid over her eyes, and I gently plucked it away.

When late morning struck, I snuck out of bed and went full-on breakfast mode. All her favorites prepped, I filled her favorite mug with coffee when she appeared by the pantry door, hands on her hips, the ultimate Superwoman stance.

"You left me alone. Unacceptable." She had that piercing stare, but her smile gave her away. I got hard at the sight of her swollen lips.

"You need carbs. I plan to feed you and then drain you," I teased, pulling her into a hug.

"Sorry," she hissed, "but I have to go to work."

"Damn it, I keep forgetting we're not some rich people who can afford to spend a day or two in bed. Oh, wait," I derided, my tongue marking the length of her lower lip. I couldn't help but notice the way she pulled her thighs together, arousing the challenger in me.

"Funny." She looked over my shoulder. "Mmmmm, I smell bacon."

Bacon more appealing than her husband?

That won't do.

"Hold your horses, woman," I whispered in her ear, my hand slowly dripping downward while the other slid the coffee over the counter to her.

"Thank you. This is nice." She took the mug, drawing it to her mouth, then she smelled the brew, inhaling the steam before taking a long sip. How such a simple action made me harder was beyond me, but there I was…in the middle of our kitchen, sporting a tent. So naturally, I took the mug from her hand, placed it back on the counter, and in one quick twirl, I had her lips on mine.

"Damn, I always knew these lips were deadly."

She let out a laugh, opening her mouth so our tongues could intertwine in a game of Twister.

Later that night, Aria coerced me into going out with her, Sabrina, and Mateo. One question I couldn't answer was how we ended up in a club instead of having dinner. Scratch that, it was all Aria's doing, the persuasive little minx. When we were younger, she would use dare tactics to get me to do something; now, all she had to do was bat her lashes, and I was her willing puppet.

So yeah, she took me clubbing—Aria's words, not mine.

Nala had saved a VIP area for us at The Brick, saying she would join us after her shift. When we arrived, the girls immediately went to the bar to greet their friend, while Mateo and I continued up the stairs to our separate section.

Soon, a waiter came with a filled tray, Sabrina and Aria in tow. The guy smiled and set the round of shots on the small table between the leather chairs, forming a semicircle.

"Forget your morals, lock away your troubles, lady and gentlemen. Let's get this party started," Sabrina screamed and downed her shot in one quick swig. Aria shook her head, and so did Mateo. I just stared. In all the times I've known Sabrina, I've never seen her so—for lack of a better word—unleashed. And yet, her husband looked at her like he was the luckiest person on the planet. I knew the feeling.

Under Sabrina's intense coercion, we entered a drinking

contest—she won, by a long shot. The girl could hold her liquor.

When Nala finally joined us, Aria was in the middle of singing her lungs out to another 'I love this song' song. The spotlight turned its attention the moment the three best friends took over the dance floor. My eyes locked on the champagne blonde goddess, wearing jeans over her boot-looking heels, with an off-the-shoulder, tight black t-shirt, and her hair finally down. I sharpened my vision, watching Aria's siren dance in slow motion. The movement she was doing might as well be called 'The Lambada'—as in, it should be forbidden. She waved her entire body, making circular motions, her beautifully sunny hair following the rhythm. Each time her hips tipped to the side, my cock jerked in the same direction.

Somewhere in the middle of the song, Sabrina separated from the trio to jump on Mateo in what seemed to be a dry-humping session. I'd known Sabrina my whole life, though not as extensively as I knew Aria; however, I was well acquainted with all her kinky behavior. Sabrina was never the one to hide her desires. Luckily, it seemed she had found the right person to satisfy them all.

As messed up as the whole situation got, it gave me clarity. Sure, they were horny dogs, but the way they looked at each other was pure love; that once-in-a-lifetime kind of love.

Throughout my life, at certain points, I was steered, switched to another lane or path, taking me in a different direction. It never mattered to me that it did. I thrived in each new surrounding, each new challenge. But I never had hopes for the future, knowing Aria would never be a part of it. And seeing a twisted love of two people who'd risked their all gave me a glimpse of something I never knew existed. And with that knowledge, all I could do was look forward to whatever was coming as long as Aria was there, right by my side.

Chapter 51

Cillian

Today marked twenty-five years of this earth being lucky enough to have Aria walking on it.

"What do you think you're doing?" She smiled through her still sleepy eyes while I slowly pulled down her underwear.

"Giving you your first birthday present," I smirked, trapping my head between her silk thighs.

"That is so not fair; I wanted to sleep in today," she whined, pulling the covers over her face, giggling.

"Tough luck." I wrestled them away, tossing everything on the floor. "This is only a warm-up; I am easing you into today."

"What's that supposed to mean?" she quipped, her fingers tangling in my hair.

"That's for me to know and you to *not* find out—*yet.*"

She released a grunt and covered her face with her arm. She couldn't hide the bite of her lower lip when my tongue found her ready for me.

"Having wet dreams about me?"

"What makes you think my dreams were about you?"

I bit down in response.

"Auch!"

"That's what you get." I positioned myself above her, grabbing her chin, making her see my half-deadly eyes.

"Don't you dare dream of anyone other than me!"

"Is that a threat? How do you expect to beat up my imagination?"

"Oh, I have my ways, so don't tempt me," I practically barked.

Having this woman in my bed, our bed, was an addiction I never knew existed. I never wanted to leave, but alas, plans were made, and we were on a schedule. Not that she had any knowledge of it.

"You know I like a good challenge." She revealed her deadliest, devilish smile.

"I mean it," I snarled, those deep blues trying to read the level on the seriousness scale.

It took one stroke over her folds to get her back to curl. It amazed me how well I already knew her body.

Every move I made, every section of skin I touched, every part I licked made her moan. The way her body reacted to mine was mesmerizing, making my sole purpose in life to unravel her, break down all the bricks that formed the massive wall around her. To set fire to the bridge we had made between us and to watch it burn, leaving the smoke to erase all the mistakes. I wanted nothing to remain, except the ashes, with the two of us standing on top of them together, finally set free.

Her second orgasm of the day wasn't planned until later, but the deviation was more than welcome.

After she'd ridden the tidewave, I pulled a small gift box from the closet and handed it over to her. She opened it, eyes filled with wonder, then her lips revealed a sexy grin. She lifted the silky velvet blindfold, dangling it between us.

"Well, Mister Wright, are you gonna go all Mr. Grey on me now?"

She moved her tongue over the tips of her upper teeth with a new kind of sparkle lighting up in her eyes.

"Maybe later if you're a good girl; right now we have somewhere else to be. The real question is..." I paused for dramatic effect. "Do you want to do the honors yourself, or will you let me hide those beautiful eyes?"

"You say the sweetest things to me."

I gave her wrinkled forehead a quick peck and started getting dressed. She frowned, not moving while she watched me cover my body with layers of clothes.

"How about a hint on what to wear?"

"Whatever makes you feel comfortable."

Okay, I walked into that one because the next thing she did was cruel. We had to leave in the next five minutes, and looking at her naked body, one she put on display after tossing off the shirt, wasn't going to distract me. Nope, no way was that going to happen. My eyes were most certainly not tracing every curve of her silhouette, and my dick was definitely not getting hard at the sight of her exposed...

After what felt like the longest minute of my life, she finally admitted defeat and got dressed in a tight pair of jeans and a simple white t-shirt. I was rewarded with a hard scold, but I should have gotten a Nobel Prize for restraining, if such a thing existed. Add to that an Oscar for pretending not to get fully aroused while tying a fucking blindfold around her head.

I couldn't tell you how I got to the car, but I did...

Aria had been protesting in the back seat the entire ride to our destination.

A quick drive turned into a helicopter ride, during which I'd spent two hours assuring her we weren't going to skydive. She kept threatening to get back at me for it. Though her mean mug had frightening flair, I was sure she would forget all about it the second she felt the rush.

We arrived at the track, where I guided her to the circuit. Though happy that her feet touched the ground of Alton, Virginia, she still cursed me with each step, and I laughed at the sight of her cute, scrawny face. I shook hands with the instructor, making no sound as I guided her to take a seat inside. She took a deep breath when the realization hit.

"You didn't?"

"I did," I whispered, untying the blindfold.

Her eyes flared, and her hands immediately took the wheel, all the while drinking in the interior, speechless.

"Mrs. Wright?" The instructor arrived, and Aria stepped outside with her hand raised. "That's me."

"My name is Jesse." They smiled at each other through the handshake. "Ready for the time of your life?"

"You have no idea."

The lesson didn't take long, with Aria practically born for the task. In less than an hour, she was whooshing down the racetrack, mastering each turn while I watched her rush by from the sidelines.

"What is she?" Jesse asked, "Some sort of mutant?"

I looked at him with narrowed eyes.

317

"No man that ever came here for a ride has driven like that, ever! She makes it look like the car is a part of her, not the other way around."

I smiled because I   had witnessed it once before.

For my 15th birthday, we spent the day having fun at the carnival. Most of the time, we were at the bumper cars, smashing into each other. When we got tired of it, we walked around, searching. She had one quarter left, one that she was saving for something special.

"What is that?" Aria stopped at a Formula 1 simulation car.

She inserted the coin and took her seat, transforming into a different person. Her smile was unmistakable, her freedom so loud, and I loved watching every second of it.

When we arrived at the house, my dad took out an old VCR and an old VHS tape, then sat us down in front of the TV. He put in the tape of the 1984 Monaco Grand Prix. Aria's glossy eyes were glued to the screen while my dad recalled that he and Peter had watched it from the front row in the rain. Aria's eyes barely blinked, and I knew she was holding her breath. I had a front row seat to her falling in love with it.

She always loved driving, even when it was on our bikes down the street, and I loved the fact that I had witnessed the first spark the moment it ignited.

A loud screeching noise filled the air when Aria hit the brakes at the pit stop. All too gracefully, she stepped out and walked straight to us, taking off her helmet. Jesse's outstretched hand held a bottle of water for her, and she took it, her smile undeniable.

"Can I live here? Is that allowed?" she bellowed, making the small crowd burst into laughter. Gulping half a bottle, she took two steps that separated us, locking her eyes on mine.

"Thank you for this." Her brows furrowed. "It's funny…it never even occurred to me that this place existed; that I could just come and pay for the rush."

I grabbed her face, tucking the loose strands behind her ears on both sides. "Yeah, well, you're not used to thinking about yourself; you're too busy thinking about others."

When her face scrunched up, I added, "That's not a bad thing; plus, it makes it easier for me to do it for you."

She smiled and tiptoed upwards, kissing me through a whispered "Smart-ass."

"Takes one to know one." I returned the kiss, deepening it. Before it got too heated, I found her ear, a whisper escaping, "Ready for the fun part?"

"This was not the fun part?" She looked around, confused.

"Not even close."

"That was the best day of my life," she said on the ride back, curled up on my lap. "No one has ever done something like this for me, and I honestly don't know what to say or how to thank you or…"

"Stop it," I blurted. "Seeing you so fucking happy is the best thank you possible."

We'd ended the day at the track by recreating the '94 Grand Prix: Aria in the white/red McLaren and hers truly in the black Lotus. Regardless of the speed, I could still see that spark while she mopped the track with me, leaving me to taste the dust.

I tangled my fingers in her loose hair, the sight of it igniting something within me. "I love when you let your hair down, literally and figuratively. There is no better feeling in the world than the one I get watching you let it all go."

She connected her hands around my neck and kissed me so deeply, every inch of me feeling its power. 'Cause that's what her kiss did, made me powerless and almighty all at once.

The second we got home, we jumped into the shower, where she thanked me thoroughly with her mouth around my cock, making me the luckiest fucking man alive.

Knowing Aria wasn't so big on surprise parties, we settled on a quiet family dinner, followed by a girls' night out I was graciously excluded from. Ok, it wasn't so gracious as it was menacing, with both Sabrina and Nala giving me a get-lost glare.

Dinner went great, especially since my mother saw right through us and started jumping with excitement. It took the others only a minute to join in. All at once, we were being suffocated by hugs and gushes, with the word 'finally' being the all-around theme. My mother cried, Helen sobbed extra thanks to her pregnancy hormones, and Peter, well, he gave me a look. After Aria went to join her friends, I stayed with my family. Peter then decided to give me *the talk* after dinner. Somehow, I ended up in my father's study, where both he and Peter gave me a lecture on how to take care of my wife.

It was funny, really.

Still, I contained my laugh and gave them reassuring nods, all serious. My father brought out a pack of rare Cohiba Behike Cuban cigars to mark the special occasion. The rich, full-bodied flavor filled the room, and we stayed silent, savoring the blend.

Before we went home, my mother gave me an extra-long hug, letting me know how happy she was about the turn of events. I was as well, and the feeling went on the rest of the night... that was until Aria stumbled in the middle of it, inebriated, trying to jump my bones.

The woman was a horny drunk, clinging to me while I fought away my protesting dick. Though my conscience cared that she wasn't all herself, the throbbing idiot in my pants disagreed, hard pun intended. It took everything in me to unglue her from me.

When she finally tired, I tucked her in bed, and she snored so loudly I could only imagine she was dreaming about being a freaking tractor. I couldn't comprehend why her snoring was so appealing. It was so charming that I had to record it on my phone—not to hold it against her, but to have it with me at all times.

The sharp noise filled the air, lulling me in. So I pulled her onto me and fell asleep, my wife wrapped in my arms, where she belonged.

Chapter 52

Cillian

Waking up with Aria in my arms was the best thing ever. Lingering, I took my time, drinking her in. Her hair all disheveled, mouth open, leg spread across my chest - perfect. I carefully wiggled out of her hold and tiptoed to the gym.

After a quick workout, I took a shower and got to the kitchen with the sole purpose of spoiling Aria with breakfast in bed. Naturally, the woman had different plans.

"Hi." Her soft voice reverberated, sending a rush through my insides.

"Coffee?" I asked over my shoulder.

"Always."

Pressed to my back, her hands flew around me, holding me while I whisked the eggs.

I turned to look at her, my insides fluttering at her beam. Raising on her tiptoes, she wrapped her hands around my neck and pulled me down for a kiss.

She stiffened at my slight flinch. "Are you okay?"

"Yeah, it's nothing; nerves reacting."

Her face flooded with worry. "Sit," she commanded, pointing at the chair.

Not wanting to fight her, I did what she'd asked and

pulled her onto my lap. When she didn't give me her full weight, I grabbed her legs and pulled them off the floor, letting her know I could handle it.

"Does it hurt?" she grilled, her fingers raking through my hair.

"Sometimes, but it's not pain; more like a jolt here and there."

Her concern only grew, and I tried to reassure her, "I overdid it, that's all. I've been spending more time at the gym than usual."

She placed her hands in her lap and started fidgeting with her fingers. "Am I the reason for that?"

Yes.

When I didn't answer, she continued, "You were avoiding me and…"

I quickly grabbed her hands. "I wasn't avoiding you."

Her face disagreed with me, and she was not entirely wrong. "I was at the beginning, but later it was more of a distraction." Her eyes narrowed, and I snuck my hand below her, groping her ass.

"There were times I couldn't handle the sexual tension, and the nights spent with my hand weren't cutting it, so I resorted to working out more."

She swallowed, her breath deepening. I knew where her mind was taking her, that stupid Playboy label finding its way to blow up in my face. It didn't matter that it was far from the truth. It was out there, and unfortunately, Aria was one of the believers.

"You were the sole source of it," I assured her, grazing a finger over her cheek.

"But all the tabloids…" She trailed off, to which I attested, "Don't trust everything you read."

I took off her hair tie and tossed it, unraveling the strands with my fingers, making her chest rise higher. I grabbed her behind her neck and pushed our mouths together. In a swift response, she rearranged herself, wrapping her long legs around me, fingers grabbing hold of my hair to deepen the kiss. Our tongues danced as she moved around my hard dick.

As much as I wanted to keep this going, the subject needed to be closed, so I pulled back. She frowned, pursing her lips.

"Let's clear the air once and for all."

"Okay," she drawled, unsure.

"Though I am far from a prude, most of those tabloids were taken out of context. I haven't even talked to half of the women I've been photographed with, let alone done anything else."

She bobbed her head, taking it all in. I brushed my hand down her back, soothing, reassuring. Begging her with my touch to believe me. I could see her wheels spinning, and just as I started to think she'd recoil, she blurted, "And what's with the NDAs?"

I should've seen that one coming. It was my nickname after all. And it wasn't even funny. It was quite the opposite.

"You can thank Mario for that. After what happened, my family's legal team coerced me into handing them out like they were flyers whenever I was at a club."

She raked her teeth over her lower lip, hunger screaming out of her eyes. How we've turned the mood back around was a question I didn't care to answer, happy with the development.

She dropped to her knees, and without breaking eye contact, tugged down my pants and boxers, setting my hard cock free. The act of her wetting her lips nearly combusted me right before she took me in her mouth.

"Fuck," I groaned, grabbing her loose hair while she sucked, licked, and grazed my cock with her teeth, making me lose all control. Those devilish lashes lifted, eating on my moans. Her eyes watered as she struggled with my length, but she continued until I filled her throat with my cum. I watched her swallow to the last drop before she released me with a pop.

We ate breakfast with her on my lap, soft music in the background. Something about it felt domestic, and I loved every second of it. It only got me thinking about wanting more days like this, us sharing a bed, sharing food, and bodily fluids. When a familiar song started playing, memories of the first time I realized I was in love with my best friend overwhelmed me.

Aria jumped on my ass, waking me up with a whisper-yell, "Come on, get dressed."

I rubbed my eyes. "Where are we going?"

"It's a surprise; come on, hurry!"

I put on my sweatpants and a shirt, then I snuck out the window. With a deep breath, I jumped down onto the grass where she was waiting, dangling the keys of her dad's car in the air, mischief on full display.

"Are you crazy?" I mumbled my shouting.

"You damn well know I am; now let's go." I followed her to the car and lay back on the passenger seat while she drove us off.

"Did you seriously just steal your dad's car?" I questioned her sanity at this point. She turned to face me, that devilish smile on her face beaming.

"Yeah." She shrugged.

Interesting, she admitted it so nonchalantly.

Terrified, I scanned for cops or our parents. I knew she wasn't supposed to be driving alone at this hour. Plus, she was stealing, and I was the clueless sidekick.

The car pulled up at the edge of a cliff, but I didn't dare move. She got out first, rounded the car, and opened the door for me. I reluctantly stepped out. "You're diabolical!"

"And yet, you're here." With a giggle, she grabbed my hand and dragged me to the very edge, pulling me down onto the grass.

A familiar song (perfect for the situation) played on the car radio as we lay upside down. Our heads hung over the hill, giving us a flipped view of the entire city.

Watching the lights of the cars passing by on the small bridge right above us, I soaked it all in. It was amazing—the view, the air, her...

She turned to face me, those ocean eyes gleaming, causing me to blurt out, "My favorite color is blue."

"Okay?" Her brows furrowed in question, but I didn't elaborate.

She looked so happy and peaceful with her deep blues lit up, reflecting the city and car lights. No thoughts existed at this moment, only her expression. She was so beautiful, and *at that exact moment, I knew I was in love with her. We were only sixteen and probably still knew nothing about love. Even so, the mere thought of breathing without her was unbearable.*

Lying with her, forgetting about the world—it was everything. *She* was everything, and I knew then and there that my life was forever changed.

With that, I swooped her up and carried her out of the kitchen while she clung to me with an ankle lock around my waist. I got us to the living room, happy that the firewood was already cracking with heat. I helped her to her feet and spread a large blanket out on the floor in front of the fire. When I turned around, I found Aria completely, beautifully naked. My cock jerked at the sight, my heart joined, and I lunged for her.

She yelped when I picked her up, her fingers tangled in my hair, pulling, pushing, undecided where to go or what to do. Slowly lying her on her back, I worked my way over her body, from her neck, over her nipples, down her stomach, where her skin prickled with goosebumps. I stopped right at her center. Never in my life had I tasted anything better than this woman's pussy; it made me feral. I grazed my tongue ever so gently from one opening up to the other, and when I got to her clit, I flicked, causing her to moan out, "Oh, fuck!"

Repeating the action, her panting got louder, and I could feel the pounding of her heart all the way down.

"More," she growled, and I felt her entire body shake with need, so I put two fingers inside her, grazing the inner wall. She clenched around them, my cock reacting in pure jealousy. I pumped in and out while she cried out her pleasure, feeding my need to move faster. So I did, adding another finger and prepping her for me. When she came, it was with my name accompanied by a scream. I kept the movement going until her body went from a full-on spasm to mush. Her eyes were locked on my hand while I slid it out and brought my fingers to my mouth, sucking them dry one at a time. I watched the muscles of her throat contract as she swallowed, all the while licking her lower lip. Taking that as an invitation, my teeth went right for it, biting and sucking the fullness… and when she spread her legs wider, I maneuvered out of my pants and boxers, lined my dick, and imploded inside her.

I slowed my thrusts to take a better look at her. Those glossy eyes, filled with want, stared right back. I kissed her, gently this time, and her fingers made patterns at the nape of my neck. She lifted her hips so I could get deeper, and she moaned. For good measure, I slid my hand where we connected, my thumb pressing on her clit.

"Say it!"

She smirked, her eyes piercing right through me as she gave me what I wanted, what I needed, in that raspy voice that drove me crazy. "Husband!" And with that, we both came undone.

Chapter 53

Aria

Tonight was the celebration marking the end of an era while welcoming the beginning of a new one. I'd officially defended my master's thesis today and was riding a high. Cillian had reserved a table for our friends and family at the Apollo. It was a Michelin-starred Greek restaurant, famous for its long waiting list—nothing a little name-dropping couldn't fix.

The hostess led us to the terrace, which offered a mesmerizing view of the river. When we passed a sculpture of Hades and Persephone, I couldn't contain my chuckle. I had been here before, but never paid much attention to the aesthetics. Now they were all I could focus on. Cillian traced my sight and gave me a smirk, practically reading my mind.

Fuck, he was gorgeous. I knew it was a strange thing to say about a man, but this one was on another level, a league of his own. Drop-dead beautiful and so fucking alluring, all wrapped in a tailored suit. When he stepped in front of me to drag out my chair, I couldn't help my compulsion to squeeze his ass in those oh-so-tight pants. I took my seat, and he lowered his mouth to my ear. "You'll pay for that."

I turned to face him. "Promise?"

He grinned, taking his seat next to me.

Dinner ticked by fast with everyone engaged in hushed

conversations. My head was occupied with something else, and that was fighting the urge to explode in front of my entire family. Cillian kept teasing the hell out of me, dragging callous fingers up and down my thigh.

After we toasted me and my smart-ass brain, Cillian's knee grazed mine, then his hand slid under the hem of my dress, making my chest rise with a deep breath. We both stood up simultaneously.

"I'm going to the bathroom!"

"Nature calls."

We looked at each other with confusion and then left the table, zero fucks given regarding our company. He pulled me into the staff bathroom and claimed my mouth. In a quick swoop, I was up, pinned to the wall, my legs wrapping around him on instinct, while he pulled up my dress. He attacked my neck, and I took action against his ear.

"Careful, wife, you know what that does to me," he growled, pressing his erection into me.

I hummed, not stopping my nibbling.

Without any further comments, I undid his belt, pulled out his stiff cock, thankful for going out panty-less, and guided him inside. He froze, his eyes sending daggers as he croaked, "You've been walking around without any underwear this whole time?"

Biting my inner cheek, I nodded.

A full-on sensory overload happened when he bottomed out. We were so hungry for each other that we both moaned with each touch. He held one hand under my ass, the other around the back of my neck, as I pulled on his hair. Raw, sexy, amazing... I could feel his need for me with each invasion, and when my moans grew louder, I tried to muffle them... I failed.

"Scream all you want, wife," he dared. "I will make them all sign NDAs."

Well, that was a first. Never had I ever laughed through an orgasm. By the look on his face, it was a first for him as well.

He grabbed the side of my face, grazing his thumb right under my lip. "You are always beautiful, but it's moments like these that you take my breath away, looking freshly taken in the bathroom."

"You say the sweetest things," I giggled, trying to catch my breath. He let me down, my legs wobbling while I tried to salvage my look. He took my hand and looked at me with a weird sparkle in his eyes, and I couldn't help myself when I gasped, "Let's go home."

He took a breath, smiling back at me, making me realize how much those words meant to both of us. All this time, I've never seen his place as mine, but now... let's just say, things had changed. Big time.

"Go and wait for me in the car. I will tell them that you're not feeling well."

I nodded and did what he said.

We got home and immediately tossed ourselves on the bed. I unbuttoned his shirt like it were an Olympic sport, pulling off his tie, damaging it in the process.

"That's fine, I didn't even like it anyway," he said sheepishly while I bit his earlobe.

"I'll buy you a new one, I'm rich, remember," I singsonged, moving down to his neck, devouring. This man made me insatiable.

"Slow down," he breathed, grabbing my waist to ease my greed.

"I can't, I'm hungry." I turned to the other side of his neck.

"We just ate."

Yeah, the dinner was delish.

"Not what I meant."

"I know," he grinned.

The little tease.

"You always do. I hate that."

Lie! It was my favorite of his superpowers.

"You love that," he growled, and I chuckled.

Bastard.

I loved how he knew me better than I knew myself, how he made me feel, how he freed me... his kindness, care, wit, but most of all, his heart. I loved how he possessed mine in its entirety.

I pushed him onto his back and straddled him.

I've never liked being on top during sex. It felt too exposed. But now in this moment, all I wanted was to feel him under me, show him how much I trusted him, and that was precisely what I did. With each movement, each thrust, each moan, I exhibited everything for him. The way he looked at me... Damn, it was hard to breathe. Like a starved animal, I moved in every direction, taking him to new depths. An unfamiliar sensation started its culmination in the pit of my stomach. Only it didn't stop there; it kept on going. As my orgasm prolonged, desperation took over while my body went into shock, every part of me curling or spasming or whatever the hell was happening. And then I felt it, his eruption, while I continued waving my own blast. Catching my breath was pointless, and so was steadying my heartbeat.

"That was new."

Fuck, I said that out loud.

"Elaborate."

"I don't know, it was long. Longer than any orgasm I've experienced." I covered my chest with my hand, feeling the hard pumping of my heart. "I want more of those."

"Your wish is my command." He pulled me closer, and I cuddled up in my new favorite place. "Rest first."

His fingers made circles over my shoulder, the movement entrancing me. My mind wandered to that dark place where it felt most comfortable. Somehow, he felt me drift, so he lifted his head, turning it to face me.

"Is this about the word that shall not be named?"

I let out a laugh. "It's just my insecurities."

"New addendum. You are never allowed to feel that way." He turned on his side, elbow digging into the mattress as he propped his head on his hand—the position ideal for gaining my full attention.

His fingers combed through my hair, voice hoarse when he asked, "You know why I like your hair down and not in that stupid tight up bun you keep putting up?"

I shook my head.

"Because when it's down, it's free, every strand goes in its own direction; flawless. I love the messy bun too, like the

333

one you had when you danced in our kitchen."

His eyes widened at the slip, and I gasped, "What?"

"The night I was at the hotel, I came home first. You didn't hear me over the music, too busy baking while dancing and singing…" he trailed off, biting his lower lip.

"You saw that?" I covered my face, humiliated.

"Don't you dare hide from me." He pulled my hands away, and I would bet I was as red as a pepper.

"Right there in the kitchen, that was my definition of perfection."

"You liked that?" Disbelief took over, and so did a whole new kind of shiver that invaded my entire body.

"Why wouldn't I? What could be better than seeing you happy? I wish you wouldn't limit yourself to being like that solely when you're alone."

"You really know how to make a girl…" I paused, and our eyes met. I swallowed excruciatingly slowly. "You really know how to make a girl love you."

He stopped any movement, eyes locked on mine, scanning for any indication of a lie. I knew he'd seen it, the look that said I meant it with all my heart, because the next thing I noticed were tears forming in his widened, blurry eyes.

He sat up, and I followed, biting on my inner cheek. Gazes locked, he framed my face between his hands, and I felt his breath hitch when our foreheads met.

"I waited my whole life to hear you say those words, to feel those words. I've loved you ever since I first saw you."

"I was a baby when you first saw me." I didn't know why I rebutted there; still, it happened, and he tilted his head, a bit annoyed.

"You know what I mean."

I did—the first time he saw me for me, not as a friend, not some family pushed into his life, but me—all of me, the good and the bad.

He took my hand and slid off my engagement ring. I suddenly felt naked without it.

"It wasn't just a point of a finger, you know?" He revealed a soft smile, making my heart skip another beat. I gaped at him, confused, as he kept going, "I looked hard for a ring, and when I saw this one, it screamed Aria. For a short minute, I didn't want to give it to you, I wanted to save it for…" He took a deep breath, and I read between the lines. "I wanted to buy another one to give you, but then I thought it would be the only chance for you to wear it…"

The most beautiful tear imaginable slid down his cheek, all the way to the curve of his lips.

"I want it to be real, for this ring to represent how much I love you, how much I want you."

My breath hitched, my heart going into overdrive, seconds from bursting out of my chest.

Pinched between his thumb and forefinger, he lifted the ring between us. "I want to marry you, for you to be mine forever and beyond that."

"We *are* married, you idiot," I joshed. The tick of his jaw indicated he was not happy with my take on it. So I cleared my throat, letting him know I was taking this seriously.

"I mean for real, here in the city you love so much. I want to kiss you with my entire being after we read the vows we wrote for each other. I want to dance to a song that defines our love, not our animosity."

Sobs were set free, my heart wide open as I stared at him, dumbfounded.

"Aria, merry me. Let me love you; the good, the bad, the damaged?"

And just like that, he managed to glue all the pieces together, giving the word I hated most a whole new meaning. He mended me...mended us.

"One condition..." I hovered above him, and he read my face while my fingers played with the locket around my neck.

"Of course, I couldn't think of a better place."

Damn this man, how lucky was I to have a mind reader? There would be times I would surely regret it, but at this moment, I loved him for it.

We sealed it with a kiss, and he pulled back. "I also have a condition!"

"I'm listening," I faltered, preparing myself for the worst.

"This time I get to pick the song," he declared, making me uneasy, but I caved.

"Fine."

"Fine."

Chapter 54

Aria

(five months later)

My closest girls were with me in the bridal suite, a photographer taking our pictures, when a knock at the door interrupted our posing. The door cracked open, and my dad peeked through it with his hand covering his eyes.

"Everybody decent?"

We burst into laughter.

"Come in, Mr. Brooks," Nala said, dragging him in. Reading his face, she waved her hand. "Come on, girls, let's give them a minute." The room cleared, and my father gasped, covering his mouth with both hands.

"Oh, Peanut, you look so beautiful; just like your mother."

The words warmed my heart and melted his, and hearing him say them without the pain that had once accompanied them, I almost combusted.

"She gave me this to give you on your wedding day." He handed me two envelopes, my name written on the first one and Cillian's on the other. Confusion overwhelmed me. "Why didn't you give it to me in the Seychelles?"

He kissed my forehead. "You know the answer to that."

Yeah, he had a point.

"Anyway, I'll leave you to it. I love you, Peanut."

"I love you too, Dad."

337

I opened my envelope and teared up at the sight of my mother's handwriting.

My sweetie,
The other love of my life.
Today is your wedding day, and as much as I wish to be there beside you, I know that you will walk through this day without me physically present. But I will be there in spirit. You made the right choice. You and Cillian were meant for each other from the start. It may not always be easy; it likely got bumpy along the way, but you're here. It will only get easier with every challenge you face because you will face it together. I am proud of you, the amazing woman I am sure you have become, and I know your pure heart deserves all the happiness it can find.

As I write this, I imagine the two of you embarking on your journey and starting your family. I am confident that both of you will be amazing parents, and I will be there, supporting you every step of the way, waiting for the stories you'll tell me, because I know you, and so does he.

I love you, always and forever.
Mom

Thankful to whoever invented waterproof mascara, I dried my eyes. Blessed for her words, grateful for her faith in us, and bewildered by the fact that she'd known all along, I stepped out and knocked on the groom's suit. Marco popped out, and I handed him the other letter to give to Cillian before my nosy ass opened it.

I stared at my reflection in the mirror, my smile unfaltering. I didn't think life could get to this point, that I could feel this happy. All I knew was that it was only going to get better.

Marco closed the door and handed me an envelope with my name on it. I recognized the handwriting immediately and tore it open at super speed.

My dear future son-in-law,
Yes, you are now ten years old, but beyond any doubt, I know that you will be the one waiting for her at the end of the aisle. You have always protected my little girl, and knowing your heart, I am sure you will continue to do so. I knew it from the first time I held you that you two would be each other's worlds.
And as I lie in my hospital bed, I am at peace, knowing she is safe with you. And for that, I thank you. She has a special kind of soul, an honest heart, and an abundance of liveliness. My only plea is for you to allow and encourage her to be just that: herself. You always manage to bring out the best in one another, so continue doing so, and you will be fine.
I love you, you little rascal.

Your mother-in-law, Nicole

"You okay, brother?" Marco grabbed my shoulder, seeing me wiping my tears.

"Her mother, man..." I shook my head with incredulity. "She wrote this letter when we were ten years old. She knew we would end up here, anticipated it even then." I let out a laugh, amazed.

"One hell of a woman. Both of them," Marco stated, then tapped my back. "Let's get you married," he paused, smirking, "again."

I stood up, pulling him in for a hug. "Thank you, man, for being a true friend, the kind I need."

"Same man, same." He pushed me away, a full grin on, "Now stop with the sob fest; we'll ruin our makeup."

We burst out laughing and stepped into the chapel.

The moment the double door swung open, revealing Aria, I stopped breathing. She had her hair down, and the sight took me straight to cloud nine. The more she approached, the louder my heart pounded. My mother's dress suited her perfectly, and she radiated with something greater than joy, something I couldn't quite identify.

The first time around, I couldn't let her wear a dress that stood for true love, since the wedding wasn't real and all... But now... My God. She was breathtaking, her eyes glowing with love for everyone around us, including me. The church was small, but big enough for the most important people in our lives. It was the same place where both her parents and mine had gotten married; Helen as well. Aria loved it, the colorful stained glass, the pictures of the saints on the wall, each with a different frame. She'd always say it had a soul, unlike the modern churches. This one had life, and I felt it. I also knew her mother was with us, her words warming my heart as Aria stood across from me, her hands in mine.

"I really tried to come up with a cheesy line. You know, that big movie moment, like a Jerry Maguire declaration. But my mind was full of clichés, and none felt right." She lifted those blue eyes from the paper and looked right at me. "Then it got me thinking... Do you remember when we were teenagers discussing this place? How one day we'd buy our little vineyard where you would make me the perfect blend of wine..." She paused, waiting for me to confirm. I nodded, the memory of us sneaking into the cellar and trying wine for the first time lighting up my core. For Aria, it was love at first sip. We were only fifteen when she concocted the entire plan: a small blue house and a giant vineyard in the back. Little did she know that the next day, I went to my parents and had it included in my trust's clause. They found a piece of land and bought it straight away. It was there, patiently waiting for a family to claim it.

"Then it hit me. How simple, how perfect... You ready?" Her eyes widened, anticipation evident.

"Yes," I replied, not knowing why I was alarmed by it.

"You had me at Merlot."

I shook my head, trying not to kiss her before we were

allowed to by the man between us.

God, how I love this woman.

She bit her lower lip before she continued. "I promise to let my hair down, to sing your ears off, and make you vanilla chocolate chip cookies. I promise to always be there, through the good and the bad, to cherish each moment, and to give my all. Now and forever to be yours, be your friend, your everything. But most of all, I promise to always be right."

Laughter echoed around us because, of course, she'd go there.

Now it was my turn.

"I promise to toss away all your hair ties, to let you be you, to see you and read your mind, because we both know I'm good at it. With me, you get an unconditional support system, someone to root for you as you take over the world. I promise to always carry an extra EpiPen, but most of all, I promise to let you be right."

The chapel echoed with laughter, but all I noticed was my beautiful wife mouthing 'I love you.' I returned the sentiment, waiting for the priest's go-ahead. When he pronounced us husband and wife, we kissed, and this time it lasted more than five seconds. Tongues were involved as well, but that could be our little secret.

Chapter 55

Aria

Everyone was crying, and I do mean everyone—my dad and Marco included. I couldn't fight my tears either. Cillian intertwined our fingers, guiding us outside as a few sprinklers illuminated the darkened sky. We all took a stroll to the tent that sat upright next to my tree. It was a mere five-minute walk, and we all decided to make it into a parade. Laughter escaped us all when Cillian started yell-singing "Left. Left. Left. Right. Left."

The sight of the twinkling lights surrounding the large tent was fairytale-like. Gold hugged the trunk of the tree, tassels trailing down over the branches. The bushes circling the tent were also covered with them, every bulb in the right place. A large number of diamond stars made an arch around the entry. Cillian had the idea of making it Christmas-themed in the spring, given how much I loved stars and Christmas. And with what the cold did to me, it was a no-brainer.

Inside the tent was a scene out of a dream. Twinkling lights lined the edges, and Christmas trees stood in every corner, decorated in sky blue and wine red. Everything was perfectly put together, as if telling a story—our story.

And even though everything was as pretty as a picture, the happiness on our loved ones' faces was the best thing imaginable. I hadn't seen Loren's eyes dry once the entire day. Each time her gaze met mine, she looked at me with so much love. We all gathered inside and took our seats. There were about ten tables, including ours, for our closest friends and family.

The band called us for our first dance, and Cillian opened his hand in front of me, waiting. My breath wheezed out of me when our hands tangled. Almost half a year together, and my heart still dove into my stomach in response to his touch. We reached the middle of the dance floor, and I sank into his hold. Familiar opening notes widened my eyes as Cillian grabbed the small of my back with one hand, pulling mine behind his neck, then he took my other hand and brought it to his chest.

"How did you know?" I looked at my husband, my brows twitched, and his eyes narrowed.

"Know what?"

The male singer started singing 'Chasing Cars' by Snow Patrol.

"That this is my favorite song?"

He smiled at me in that knowing way I love-hated.

"I didn't." We swayed in circles, my face begging for an answer.

"It was the song playing on the radio the night you stole your dad's car."

"You mean when *we* stole my dad's car?" I stretched out the 'we' part.

"I will neither confirm nor deny my implication in your shenanigans." He smirked, but his eyes twinkled. Even in my favorite heels, I had to stretch out to give him a soft kiss.

"It was playing the moment I realized I loved you." His words made my whole body shiver; goosebumps covered me.

"Funny. It was playing the moment I realized I loved you," I confessed, and he smiled at me before he lifted me so he could twirl me. I burst out in a squeak.

"Tell me something…" he waited for my eyes to meet his before he continued, "Why is blue your favorite color?"

"A weird question to ask someone you've known your entire life," I deadpanned.

"Humor me."

"Because that night you said it was your favorite."

Satisfaction washed over him, making one of my brows twitch upward.

"It still is. Do you know why?"

I shook my head.

"Your eyes, Aria, they're my favorite thing about you. I can see your heart in them."

Well, that turned me into a puddle.

He pressed his lips on mine, and I tasted the vanilla on his tongue as I deepened our kiss.

That got me thinking out loud.

"You switched your drink for me?"

God, what a fool I had been. His favorite whiskey had a nutty taste that used to make me gag whenever I smelled his breath.

He bobbed his head.

"So you knew we would be kissing?" I wiggled my brows.

"Had high hopes is more like it."

The rest of the people joined us on the dance floor when the next song faded in.

"May I cut in?" John pushed Cillian out of the way and twirled me into the ballroom stance. It was our Christmas tradition. When I was too small, he would let me stand on his feet, but I soon grew out of it and learned to follow his lead.

"You still got it, Mr. Wright." I smiled with amazement. "I believe it's about time you start calling me Dad." He pushed me into another twirl. "Okay, Dad; it's a deal." My words lit up his face, and a sense of pride rushed through me.

Loren and my father came up next to us, exchanging weird looks. "We did good, ha?" my mother-in-law said, winking at John.

"What does that mean?"

"Nothing," they all blurted in unison.

The music stopped, and the band announced the dinner as we all took our seats.

I turned to Cillian, whispering, "We have been hoodwinked."

He grinned. "You just figured that out? For a smart person, you can sometimes be so—" I gagged his mouth with my palm. "Don't you dare finish that sentence."

His whole body shook with his mocking titter.

"How long have you known?" I could feel my eyes sending lasers at him, trying to make his head explode.

"Since they delivered a prenup on day two."

"What?" I dragged it out, raising my voice, "I never got a prenup."

He kept smirkingly laughing. "I think that was the point."

No way would our parents ever make us sign a prenup, fake marriage or not.

They all played me.

Loren came between us. "Sorry, honey, but we couldn't wait any longer for you two to figure out what we all knew all along."

She wrapped her arms around us, squeezing us into a sandwich, and left, knowing I was about to raise some hell.

Alone again, I glared at my husband. "But if you knew all along, why did you go along with it?"

"You can blame yourself for that one. I was ready to decline it all when you came to my place with your master plan."

"What does my plan have to do with it when it wasn't even necessary?" At this point, I was yelling, making every head turn my way. I raised my arm and mouthed the word 'sorry.'

"It wasn't the plan; it was the woman. When you barged in, all demanding, assured, funny… The old you, not the stuck-up version you pretended to be… The game changed."

"So you duped me?"

"Yes."

"No elaboration?"

"Not necessary. It got us here, don't dig into it. You love me, I love you. Bada bing, bada boom."

God, I love this man.

"Bada bing, bada boom?"

"Yeah, whatcha gonna do about it?"

I pulled him closer, capturing his lips before I whispered, "God, I hope this kid takes after me."

He pulled back, switching his gaze between my eyes and my mouth, and when a small curve escaped my seriousness, he gasped.

"No," he breathed, his smile widening. "Seriously?" he murmured, and I nodded.

I've been off birth control for a few months now, but I had no idea Cillian's sperm also had his overachieving tendencies.

My face framed between his palms, he lowered his head to get a better look, to make sure. When he received the confirmation he needed, he pulled me into his arms and twirled me around, making my stomach protest.

"Stop it, I'll get sick." He stopped right away, putting me down; then he started jumping like a kid who got his Christmas wish.

In mere seconds, we were surrounded by everyone realizing what was happening.

"I'm gonna be a grandpa?" My dad grabbed me by my shoulders, his eyes filled with tears, his smile the widest I had ever seen. I nodded, unable to speak, before he pulled me into a hug, squeezing me gently.

"I call godmother," Nala shouted, her hand up in the air, volunteering. Followed by Marco's deep, commanding voice, "I call godfather."

I took a mental picture, hearing my mind make the click sound. Who cared how we got here... I was so freakin' happy; we all were, and that was that.

Epilogue

Aria

FIVE YEARS LATER

I sat in my office chair, gazing out at the city I loved. It had given me everything. Then, the intercom buzzed. My assistant Tina's voice came through, "Incoming." I turned around just as the door opened. "Mrs. Wright, are you ready for us?" Derek, the firm's lawyer, picked me up to head to the conference room. "Born ready," I said, smiling lightly.

In the room, ten board members awaited, my father, standing at the very edge of the large table, a stack of papers laid out before him. John stood right beside him, ready to cry, the big old softy.

I closed in on them, shook my father's hand, and signed my name on the dotted line. I was now officially the CEO of the W&B Group. A small ping struck my chest when each set of hands echoed a clap, followed by a standing ovation. Everyone shook my hand in congratulations, right before the popping of the champagne cued my short speech. I contemplated for a long time what to say, so I chose a simple shout-out: "There is a new bitch in town."

Another round of applause led the way, followed by a burst of laughter. Tina popped in and whispered, "They're here."

I jolted, hurrying out, and then I heard Nicky shout,

"Mommy!"

He sprinted into my arms, and I squished him tight. This little rascal had refused to get out of me, paining me for 12 hours straight. He was my biggest challenge, but it was so worth it. He had his father's eyes, a bit lighter skin, and all of my smarts. It was Cillian's idea to name him after my mother, one of many reasons why that man was my everything.

"Hi, Boss!" Cillian hovered over us, Gaby hiding behind him.

"Come here, sweetheart," I told her, and she jumped into my arms. We had adopted her at the beginning of the year.

After having Nicky, I'd decided to take out my ovaries and undertook a double mastectomy. Cillian had been supportive of my decision, and I've never regretted it. We'd also agreed to adopt before my operations, so it was an easy choice.

Gaby was 12 years old. She'd lost her parents in a fire, and it took one look between Cillian and me to know that she was our missing piece. She was still closed off, but Nala got her into reading. Fuck, she got me into it. We were currently reading 'The Prisoner of Azkaban'. I was determined to make Gaby a Potterhead, and so far, I had been succeeding. What a weird thing to say, but she had a lot of me in her. She loved music like me... She would join me whenever a song hit a certain dance mood, whether it was in the car, a store, or on the street.

Cillian had taken a back seat, making me the only CEO, knowing I could handle it all. No need to worry, he'd turned to something he actually loved. He was now a badass basketball coach. After our real wedding, he'd returned to college and graduated in record time, all the while coaching a high school girls' team. Last year, he'd gotten called out for an assistant coaching job with the Celtics. Soon after, he had earned the head position. His team was undefeated, and even though he wasn't playing, the spark was there. He loved coordinating it; he was terrific at delivering inspirational speeches, and the whole team loved him. He got Gaby into it as well; they played in the backyard whenever they could. It was one of my favorite sights.

Cillian

"Coach," I turned to face my point guard. "Yes, Derek, what can I do for you?" I was more than a coach; I was their mentor, their friend, sometimes, even their shrink. Pride warmed my chest at the notion that the players felt free to come to me with any problem. "I wanted to say congratulations again."

We had just won the NBA Championship.

"Thank you, and you too, good game," I echoed before he disappeared down the hall, just as a vision came into view.

"Well, hello there, NBA-winning coach. Are you free tonight to celebrate with this little hoop bunny?"

Her voice made my dick instantly hard. I went around the table and trapped her against the wall, my hands on each side of her head, pinned.

"I don't know, my wife will be pretty mad. You don't want

to mess with her."

She nodded, smirking up at me. "We wouldn't want to have that, now would we?" Taking my whistle in her hand, she pulled me in for a kiss. "I am so proud of you; we all are."

I focused on the most breathtaking blue eyes staring back at me, filled with love, and right there in those eyes was my everything. This woman was my lifeline, my heart, my soul, my lungs… Everything I needed to—just *be*.

"I love you, wife," I said, leaning in to lock the door. Thankfully, the blinds were down, so I picked Aria up with one hand. Her pencil skirt rose when her legs wrapped around me. It was a reflex, really; so was it when her fingers found my hair.

"Good thing I went commando." She bit my ear, making me groan.

"Damn, the things you do to me."

She pulled down my pants enough to set me free. Her hand aligned my cock to her entrance, and I busted in; hungry for her, needy. I hadn't seen her for two days, and it might as well be like forever. Every minute without her was pure torture. She was on the top of the corporate world, owning the boardroom, and executing new ideas daily. But she still let out her goofy self. Gaby had been joining in with her more and more each day. Last week, they'd started dancing in the middle of Barnes & Noble when someone's phone rang to a song that apparently both of them loved. It was the most beautiful thing I'd ever seen. Aria had been keeping her promise of letting her hair down every chance she could.

Her hair was currently tangled with my fingers, let down in

the best way. After her surgeries, I had assured her I would love her body and proved it to her every day. She'd had breast reconstruction surgery. At first, she had struggled to embrace them. My mouth and tongue had worked overtime, and she relaxed into it with each lick and kiss. It didn't take long to gain back her cocky side. She'd once told me how I mended all the pieces back and glued them with my words. But she did that all on her own by accepting herself. I simply gave her a gentle nudge.

"I love you, wife," I said under my breath, and we both combusted.

"Oh, come on, say it like you mean it!"

"I always do!"

"Fine!"

"Fine!"

The end!

Also by Lena Knight

Brick-ed series
Averted
(Sabrina and Mateo)
Anticipated
(Aria and Cillian)
Allured
(Nala's story - coming soon)

Fostered H(e)arts series
Nothing's fair in Love & Basketball
(Tyler and MJ)
Nothing's fair in Love & Marriage
(Luka and Nora)

Flip the page for EXCERPTS

EXCERPT - Averted - Book 1 - Brick-ed Series

Chapter 1

Sabrina

Kesha's voice shouted as my alarm woke me up, the lyrics of 'Tik Tok' reverberating. With eyes wide open, I leaped out of bed, threw on my clothes, and brushed my teeth. I descended the marble stairs of my prison to sneak out the back door before Rea, our maid, made her dusting rounds. I ran through the literal maze that was our backyard and shimmied myself through a small crack in the hedge until I was touching concrete. The moon was still at its peak as dawn began to fade. I got in my hidden Jeep and started the engine, setting the checklist on the passenger seat.

Our garage had over a dozen cars at my disposal, but every single one of them was unique and easy to spot. And for my task at hand, I had to be incognito.

This Jeep was mine, not theirs - my version of a getaway car. With the first address entered in my Google Maps app, I drove off into the literal sunrise coming up before me. Passing by the iron gate surrounding my prison, I cringed at the family crest in the center of it, and yes, we had one of those - a symbol that used to represent power. Now, all I could see were the lies associated with the name plastered above it.

The name itself - a deception. My parents were clever. Well, my father was.

When they'd emigrated from Dubrovnik during the Croatian War of Independence, my father, being the respected man we all thought he was, used his connections and fled to the US, taking his newly wedded wife with him. They made a new life here with high expectations. Our original family name used to be Knezovic, meaning something akin to a title of a monarch's son, similar to a prince. My father wanted to keep the meaning, and he chose the German translation to mark the new beginning.

Drum roll, please...

The Family Furst was born, making it our new history.

By the time I'd arrived, they had already established their empire, hiding behind fake smiles to maintain the well-respected, rich, and famous act. The name meant something in this city. I was born into it, the title it came with, a silver spoon, and all.

Now, my billionaire parents owned more houses than they could count, as well as cars, boats, and planes... They practically owned the air we breathed, and once upon a time, I admired them for everything they had accomplished. My ignorant self didn't know better.

As I cranked up the stereo, one I had installed myself in this beat-up, sorry excuse of a car, a smile spread across my face. It was no ordinary smile, oh no. This one was special, one that I didn't have the luxury of producing much often. This particular smile had only one mission, one definition, and one meaning.

Vengeance!

The path I have chosen was not an easy one. Especially for a 20-year-old, soon to be 21, who still lived with her parents in the castle they made to flaunt her away in. The Barbie doll, who's heard the saying 'smile for the camera' more than any other. The same girl who was her mommy and daddy's perfect little princess. So, why was I sneaking out of this so-called castle and driving a rust-infested Jeep, you ask? Well, it's a long story, and lucky for you, I like 'em long.

This one had started a year ago when I uncovered some disturbing facts regarding my father. It opened a can of worms, and my curiosity got the best of me, so I kept on digging. Behind my parents' backs, I did a complete 180 and switched my concentration to law. At the time, I was a 'proud' student of Harvard Business and Economics, while taking online courses at the Harvard Graduate School of Design. I had to keep it secret for two reasons. Reason numero uno: my mother. For her, the notion itself would be unacceptable, because God forbid her daughter did something meaningful. Nooooo. I had to be the mirror of society; our family name was at stake here. And reason number two, my father. To uncover all the dirt on him, I had to obtain a lot of legal files, and what better way to do it than to infiltrate myself in the circle. What I didn't realize at that time was how much I would love all the legal bullshit. Now, I could even picture myself in a courtroom defending the innocent. And on some weird level, I had my father to thank for that. Because if it weren't for his secrets, I would still live in the bubble, happy to do as I was told, and I would never have discovered myself.

The anchor keepsake dangled from the rearview mirror, the memory of the only place that shielded me from the flashes that my eyes had grown accustomed to by the age of one. I came out of my mother's womb a model, and I mean that literally. Two minutes old, that's how old I was when I got on the cover of Boston Common, cradled in the Amelie scarf. And yes, you guessed it - the empire was Fashion. I was born into that world and lived in the spotlight, where I learned how to do my makeup before I could walk. I never resented it or hated it much; it was simply all I knew. Thankfully, I wasn't world-renowned. My so-called fame stayed inside the city limits. I didn't do any modeling for anything other than promoting my family brand.

With the sight of a red light, I hit the brake and turned up the stereo, bobbing my head and letting Little Mix's 'Power' transform me into a tone-deaf siren.

EXCERPT - NFILAB

Chapter 1

Ty

"Come on, dude, you've got 2 minutes to shower, and we need to sprint out!" Ben yells as he breezes by me to get the first empty cubicle.

"Where's the fire? The class is not for another..." I look at my watch: 35 minutes.

"Yeah, but theirs is still going on, so we have to hurry!" he shouts back. The room is filled with the whole team, each under a showerhead, scrubbing at full speed.

"Whose?" I remove my shirt and toss it on the bench by the wall.

"The girls, dumb-ass," someone screams from the showers.

Now it all makes sense.

"You guys are crazy." I shake my head, turning on the water, setting it to just the right of lukewarm.

"Trust me, Ty, you *want* to be there," Cole says, his brows dancing up and down.

"I am nothing if not a team player." I give in and join their fast pace.

"That's the spirit," Parker yells from across the room.

"I thought you were gay?" I quickly work, scrubbing my hair, loving the sensation on my scalp.

"True, but I am nothing if not a team player!"

"Touche!" I holler back.

All at once, as if an alarm has gone off, we turn the taps and start getting dressed. The next thing I know, we're power walking to the performing arts hall.

"Thank God it's still not over," Ben sighs with relief the second we get in the hall overlooking the large mirrored studio, filled with girls in the middle of a dance. The entire Basketball team is glued to the glass, focusing on said girls. Amused, I join them, allowing my eyes to be blessed by the view. Girls in short shorts, tights, tops, tight shirts... Girls with different body types, hair colors, all hot in their own ways... following Ms. Lynch at the front.

The team is well acquainted with Ms. Lynch, the woman assigned to carry out our punishment for the fight we caused during the first game of the season. The only thing the coach could think of to punish us was to embarrass us; his words were around *'If you can't act like men, then maybe I should indulge you'* right before he laid out his master plan.

Subjected to two and a half months of dance lessons, all so that we can perform a formation-type choreography in front of our friends and family at the Christmas benefit. For the last month, we've been practicing the cha-cha twice a week, and today is the day we're supposed to have our first practice with our forced-on dance partners.

Right now, I am looking at all the potentials focused on their reflections.

Well, all except one.

Love at first sight. I've heard of it, read about it, seen it on multiple screens, and witnessed it happen to my brother. On the other hand, I haven't had the pleasure of experiencing it. That is, until I laid my eyes on a blonde wonder.

Right there, overlooking a crowded room with bright lights and loud music, I get struck.

Experienced symptoms: all-around butterflies, shortness of breath, stopping of the heart, stiffness of the muscles, chest pains, temporary focused blindness (as in - not able to see anyone or anything else other than her), tightening of the throat, arousal, and spiking high temperature. To sum it all up - the whole nine yards.

A special kind of lighting strikes me, and my body goes into shock. It's that kind of thing that no doctor can fix, no remedy for the illness, no cure, no way of ever going back. In all honesty, I'm not planning on going back. I like the feeling, the moment it has its hand in consuming me, I am done for. The problem is that I want, need, and am determined to get more.

The entire room blurs out, making her the sole focus of my view. She is the only one not showing off her body, wearing a loose t-shirt with her sleeves pulled up over her shoulders and basketball shorts. Her blonde hair is tied in a ponytail, swinging from side to side. Her mouth opens to the lyrics, and she moves in sync with each beat. It's as if she's feeling the music, immersed in it with closed eyes, all the while nailing every step. I forget how to breathe, looking at her, transfixed, and I swear, time stands still for a moment. A bit of frustration comes over me due to her closed eyes, making me desperate to see them - the color, the shape, her soul.

Noticing the direction of my stare, Ben snaps me out of the trance. "Don't even think about it, man."

"What's the story there?"

Ben takes a deep breath, the warning kind, before he says, "That's Maddie, the volleyball captain, and you don't stand a chance. No offense."

"Some taken, but tell me more," I demand, intrigued.

"Look, Johnny, trust me when I tell you, don't go there."

I chuckle at the name drop from before either of us was born and fight the urge to sing out the timeless tune.

"Points for the reference, but if you don't mind, indulge me." I am practically begging, ready to go down on my knees even.

"Fine, your funeral," he gasps, then gives me what I need, placing his arm around my shoulder. "She's the all-around player of the year, number one in the state, and doesn't do basketball players. Trust me, we all tried and failed miserably."

Of course, she isn't going to make it easy, and we haven't even met.

"Minor setback," I deflect. "Keep going."

"You have a death wish, I see," Ben sighs, shaking his head. "She got here on a basketball scholarship."

"But I thought you said she plays volleyball?"

"Patience, brother, patience, I was about to get there." He rolls his eyes for emphasis.

"Did you ever read about a big-shot high school player that all the majors wanted to draft, and she turned them *all* down?"

"Yeah, from Chicago, Stevens something."

I stare at the beauty, her eyes still closed, entranced in her world. She looks breathtaking, and the info dump I was just overstimulated with makes her unreal. But there she is, flesh and bone, intimidating and inviting all at once.

Ben squeezes my shoulder and points at the person I'm developing an obsession with. "Meet Maddison Stevens."

"Damn," I mutter.

"Yeah, bro," Ben agrees, praising how she quit basketball and turned to volleyball to keep her scholarship. He didn't say anything about the reason she quit basketball, only how she spent the summer training for a whole new sport before trying out for the volleyball team and making the second string. By the following season, she was crowned captain.

Impressive is too small a word to describe her.

The music stops, and all the girls scatter to the corners, grabbing their towels and bottles. I check the time; it's probably just a break, since there are fifteen more minutes till our torture starts. Unable to look away, I soak her in, and the switch. Taking a place in the right corner, she grabs a blue bottle and chugs it right before she spits some of it out, bursting into laughter over something a tall redhead says. Her smile is even more captivating than I imagined.

The clapping of Ms. Lynch's hands gets all the girls to momentarily stiffen before they go back to their former places. The redhead and Maddie do a cute handshake with wiggling fingers and their tongues sticking out right before they take their positions. Her eyes close the moment the music starts, and her fingers start drumming to the beat, tapping the side of her thigh, and when she begins her steps, I can't look away. Diverging from the dance before the break, she moves more sensually, swaying her hips, deep diving into the salsa rhythm, and it is the worst - slash - best thing any man could witness.

"Does she have a boyfriend?" I turn the question to Cole.

"Are you deaf or just need an ear cleanse?" It's Ben who drawls, "It doesn't matter; she does not do basketball players."

"Not what I asked, Ben."

"As far as I know, she's a free woman."

That she sure is!

About the Author

Lena is a wife, a mother of two, and somewhere along the way, she lost herself in her roles. She has a master's degree in Physical Education, but after her son was diagnosed with autism, she proudly pulled on her stay-at-home-mom shoes. She rediscovered herself through books and the new worlds they opened up. Reading turned into writing, and a new passion was born. Lena grew up never believing in herself, but thankfully, there are people in her life who gave her the necessary push to try... so this is her... trying.

You can find her on:
Tik Tok -   authorlenaknight
Instagram - authorlenak

Acknowledgements

First, I want to thank my only support system - my husband. Without you, I never would've taken this step. Thank you for believing in me and being my rock.

To my kids who made my dreams of becoming a mother come true... Mommy loves you the mostes.

I want to thank each person who took the time to read my words.

To Sunny, the first person who read my stories and gave me the push I needed to continue my journey.

To my beta readers and editors for helping me make the story better

And last but not least, I want to thank the Holy Trinity of BookTok for getting me back into reading, which eventually turned into me writing...

Lena